CHOOSE COSTA RICA

CHOOSE COSTA RICA

A GUIDE TO WINTERING OR RETIREMENT

John Howells

GATEWAY BOOKS

Printed in the United States of America

Gateway Books
San Rafael, CA

Distributed by Publishers Group West

Library of Congress Cataloging-in Publication Data

Howells, John, 1928-
    Choose Costa Rica : a guide to wintering or retiring / by John
Howells.
        p.   cm.
    Includes bibliographical references and index.
    ISBN 0-933469-14-4 : $12.95
        1. Retirement, Places of —Costa Rica.   2. Retirement. Places of-
    -Guatemala. 3. Costa Rica—Guidebooks 4. Guatemala--Guidebooks
    I. Title
    HQ1063.2.C8H69   1992
    646.7'9' 097286—dc20   92-27009
                                                                      CIP

10 9 8 7 6 5 4 3 2

Contents

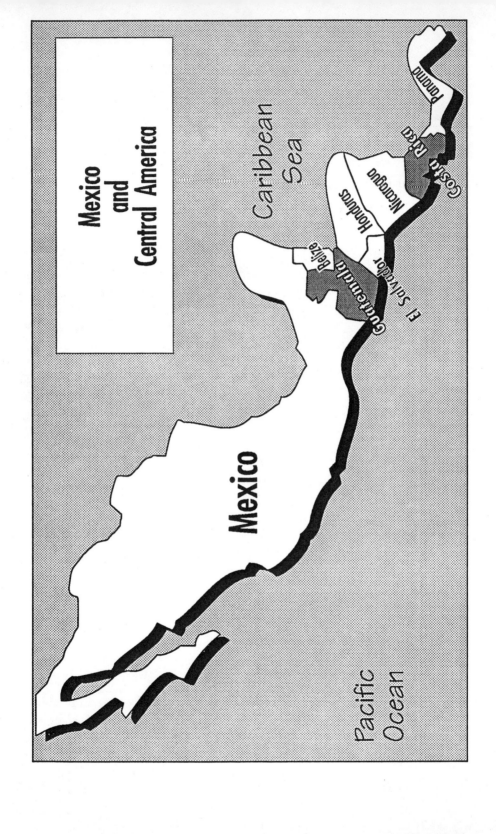

Mexico
and
Central America

Mexico

Pacific Ocean

Caribbean Sea

Belize

Guatemala

El Salvador

Honduras

Nicaragua

Costa Rica

Panama

Introduction

This book is the result of 20 years of travel in and writing about Central America. Before I began doing nonfiction books, I was a freelance writer; my specialty was writing travel articles on Mexico, Costa Rica, Guatemala and other Latin American countries. Why Latin America? Partly because of the warm climates (I hate cold weather) but mostly because of the gorgeous scenery, exotic foods and the friendly people who live there. Places like Mexico, Guatemala and Costa Rica naturally beckoned with tropical warmth and picturesque surroundings. I always hated it when my research was completed and I had to return home!

My first book on seasonal travel and retirement was about Mexico—co-authored with Donald Merwin—published almost ten years ago when that country was in the beginning of a travel/retirement boom. People were eager for information about how to winter in Mexico or how to retire there, so the book did rather well. Since that time, my wife and I have taken our advice to heart, spending several winters in Mexico, and enjoying the good things Mexico has to offer. Lately, however, we've broadened our seasonal focus to include Central America— specifically Costa Rica and Guatemala.

Unfortunately, most Central American countries underwent some rather stormy times throughout the last decade due to civil strife and unrest. Today, however, rays of hope are breaking through the clouds. Restoration of peace and tranquility have returned large portions of Central America to places where North Americans feel comfortable traveling and investing.

Only Costa Rica avoided the problems that mired her sister republics in a quicksand of turmoil and tragedy. Costa Rica's devotion to democracy and peaceful cooperation with its neighbors enabled the country to retain its enviable position as a showcase of prosperity, respect for law and personal freedoms.

Guatemala was not so fortunate; it underwent a long period of military-civilian strife which is only now being resolved. However, many North Americans calmly lived in Guatemala throughout the times of trouble and felt secure, since both government soldiers and rebel guerrillas scrupulously avoided involving them in the conflict. They learned of the problems mostly from reading foreign news magazines. Today, a peaceful reconciliation seems to be settling over the countryside, promising to make Guatemala once again a viable retirement option just as it was before the problems began. The number of visitors and retirees grows daily, with the government making sincere efforts to attract foreign residents.

According to a U.S. State Department source, about 40,000 American citizens live in Central America, most of them either in Costa Rica or Guatemala. A few North Americans live in other Central American countries—Honduras, Belize, and even El Salvador and Nicaragua—but their ranks are scanty. From my perspective, there are too many drawbacks for the average North American to consider living in any of the countries except Costa Rica and Guatemala.

A New Prosperity

For the past several years, North American tourism overseas has been on the decline, particularly travel to Europe. Out-of-sight prices, vague threats of terrorism, hostage-taking and a war in the Persian Gulf discouraged Americans from traveling or living overseas. In Britain, for example, the number of North American tourists dropped 30 percent recently while the number of visitors from neighboring Western European countries increased by 18 percent. At one time, Europe was considered a bargain place for travel and retirement—but prices in many

European countries have risen steadily, and now prices exceed those in North America.

In the midst of this softening of foreign travel and retirement, Costa Rica and Guatemala are becoming more and more popular. In Costa Rica, for example, tourism is up *336 percent* over the past six years! The larger U.S. airlines and European charter services are gearing up to handle the hordes of travelers who are discovering the joys of pocketbook-friendly vacations in Costa Rica and Guatemala.

Like Mexico, these countries eagerly welcome tourists, seasonal residents and retirees, but Costa Rica and Guatemala place fewer restrictions on newcomers and make it very easy to buy property or start a business. To become a *pensionado* in Costa Rica, one only needs to prove a $600 a month retirement income. In Guatemala, the requirement is just $300 a month! Happily, these amounts easily cover a couple's basic living expenses, something unthinkable in most parts of the world. Red tape for entering these countries is minimal; a passport is all one needs to spend an entire winter or summer season, with extensions easily obtained.

Two other conditions make Costa Rica and Guatemala special as destinations for part-time or full-time living. The first is the evenness of the climate. The central plateaus of both countries are wonderfully temperate, with thermometer readings virtually the same the year around. A second favorable condition is the exciting investment climate, particularly in Costa Rica. Instead of placing barriers to prevent foreigners from going into business, as do most countries in the world, Costa Rica and Guatemala *encourage* investments. To encourage investment and year-round retirement, both governments offer tax incentives and duty-free imports. You don't have to be a citizen or even a legal resident to own property or conduct a business.

Choose Costa Rica is intended not only for retirees searching for an affordable, interesting lifestyle after leaving the workplace, but for those nearing retirement age, who are casting about for ideas for the future. This book is also designed as a guide for those individuals who manage to have part or all of the year free for doing exactly what they feel like doing. It's for the professor on sabbatical; the school teacher on a summer vacation; the construction worker with chronic winter unemployment; the executive who can take a leave of absence. This book is for the self-employed individual who can trust his business to others while he enjoys life *now* instead of waiting for that "someday" which may never come. This book is specially oriented toward those who seek a "new start," who might wish to invest their time and resources into launching a new business career as well as a fascinating lifestyle in an exotic foreign country.

Although this is partly a travel book, the emphasis is on "how to do it" rather than "where to go." A few hotels or restaurants may be mentioned from time to time, but these are only incidental to a description, and should not be taken as recommendations. That's the job of the many excellent travel publications such as Frommer's *Costa Rica, Guatemala & Belize on $35 a Day*, Blake and Becher's *The New Key to Costa Rica*, Ellen Searby's *Costa Rica Traveler* or Fodor's *South America on $25 a Day*.

A final note on prices quoted throughout this book: they are accurate as of the writing, based on the current dollar exchange rates in Costa Rica and Guatemala. As of spring of 1992, the Costa Rica currency, the *colón* was valued at 138 to the dollar, the Guatemalan *quetzal* at five to the dollar. These rates surely will change by publication time, since the Costa Rican government lifted currency controls in early 1992, and the Guatemalan government was considering changing the official rate to bring the dollar and quetzal into a better alignment.

Chapter One

Switzerland of the Americas

As the jet liner droned over the Nicaraguan border, crossing into Costa Rica, I eagerly looked forward to touching down at the Santa María Airport for my fifth visit to Costa Rica. As I tried to identify landmarks below, anxious to catch a glimpse of the bowl-like mountain valley that contains the sprawling city of San José, I heard the lady in the aisle seat sniff disgustedly as she tossed aside a guidebook on Costa Rica.

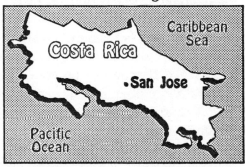

"Why can't these books simply describe Costa Rica?" she complained peevishly. "Every place is described in superlatives or else it is 'just too beautiful to describe.' You'd think the authors were poets instead of travel writers! Give me a break!" The empty seat between us held four discarded books, all travel guides to Costa Rica.

A frown creased my forehead as I realized that my mission on this trip was to complete the research for yet *another* book on Costa Rica to add to the stack. Perhaps her complaint was a message I needed to take to heart; clearly, I wouldn't want to evoke similar reactions from my readers. But after a few moments of thought, a truth dawned upon me: it's *impossible* to describe Costa Rica without using superlatives, because the country *is* a superlative!

People who have traveled all over the world affirm that Costa Rica's beaches are unsurpassed anywhere. Its various climates offer choices of weather as perfect as you could hope to find any place on earth (unless you are a skier, of course). Steep-sloped mountains, topped with cloud forests, ferns and exotic wildlife, tower over fertile farmlands dotted with hundreds of neatly maintained homesteads. Flowers bloom everywhere; often entire trees bear so many colorful, scented blossoms that green leaves are hidden. As if this weren't enough, the cities and towns are every bit as neat and clean as the countryside, and blessed with friendly Costa Rican hospitality. How can this country be described except by superlatives?

One of the more common descriptions of Costa Rica is "the Switzerland of the Americas." At first glance, Costa Rica differs so much from Switzerland that one might wonder how it earned this title. True, both countries are of similar size (although Switzerland is actually a bit smaller—one of the world's few countries with that distinction). But Costa Rica is lushly tropical, continually swathed in luxurious green vegetation, a place where coffee, sugar cane and mangoes thrive, and where snow never falls. Costa Rica would seem to be totally opposite from Switzerland, with its snowcapped peaks and rocky terrain.

Yet, the more one travels in Costa Rica, the more apparent are the parallels with Switzerland. Both are peaceful, progressive countries where democracy and stability are hallmarks. Although Costa Rica's tropical beaches are incongruent with the Swiss terrain, the higher mountains rival the rugged beauty of the Alps. The lake area around the Arenal Volcano could easily pass for parts of Switzerland—during the Swiss summertime, at any rate.

Even closer similarities between the two countries appear in their philosophy of life and economic structures. Both are places of small farms, small businesses, with an air of prosperity and a feeling of equality among citizens. Both countries have renounced aggressive militarism, diverting resources—that otherwise would be consumed by wars—toward education, medical care and services for the good of all. In short, both places are affluent, happy and tranquil. Both are locations where North Americans can feel at home, safe and welcome.

There are differences, of course. Costa Rica is closer to the United States and Canada, making it more accessible than Europe. Costa Rica enjoys a dramatically lower cost of living. And, best of all, Costa Rica has a climate that can be enjoyed year round by those of us who hate wearing snow boots and earmuffs. The higher elevations enjoy spring-like temperatures all year; flowers bloom everywhere and seem to glow in the crystal-clear atmosphere. The countryside is so fertile that fence posts sprout and become trees despite all the farmers' efforts to keep them as fence posts. Crossing over the mountains, you drop down to tropical lowlands where North Americans own plantations of coffee, macadamia nuts, black pepper and other exotic crops for export. Costa Rican beaches are world-renowned and just too beautiful to describe. Oh boy—now *I'm* writing in superlatives!

A Unique History

Costa Rica stands out in this hemisphere in many ways, but its biggest contrast is with its Central American neighbors. When you drive across the border into Costa Rica, or when you step off an airplane arriving from another Central American country, you know immediately that you are in a special place. The neighboring republics all point to Costa Rica as an example of the kind of world they would hope to imitate. "If Costa Rica can be prosperous, democratic and free," the envious neighbors ask, "why can't we?"

Clearly, there are light-years of difference between Costa Rica and the other Central American countries. How did it get that way? Why is there so little poverty and so large a middle class in comparison with neighboring countries? The answer to this question can be found in a series of historical events, some accidental, some planned. Let's take a quick look at the country's history as a means toward understanding where Costa Rica is today.

In 1502, when Columbus happened upon Costa Rica during his last voyage to this hemisphere, he anchored at present-day Limón and dispatched an expedition ashore to determine what kind of country they had discovered. By the way, there is a question as to whether Columbus actually set foot ashore. Chances are, he waited on the ship for a report from his landing party. His explorers returned to report an inhospitable jungle, impossible swamps, plus ferocious natives who wore a few paltry ornaments of thinly-pounded gold. In short, the Limón Coast offered little to excite the imagination of these early explorers. They quickly moved on without making any attempt at colonization.

According to legend, Columbus gave his new discovery the name *Costa Rica* or "rich coast." Actually, the name probably came from another explorer, Fernández de Córdoba, as he charted the *Pacific* side of the isthmus some 30 years later. Impressed by the magnificent forests, fertile lands and abundant wildlife of the Nicoya peninsula, he coined the term "Costa Rica" as he established a settlement in 1539. The coast that Columbus discovered was left virtually untouched and ignored by Europeans for several more centuries. The earliest settlements were planted on the Pacific side. But in contrast with the fast colonization of other parts of the new world, Costa Rica grew very slowly.

After the Spanish conquered the New World, the Spanish Crown granted huge tracts of land to the conquistadores as a reward for their services. Indians were considered a part of the land, and although not exactly slaves, the Indians essentially belonged to the enormous haciendas, forced to work as peons for the aristocratic conquerors. In other places, such as Peru, Mexico or Guatemala, the Indians meekly accepted their new rulers and continued working the same lands as before, paying tribute to new overlords. However, the Indians of Costa Rica (like their cousins in North America) proved to be determined, fierce fighters who refused to accept the intruders as their superiors. Experts in defending their heavily forested lands, the Indians simply withdrew farther into the jungle when defeated. Archaeological evidence suggests that at least some tribes were headhunters, possibly related to the Jívaros of Colombia whose warriors dangle their enemies' shrunken heads around their necks as ornaments. In short, these Indians were definitely not likely candidates to become docile field laborers.

This left the newcomers in a position they hadn't counted on. Instead of being lords over huge estates and overseeing gangs of laboring peons, the Spanish conquistadores were forced to work the land for themselves! This required hard work and marginal existence on small, family-run farms. From the beginning, all were equal in their struggle for existence. Even the royal governors had to tend their own gardens to avoid starvation. Small wonder most early settlers moved on to easier pickings while still others ignored the country completely.

Therefore, Costa Rica's development got off to an unauspicious start. The country remained a backwash of Spanish colonization, all but forgotten over the ensuing centuries. It grew in its own way, ignoring the ineffective Spanish governors, the royal court of Madrid, and unaffected by events in other colonies. In fact, in 1821, when Spain granted independence to the Spanish colonies, Costa Rica was the last to know (and probably cared the least). For all practical purposes, it had always been on its own. Independence was no novelty.

Fortunately, Costa Rica's first president turned out to be a progressive leader, a visionary who wanted to see the country develop socially and economically. He was convinced that growing coffee for export could be a major economic breakthrough, a key to modernization. Coffee could build roads, schools and cities.

But Costa Rica was scantily populated. More people were needed to grow coffee in order to fulfill the president's dream. Consequently, free land grants were offered to anyone willing to plant coffee trees. Since coffee production in Costa Rica is ideally suited to small farms, European families began immigrating to take advantage of Costa Rica's opportunities. They came from Italy and France as well as from Spain. Rather than developing huge coffee plantations owned by a few wealthy families, as happened in other Central American republics, thousands of small farms sprang up, selling coffee beans to merchants who processed and exported the product. This resulted in a tradition of independence and equality, with a preponderance of middle-class farmers and a few moderately wealthy coffee-exporting families. The spread between rich, middle class and poor was much narrower than anywhere in the hemisphere, and remains so to this day.

Troubled times in the last half of the 19th century sent new waves of European economic and political refugees to the Americas, seeking a chance to "start over." The standing offer of free land to grow coffee was irresistible. The ranks of small farmers grew even larger. These refugees, often imbued with contemporary Europe's liberal intellectual and political philosophy, contributed heavily to the notions of freedom, democracy and individual rights that were already in place.

This is not to say that Costa Rica didn't develop a wealthy oligarchy of elite families whose position rested upon their control of coffee exports. But because of their tradition of being "self-made" families and their respect for hard work, their mentality evolved differently from the arrogant Spanish conquistadores who worshiped royalty and privilege.

Free and compulsory education was an early development, starting in 1869 and setting a tradition of literacy that ranks Costa Rica higher than most countries of the world—including the United States. A university was founded in 1844, staffed in part by intellectuals who fled Europe's political and economic maelstrom. Modern European traditions developed in Costa Rica in stark contrast with the medieval, feudal heritage of Mexico and other Central American countries.

A century-and-a-half tradition of free and honest elections forms the basis for today's political life. Instead of frequent coups d'etat, so common in neighboring countries, Costa Rican governments change by balloting. Although members of the same, affluent families win office frequently, they tend to be civilians, intellectuals and for the most part, working for the good of the country as a whole, not just for one particular class. In 1889, the population survived a potential revolution when the defeated incumbents almost refused to recognize the election results. But at the last minute they decided to accept the will of the people, thus reinforcing a tradition of democratic process.

A truly significant event that totally separated Costa Rica from the ranks of other Central American nations occurred in 1948. The ruling party decided not to recognize the results of a disputed election and refused to give up power, ordering new elections because of the closeness of the vote and accusations of fraud. A crisis of democracy threatened. Pepe Figueres, a charismatic member of one of the wealthy families, stepped forward to lead an uprising against the illegal government and its attempt to use the army to hold on to power. The result of this successful action was a movement to abolish the army and replace it with the *Guardia Civil*, a civilian-controlled police force comparable to a city police or state patrol in the United States.

This was a brilliant and bold step. Barracks were turned into schools. Ex-soldiers were given jobs building roads. Money which would normally be absorbed by military corruption and graft was devoted to highways, education and medical care. Today, 27 percent of the national budget goes to education and culture. Public money pays for four universities, three symphony orchestras, and five autonomous state publishing houses. Of the gross national product, about 10 per cent is spent on medical care, and there is a physician for every 700 inhabitants.

Many North Americans shake their heads in dismay at the lack of a standing army. They ask, "Without a military, how can you defend your country from aggression?" The answer is simple. The function of a Central American military has never been to deter aggression; its duty is to protect the *rulers* of the country from its *citizens*, to keep the people in line and protect privileges for the military and the country's financial elite. The truth is, democracy doesn't stand a chance when armed soldiers threaten voters, bully candidates, conduct the elections and count ballots.

Election day is Costa Rica's most important holiday, a riotous celebration with a joyous spirit that goes far beyond mere politics. Voting is mandatory (non-voters pay a token fine), but few citizens would think of passing up the fun and excitement of an election. For three weeks prior to election day all parties campaign vigorously, with folks everywhere waving their party's flags, cheering enthusiastically when a car displaying a favored flag drives past, or booing good-naturedly when an opposition flag passes by. On the day of election, all stores and businesses are closed. All transportation is free. Buses, taxis, even private cars are expected to stop when someone indicates they want a ride to a polling booth. In practice, most autos will stop for anyone who waves and asks for a ride in whatever direction the auto is headed. After all, this is a fiesta!

It's interesting to note that many Costa Ricans, when they move from their home towns to another part of the country, do not change their voting registration to their new address. Because transportation is free, this is an opportunity to return to their home towns to vote and to visit friends and family at the same time. Parties, reunions and celebrations are a most important part of election day.

Voters must dunk their thumbs into indelible ink, to prove they've voted (and cannot vote again), and this purple digit is worn as a proud badge of civic duty. Automobile drivers honk their horns and wave their discolored thumbs in the air as they drive along the streets, to show everyone they have voted and to ask "have *you* voted yet?" There are so many horns blowing on election day that it sounds like New Year's Eve at midnight, all day long.

The result is a country intensely dedicated to notions of democracy. All segments of the political spectrum, from extreme right to far out left are represented; all are totally legal. Yet middle-of-the road parties always seem to garner most of the votes. Despite vigorous campaigning, the Communists used to garner 2 percent of the vote, but have fallen to around 1 percent as party members become disenchanted with failed Marxist experiments in Nicaragua and elsewhere.

This is not to imply that there is no poverty in the country, or that Costa Rican workers are among the world's best-paid. But compared to most Latin American countries, workers here enjoy excellent working conditions and government guarantees of fair treatment from employers. Even those living below the poverty level live far better than in most other countries, including the United States. You don't see "street people" or panhandlers on Costa Rican streets. As a friend observed, "Among the world's poor, Costa Rican poor are probably the best off." Food is plentiful, medical care and education are free and there is always a network of government, family and friends to act as a safety net. Open-air markets have a tradition of giving food to the poor, with vendors handing out surplus to those asking. If a family wants land to grow food, the government does its best to comply.

Yet, wages appear to be extraordinary low. How can a worker be expected to survive on as little as $150 a month, much less be considered well off? The answer is that even though the cash salary is small, fringe benefits connected with the job make a big difference. In addition to this $150 a month in cash salary, a worker is guaranteed items such as sick leave at the rate of 50% of his salary, from the first day of illness up to a lifetime of disability. All employees receive a month's *aguinaldo* or Christmas bonus every year. Workers earn from two to three weeks paid vacation every year, plus free medical care. Women receive six weeks maternity leave (at full salary), and all receive a pension upon retirement. It isn't necessary to put aside money for the children's college education; tuition is free, a service provided by the government. A worker can spend his salary on living expenses instead of having to put a portion aside for illness or medical emergencies. These benefits are guaranteed by *law*, and everybody knows exactly what their rights are.

When you measure these benefits and put a cash value on them, you'll find that Costa Rican workers are ahead of many North American workers. In the United States a pitifully inadequate medical insurance policy costs a worker twice as much as a Costa Rican worker's total earnings. Since few low-paid U.S. workers can afford insurance, one short visit to a hospital pushes them into hopeless poverty. Sick leave? Only higher-paid employees in the United States enjoy that luxury.

Why 'Ticos'?

Throughout this book and in other guidebooks, you'll continually see the term *Tico* used when speaking of Costa Ricans. This is a nickname for a Costa Rica citizen, much as *Gringo* is used for North Americans in general, and *Yankee* for a citizen of the United States. It's an affectionate nickname, and no one gets upset by it. They call themselves Ticos when distinguishing themselves from foreigners, instead of the more cumbersome *Costariquense*. The name *Tico* comes from an archaic practice of using the sound

-*tico* on the end of a word as a diminutive instead of the normal -*tito*. For example: whereas a Mexican would say *momentito* for "just a tiny moment," some Costa Ricans (not all) might say *momentico*. Thus a kitten would be a *gatico* in Costa Rica, but a *gatito* in Mexico.

Although guidebooks and tourist literature suggest that Costa Ricans *always* use the "tico" ending, my personal observation is that many, if not most, do not say "tico". I have a feeling that this may be a speech pattern which is falling out of favor.

One uniquely Costa Rican term, solidly ingrained into the language, is *pura vida*. I suppose this would translate as "that's life" or "great life," but today it means "all right," or "okay," or often an emphatic "aw-right"! A clerk in a store, instead of asking, "Would you like anything else?" might ask instead, "Pura vida?" A gas station attendant may ask, "Is your oil *pura vida* or should I check it for you?"

A Comfortable Country

Costa Rica is a country where North Americans feel very much at home. Costa Rica is a country of law-abiding citizens, a place where you don't feel shivers of apprehension at the approach of a policeman. This is a country where juvenile gangs and graffiti are all but unknown. It's a place where your conscience isn't continually assaulted by obvious poverty, beggars in the streets or social injustice. It's a place where North Americans feel comfortable living in just about any neighborhood, not forced to huddle together in enclaves of other expatriates for mutual support.

The fact is, North Americans like Costa Rica so much because Costa Ricans are so much like us. They look like us, act like us and, importantly, think like we do. Costa Rica is a place where North Americans can feel at home. It is a country of superlatives.

Visas and Passports

Another thing North Americans like about Costa Rica is the ease with which they can enter the country. A Canadian or

American tourist traveling with a valid passport has only to present it at the airport for a 90-day visit, which can be extended upon request.

Without a passport, a tourist card is needed. The only requirement is payment of a $2.00 fee plus a birth certificate and identification with a current photo, such as a driver's license. Tourist cards are available at any Costa Rican consulate, from your travel agency, from the airline, or even at the airport when you disembark from the airplane. With a tourist card, U.S. citizens are only entitled to a 30-day stay, but Canadians receive 90 days.

Extending your stay is a relatively simply matter; merely ask permission. However, if you are a single parent traveling with children, or if you are traveling with your grandchildren, there is an important consideration about extending visas. When a child stays over the 30- or 90-day limit he or she falls under the jurisdiction of the *Patronato Nacional de la Infancia,* a children's welfare organization. In order for a child to leave the country without *both* parents, you must have a permit notarized by a Costa Rican consulate in your home country. If you don't have this permit beforehand you can straighten things out at the Patronato offices on 19th Street and 6th Avenue in San José.

Required Reading for Costa Rica

There are two publications I strongly recommend for anyone considering Costa Rica for anything more than a short vacation. The first is San José's English-language newspaper, the *Tico Times*. If you read every issue, from front to back, including all advertisements, by the time you actually get to Costa Rica, you will know so much about the place you will feel as if you are returning home. The classified ads keep you up to date on rental costs, housing prices and what second-hand furniture and appliances sell for. Display ads tell you what you should pay for a hotel room or a bed and breakfast, the best places to dine or where to go for a beach excursion. The news columns are well-written, with complete and unbiased news of what's happening in Cost Rica as well as in neighboring countries—news not available in other English-language newspapers. Featured are articles relating to foreign residents, governmental actions or changes in law that may affect them, as well as news of social activities and club events. An extensive letters-to-the-editor section prints opinions of tourists and residents alike, telling of exceptionally nice places to go and which places are rip-offs, giving opinions about the country, kudos and complaints, political views, and just about anything you can imagine. By all means, start your subscription several months before you leave.

The second essential to your initial trip is the book, *The New Key to Costa Rica*, by Beatrice Blake and Anne Becher ($14.95, Ulysses Press, can be ordered from any United States or Canadian bookstore). This is a no-nonsense paperback, packed with all the information you need on bus schedules and hotel rates in accurate, non-flowery language. It's all there in one volume.

Choose Costa Rica makes no attempt to make recommendations on business services such as real estate agencies, simply because of the impossibility of being able to vouch for reliability or character. Personnel can change; agencies are sold. Your job is to investigate, make inquiries and make your own, on-the-spot selections. When realtors, business services or travel agencies are mentioned, it isn't as an endorsement of their reliability, but simply as a starting place for checking out the field. At the time I interviewed these business representatives, I was impressed by their knowledge—but that says nothing of their competence or honesty; these are judgments you must make for yourself.

Finally, I emphatically urge that you make no decisions about permanent moves or business investments without spending at least six months "on location," getting to know the country, meeting the people and learning what it's all about. And above all, find a good lawyer before making any financial moves; don't hand your money to someone simply because he or she also comes from Kansas City or Vancouver and has an honest look.

Chapter Two

What's Costa Rica Like?

Costa Rica is a small country, even though it doesn't appear so from the standpoint of the traveler who is driving a rental car from one end of the country to the other, over winding roads, uphill and down. Every turn in the road brings a new vista, something else to contemplate. Actually, the country contains a little less than 20,000 square miles. Travel articles and guidebooks traditionally describe Costa Rica as being "the size of West Virginia," but that's not really accurate. Some travel writer must have said that years ago and others automatically repeat this misinformation. The truth is, Costa Rica is smaller than West Virginia by 20 percent. To be more accurate, let's say that Costa Rica is about the size of New Hampshire and Maryland with poor little Rhode Island tossed in for good measure. Well, would it help to say that Costa Rica is about half the size of Kentucky? If that makes the place sound small and insignificant, we can balance out the equation by pointing out that Costa Rica is *larger* than either Albania, Denmark, Belgium, Holland or Switzerland (plus a handful of countries I've never heard of). Here's a final comparison for you: Costa Rica is almost two-and-a-half times the size of Israel.

Yet, few large countries offer such a diversity of scenery, climates or such a wide variety of flora and fauna. Probably no country in the world devotes as large a percentage of its territory to national parks and wildlife refuges. About 27 percent of Costa Rica's land is thus protected. These preserves range from cloud forests to tropical beaches, from volcanic craters to jungle swamps and inland waterways. A bewildering assortment of wildlife includes 850 species of birds—more than three times as many as in the United States and Canada combined. Common mammals are monkeys, coatis, jaguars and ocelots as well as sloths, tapirs and agoutis. One evening, down on the Pacific coast, a large anteater ran in front of my car, its long snout almost touching the ground in front with an equally heavy tail drooping behind, looking very prehistoric. Turtles, colorful frogs and toads of all descriptions are found, as well as crocodiles and iguanas. There are said to be more varieties of butterflies in Costa Rica than in all of the African continent. The number of orchids and bromiliads confuses the mind. This is truly a naturalist's paradise, drawing visitors from all over the world.

Many countries offer beautiful beaches and excellent vacation accommodations, but nowhere else in the world can a tourist find such a combination: delightful beaches, a safe and pleasant country, plus a tropical wonderland that's accessible year round—only in Costa Rica.

The Costa Rican government recognizes this unique asset and actively involves its citizens in both the preservation and exploitation of nature at the same time. How can you protect *and* exploit the environment? Just one example: by hiring local people to guard and preserve endangered turtle nesting beaches, jobs are created. Beach villages then become tourist attractions, complete with motels, restaurants and shops, thus creating even more jobs. Visitors from all over the world can now visit cloud forests, turtle nesting beaches and nature preserves—in comfort. In the process, they leave much-needed foreign currency with Costa Rican businesses and banks.

Many North Americans and Europeans are scrambling to join this bandwagon and, with government encouragement, are investing heavily in tourist businesses, particularly in motels, restaurants and endeavors of a like nature. Many of these enterprises become instant successes, with full bookings and plenty of business. One Canadian who started a motel on the Caribbean side of the country a few years ago, showed me the registration book for his 12-unit facility, saying proudly, "This place has an occupancy rate of 98 percent during the tourist season and over 60 percent during the off season." I asked for a room, but was told, "Not until next week. I'm booked solid." Details about starting and operating businesses in Costa Rica are presented in Chapter Nine.

A Country of Contradictions

Before readers are left with the impression that things are perfect in paradise, that Costa Rica is the best of all worlds, let's examine some contradictions. Even though the Costa Rican government is totally committed to preserving the environment and tries to control illegal deforestation, it also permits foreign companies to bulldoze forests to plant more banana fields. The government puts large tracts of land into biological and wildlife reserves, forest reserves, national parks and Indian reservations—yet, at the same time farmers and agribusiness cut down forests on private tracts at a faster rate than anywhere else in the world. The economy destroys in the name of progress while the government tries to preserve in the name of conservation. The growth of ecotourism in Costa Rica brings hundreds of thousands of visitors to enjoy the ecological wonderlands here, but these large numbers of visitors threaten to destroy the very ecological treasures that draw them.

Another problem, one which could become more serious as time passes and the population increases, is land ownership. Although the Costa Rican people are friendly, gentle and welcoming, they cannot help but harbor a certain amount of resentment as they see foreigners bid up the price of property until it is out of the locals' price range.

Visitors and foreign residents can do little to affect any changes in these situations, but they need be aware that problems do exist. The best they can do is try to minimize their impact upon the natural resources of the country. None of these problems have gotten completely out of hand, and solutions are constantly being sought by the Costa Rican government. But as is the way in any democracy, the going is slow and cumbersome. Just be aware that not everything is perfect in paradise—but it is still paradise!

Menu of Climates

For such a small country, Costa Rica has an astonishing variety of climates. From the cloud-misty mountain tops of Talamanca or Monteverde, to the almost desert-like northern Guanacaste province; from the permanent spring weather of the Arenal area to the jungle lushness of the Caribbean coast, Costa Rica has every kind of climate one might desire. The exception is frozen snow and bitter cold. But you don't want that anyway. Yes, there are seasons, but the differences between them are minimal. Unlike many other vacation spots, Costa Rica isn't a one-season destination; any time of the year is wonderful here.

In Costa Rica, people transpose the meanings of winter and summer. They call the months of December, January and February "summer," or the "dry season." These are the months that children take their "summer vacation" from school. To a Costa Rican, "winter" means June, July and August! Conversations can become very confusing when Costa Ricans and North Americans discuss the seasons, with summer and winter having opposite meanings for each of us. To avoid misunderstandings, I generally say, "June, July and August" instead of "winter"—then everybody knows what I mean.

The dry season, which actually begins around the last of November and lasts until the end of April, isn't parched and arid as the name might imply. There are always plenty of showers to keep plants and lawns pleasantly green and flowers blooming in the higher parts of the mountains, where most folks live. On the Caribbean coast and the area around Lake Arenal, the "dry season" is just a figure of speech; rain knows no seasons here. Some Pacific coastal areas are truly dry during December, January and February, looking much like California during its summer, when rain rarely falls.

The "winter" months of June, July and August—referred to as the "rainy season"—are actually cooler than the "summer" months. This is because of the almost daily rains and evaporation effect. A common misconception is that "rainy season" means continual downpours. Typically, even in the most rainy parts of the country, the day begins with glorious sunshine, with blossoms glowing in the sparkling clean air, birds singing happily. Then, rain starts falling between two and four o'clock in the afternoon. Some places you can almost set your clock by it. A heavy downpour sends people indoors for a couple of hours. Then the sunshine returns and the world is once again refreshed. Other sections of the country enjoy sunshine all day, with the rain falling at night. This is the best rain, for it makes falling to sleep to the sound of raindrops on the roof a delight. It's not often that it rains *every* day; several days in a row can be perfectly dry.

Because most North Americans customarily think of the tropics as a place to visit in their winter season—to escape the snow and ice of their homelands—they are often surprised to find that the rainy months of June, July and August are the favorite time of year for many who live in Costa Rica. "You can't really appreciate this country until you've experienced our winter months," says Graham Henshaw, an expatriate from England. "Everything is green now in January, but when the rains start in May, the grass changes to an even brighter emerald color. Flowers that only bloom in July and August are absolutely stunning. Winter is my favorite time of year." (Remember, "winter" is "summer" for us North Americans!)

To further complicate matters, what is true of the mountain valley environment around San José isn't necessarily true on the Atlantic side, which can be flooded with sunshine while the capital is awash in *aguaceros* (rainstorms) and vice versa. The truth is, no matter what time of year you choose to visit, you're guaranteed a serving of nice sunny weather—and probably some rain as well.

Weather in the tropics is largely determined by altitude. At ocean level, the climate is a year-round summer; at moderate elevations year-round spring is a better description. The higher you go, the cooler it gets. A sweater or jacket can be worn almost every evening of the year in higher elevations. Your travel wardrobe should include shirts, sweaters and jackets you can peel off or pile on, depending on whether you're dining at a beach restaurant, visiting a volcano, or traveling somewhere in between. Be sure to bring rain gear and sturdy shoes if you plan any jungle exploring, plus sunscreen for visits to mountains or beaches; the tropical sun is fierce at all altitudes.

In the northwest Pacific side, the dry season is exactly that, with very little rain falling from November until the beginning of May. The grass turns brown, and many trees lose their leaves just as they do in North America in the winter. But the reason for leaf loss is to conserve water, not frost and freezing weather. There are some evergreen trees, but even some of these lose a large portion of their leaves. It isn't as bleak as it sounds, for many of these trees replace leaves with brilliantly-colored blossoms, for this is the time of year to attract bees, butterflies and other pollinating insects.

Even on the dry Guanacaste coast you'll find microcosms of green environments tucked away in the interior valleys, where sporadic rains are coaxed from the westerly Pacific winds. Farther south along the Pacific coast, the dry-season rainfall is even more frequent, keeping things pleasantly green during the driest months.

There is a weather chart at the end of this chapter to provide an idea of the statistics.

Insects and the Tropics

An odd thing about the weather checkerboard of Costa Rica is that, contrary to what one might think, the more humid areas are not necessarily the most insect-plagued. Of course, bring your insect repellent, but I'm convinced that you need it less in most places in Costa Rica than you do in the American Midwest. Along the rain forest coast of Golfo Dulce, where the insect and animal life is abundant, mosquitoes and flies pester you far less than in the dry, almost desert-like climate of Guanacaste. On the humid Caribbean coast where rain can fall almost any time of the year, and where bugs can get so large you'd think they've been taking hormones, household cockroaches and flies are not nearly as plentiful as I've seen in Houston or New Orleans. In most parts of Costa Rica, people don't bother with screens on their windows. Of course, the rainy season in some areas will make a liar of me.

Why flies and mosquitoes are relatively scarce might seem puzzling. But the answer seems to lie in the fact that the natural environment in Costa Rica is largely intact. The innate enemies of these pests haven't yet been eliminated by pesticides, chemicals and extinction as they have back home. By day, birds of all descriptions flit back and forth, snacking on insects, keeping them in an intrinsic balance with nature. Many birds consider houseflies to be special treats. By night, squadrons of bats keep up the good work, finishing off mosquitoes before they get a chance to do damage. According to one naturalist, a small bat can catch about 600 mosquito-sized insects per hour, and a large colony of bats will consume thousands of pounds of insects every night! (There are over 30 species of bats in Costa Rica.) Meanwhile, lizards, geckos and chameleons patrol the walls and corners of the houses, cleaning up cockroaches and water bugs before they have any chance to infest the kitchen or make a condominium out of your bathroom. The fearsome looking praying mantis lurks about the edges of the rooms, snapping up bugs that the lizards miss.

Not that insects can't make one suffer. Some very small creatures made my last trip to the Pacific beaches memorable for several weeks. These were the dreaded "no-see-ums," a generic name given to any tiny bug that bites without your knowing you are being attacked but make you suffer afterwards. In this case they were probably some kind of mini-sand flea because they got me on the ankles and lower legs. However, it was my own fault, I knew better than to stroll along the beach at dusk without repellent on my bare legs.

It's claimed that Costa Rica has more species of insects than anywhere else in the world, and I believe it. Once, in Cahuita—on the Caribbean coast—I was about to enter my cabin when I encountered an enormous beetle. It was about the size of a large teacup, shaped like a giant ladybug, but the color of an army helmet: olive drab. Feeling brave, I gingerly picked it up by its back, correctly figuring that its wicked-looking legs couldn't reach around the shell. I carried it to a nearby restaurant and showed it to the people sitting at the bar, figuring that my discovery would raise a few eyebrows. The bartender looked at my discovery with a bored expression as he remarked, "Yes, those little ones are females." It turned out that I was holding a rhinoceros beetle, possibly the largest bug of the entire insect world. They told me that the male, which fortunately I never happened to confront, grows to a length of 10 inches, sports enormous horns and is colored in brilliant metallic hues.

Earthquakes

All along the mountain chains that stretch from the tip of South America to Alaska, you will feel earthquakes. As a Californian, I've become accustomed to them, and seldom experience more than a slight feeling of excitement when windows start rattling and my desk sways a bit. We Californians expect to have several minor quakes a year, and every 75 years or so, a *big* one.

So it should come as no surprise that Costa Rica has its share of shakes and tremors, actually more than its share. The really big ones here are spaced by decades instead of generations. Yet, Costa Ricans are just as calm about earthquakes as are Californians. After all, compared with the 700 or so tornadoes that slam the midwestern and eastern parts of North America, claiming 80 to 100 victims each season, an occasional shaker seems relatively mild.

The last big tremor—a whopping 7.4 on the Richter Scale—hit the Caribbean coast near the city of Limón in April of 1991. Older structures suffered most damage, particularly those not constructed to modern-day standards. However, by the beginning of the tourist season, most of the damage had been repaired, hotels were operating, roads were open to traffic and tourism was going full blast. A few months after the quake, I visited Cahuita, not too far from the epicenter. Expecting to see a lot of damage and hear horror stories, I was delighted to learn that there were no fatalities and that, except for one major building (which had been made of non-reinforced cement), the town seemed almost unscathed. Cahuita construction is of wood, which may shake, rattle and roll, but doesn't usually tumble down.

Costa Rica's 7.4 shaker claimed about 40 lives, one of the worst ever. But compare this earthquake with the one in Iran the year before; it was 7.5 on the Richter Scale and killed over *50,000* victims. A horrible 6.9 quake in Armenia in 1989 killed 25,000 people; one in Costa Rica the following year was just as strong yet *nobody* was killed. Why the difference?

One answer to this question is construction methods. Costa Rican homes and businesses are designed with earthquakes in mind. Costa Rica has prohibited the use of adobe in constructing homes for more than eighty years. This is the only nation in the hemisphere with a ban on adobe, a material with a tendency to collapse and bury earthquake victims. Wood, reinforced concrete block or stressed cement is infinitely safer. Instead of picturesque tile roofs, which can crush inhabitants under tons of heavy beams and broken tile, most Costa Rican roofs are of ordinary-looking corrugated aluminum, plastic or iron. These lightweight roofs may slide about during a quake, but they won't collapse and kill people by burying them.

An interesting feature of the 1991 quake was an uplifting of the coastline. The force raised the land as much as five feet near the town of Puerto Limón and a foot-and-a-half at Puerto Viejo. Coral reefs are now dry land at the edge of surf where fishermen once hauled in crab, shrimp and red snapper. This lifting of the land from the sea is a wonderful example of how the Central American land bridge was formed some two or three million years ago when quake activity began pushing the land ever higher. Geologists find coral fossils on mountain tops now 3,000 feet above sea level.

Temperatures and rainfall for selected Costa Rican locations.

	Avg.	Jan.	Feb.	Mar.	Apr.	May	June	July	Aug.	Sept.	Oct.	Nov.	Dec.	Year
Alajuela	Highs	81	83	85	85	82	81	81	81	80	80	80	81	81
	Lows	62	62	63	63	64	64	64	63	63	63	63	63	63
	Rain	0.3"	0.5"	0.6"	3.3"	10.8"	10.8"	7.2"	10.3"	13.9"	13.6"	19.9"	1.2"	92"
Golfito	Highs	91	92	92	91	90	89	89	90	89	89	89	90	90
	Lows	71	72	73	73	73	72	71	71	71	71	71	71	72
	Rain	6.3"	5.8"	8.2"	11.2"	19.2"	17.8"	18.4"	22.3"	28.1"	28.1"	22.6"	11.8"	200"
Cahuita	Highs	86	86	87	87	87	87	86	86	87	87	86	86	86
	Lows	68	68	69	71	71	71	71	71	71	71	69	69	69
	Rain	12.7"	8.4"	8.2"	11.0"	11.3"	11.8"	17.1"	12.5"	5.8"	8.2"	15.6"	17.8"	140"
Nicoya	Highs	91	93	95	96	91	89	89	89	87	87	87	89	87
	Lows	69	71	71	73	73	71	71	71	71	71	69	69	71
	Rain	0.2"	0.4"	1.0"	2.8"	11.0"	13.0"	9.8"	12.2"	16.0"	16.3"	4.6"	1.0"	88"
Manuel Antonio	Highs	87	87	89	89	89	87	87	87	86	86	86	86	87
	Lows	69	69	71	71	71	71	69	69	71	71	71	69	71
	Rain	2.9"	1.4"	2.4"	7.0"	15.7"	17.3"	18.4"	19.1"	21.1"	25.8"	15.5"	6.8"	153"
San José	Highs	73	75	77	78	78	78	77	77	78	77	75	77	77
	Lows	59	59	60	60	62	62	67	62	60	60	60	59	62
	Rain	0.4"	0.2"	0.5"	1.8"	9.0"	11.5"	8.6"	10.0"	13.3"	13.3"	5.7"	1.6"	75"

Chapter Three

The Meseta Central

A mountain range starts near Costa Rica's border with Nicaragua and marches south until it crosses the Panamanian border. It's known as the *Cordillera*, a picturesque complex of high ridges, valleys, peaks and tablelands, perpetually

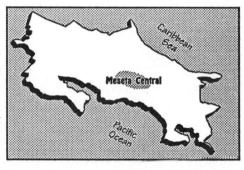

covered with green vegetation and teeming with wildlife. The mountains vary from rounded promontories to the rugged peaks of the Talamanca Range, dominated by 12,600-foot Cerro Chirripó. Valleys and rolling table lands are interspersed between steep mountains and volcanic formations, providing fertile agricultural space.

San José, the largest city in Costa Rica, nestles in a wide depression about halfway down the Cordillera, at an altitude of 3,750 feet above sea level. The city of 275,000 inhabitants is surrounded by dozens of satellite towns and villages, and with small cities such as Heredia, Alajuela, Escazú and Cartago perched at various elevations on the uneven plateau. About 15 miles wide by 40 miles long, this break in the mountains is called the *Valle Central* (Central Valley) or the *Meseta Central* (Central Plateau), depending on who is speaking. (In this book, I'll stick with *Meseta Central*.) From just about any point in this area you are treated to views of the high mountains that form a half-bowl around the Meseta Central. This is the place most folks live, and is the most heavily populated area in Central America.

The towns and villages that surround the capital have grown to the point that it is sometimes difficult to tell where exactly one ends and another begins. Although there is plenty of greenery and small farms scattered about, the Meseta Central blurs into a loose suburban complex.

Why so many choose to live in the Meseta Central is an easy question to answer: the climate is superb. This is the land of perpetual spring. San José's daily high temperatures are almost always in the 70s—creating newspaper headlines on occasions when the thermometer climbs into the 80s. Low temperatures are always in the 60s. Understand, these aren't *average* temperatures, which can give a distorted picture, but average high and low readings. Because Costa Rica is so close to the Equator, temperatures vary little between summer and winter.

Even this weather doesn't please everyone; some prefer temperatures in the 80s and even 90s, others feel more comfortable in the 60s and low 70s. Fortunately, in Costa Rica, it's possible to "fine-tune" your weather simply by moving a few kilometers in one direction or another. Temperatures and weather patterns are determined by altitude in the tropics; just a hundred feet more or less elevation makes a difference. A 15-minute drive from anywhere on the Meseta Central brings you to a slightly different climate, with more or less rainfall, warmer or cooler average temperatures. Each town or community brags of having the "best climate in the world." Each is right for at least someone. Alajuela is proud of being a few degrees warmer than San José, while Escazú is happy about being a few degrees cooler. Poas boasts about being even cooler than Escazú, and La Garita brags about its rating by *National Geographic* of having one of the three best climates in the world. The wonderful thing about all of this is that these choices, however so slight, are available for you to make. The weather chart at the end of Chapter Two illustrates this diversity of weather.

San José

San José, the capital and business center of Costa Rica, is a comfortable place to live despite its large population. Although the downtown streets throng with shoppers and automobiles, neighborhoods just a few blocks away can be tranquil residential areas. San José doesn't suffer from slum problems that plague many U.S. cities. There are modest neighborhoods, to be sure, but not the starkly depressing ghettos so apparent in the U.S.A. Truthfully, I've found few if any residential neighborhoods in San José where I would feel uncomfortable or ashamed to live. There is a slight smog problem, but very slight when compared to cities like Athens, Los Angeles or Rome.

As you might expect, the farther from the business center, the better the housing. However, this isn't because of a decaying city core, as is the case with most U.S. cities; it's because the center is taken up with businesses, hotels, restaurants and uncountable shops and stores. For some reason, people from all over the valley feel a compulsion do their shopping in downtown San José. This is mostly from habit and the fact that shopping is something of a social event. By the thousands, crowds of shoppers amble along the streets and avenues, checking out window displays, making purchases and gossiping with friends. Most could shop in their own communities and neighborhoods, but it's more fun this way. So many pedestrians pack the main downtown avenue (Avenida Central) that the city has been forced to turn part of it into a mall. During peak periods, pedestrians turn the rest of the downtown section into a virtual mall by filling the streets, forcing drivers to detour around Avenida Central.

Although just about any neighborhood in San José is comfortable, North Americans are predisposed to congregate in some of the more costly areas. This is understandable, since they tend to be more affluent than Costa Ricans and can better afford upbeat neighborhoods. The southern part of the city attracts a large percentage of foreign residents, particularly around the Sabana Sur area. Better supermarkets, nicer restaurants and amenities such as tennis clubs and parks make this a very livable part of the city. The *Tico Times* classified section always lists homes and condos for sale or rent here. Typically, rents for one-bedroom condos start around $350 and can go as high as $3,000 a month for a super-luxurious manor.

Other San José areas where North Americans choose to live are Cariari and Rohrmoser (very expensive), and Los Yoses and San Pedro (moderate). San Pedro has a university atmosphere with rentals ranging from $250 a month for an apartment to $600 for a large house. By shopping around, you can usually find places even more reasonable, and you must remember that ads in the *Tico Times* are directed toward North Americans who can afford to pay more. The less expensive places will be advertised in *La Nación*, where Ticos find their rentals. San José has several apartment complexes that rent furnished places by the day or week, that make excellent "base camps" while looking for permanent quarters or when trying out Costa Rica as a place to live.

Finding Your Way

Searching for an address in and around San José and its suburbs can be an exercise in frustration; few buildings have street numbers and no one pays attention to them when they do. Even worse, many streets have no names, or at least no street names posted on the corners. Suppose you are looking for the García residence, whose address is listed as: "From Caballo Blanco 250 mts. West, 300 South." In order to understand where this house is located, you need to know the location of a store called Caballo Blanco, then go two-and-a-half blocks (250 meters) to the west and then three blocks south (300 meters). At that point you need to ask someone which house belongs to the García family.

This confusion isn't restricted to residences; businesses use the same system. On maps, advertisements and business cards, the word *calle* is often abbreviated as "c", *avenida* as "a" and *central* as "ctl". The distance from a point is given in meters (abbreviated with an "m"), although sometimes people give it in *varas* instead of meters, both meaning a long pace or step about a yard long. A vara is technically a bit shorter than a meter, being just under our yard.

The address of the Hotel Presidente would be "c ctl, av 7-9," which translates "on Calle Central between Avenidas 7 and 9." The address of the bus terminal for Alajuela is "a 2, c 12-14," meaning "facing Avenida 2, between Calles 12 and 14." Directions and addresses can be vague to the point of impossible. This is particularly true away from the orderly grid of north-south, east-west streets. An address might be described as, "From the gasoline station, go 100 meters north and 75 varas to the east." *Which* gasoline station? My favorite address is on a real estate agent's business card. It says, "50 varas south from where the Mas Por Menos supermarket used to be."

Away from the City: Alajuela

Although many foreigners live in the city of San José, the majority prefer one of the smaller communities surrounding the city. These towns range from expensive to moderate places to live. For some mysterious reason, at least six of these towns have the same name—San Isidro—which adds to the confusion of finding your way about Costa Rica! San Antonio is another favorite place name which is scattered about like leaves in the wind.

One of the less expensive, yet pleasant places for foreigners to live, is Alajuela. Situated on the western side of San José, this small city is convenient to the airport, just a 20-minute ride from downtown San José. Clean, modern buses run every few minutes during the day, stopping at the airport on the way to and from San José.

Your first approach to Alajuela can give a misleading impression. The highway comes in on a higher level than the town, providing an unfortunate panorama of tin roofs in every direction; some new, some rusted, some painted red to resemble tile—but mostly of corrugated iron or aluminum. In the United States, a tin roof usually implies cheap construction, structures such as storage sheds or temporary buildings. But as explained in Chapter Two, this is earthquake country; those picturesque tile roofs can be deadly if they collapse. You may see occasional tile roofs, but you can be reassured that underneath all that pretty tile is a steel-reinforced concrete roof. Since the temperature never gets hot or cold, the insulation value of a heavy tile roof is beside the point.

Alajuela's focal point is a large park in the center of town (called the *Parque Central*, of course), a pleasant place shaded by tall trees, with chess boards built into some of the cement benches that surround the park. If you would like to meet North American retirees to ask information about Alajuela, this is the place to come; sometimes there seems as much English being spoken as Spanish. This is the place to find out about housing rentals, who is leaving for the States, who has a car for sale or who can recommend a gardener or a maid. A reputable money changer sits on a bench across from the bank in case you want to deal with him rather than stand in line. In the evenings, a mixture of classical and pop music can be heard by the park's bandstand where professional musicians entertain a couple of times a week.

A movie showing late run Hollywood movies faces the park as does an open-front restaurant where 80 percent of the conversations are in English. (Other common languages are German, Italian or French.) The restaurant is known as an information center—a place to find rooms or houses for rent, for the latest scoop on what's happening about town. It's operated by an

American ex-trucking company owner. Not far from the park is an excellent English-speaking dentist, a travel agency run by an ex-Floridian, and several real estate agencies with North American personnel.

One interesting business, which was in the process of opening its doors when I visited, is the Alajuela Welcome Center. Operated by two long-time Costa Rica residents, the partners offer to share their experience in agriculture, construction and property management with newcomers. The business is affiliated with a travel agency and real estate office. This might be a good place to stop for a preliminary overview of Alajuela as a place to live.

Alajuela has several rather attractive neighborhoods, none very expensive, yet classy in appearance. One area I inspected is called Trinidad, about a 15-minute walk from the park. My wife and I visited a man there who owns a very nice home with three bedrooms, two baths, a maid's room and a garage. When asked what the present-day value might be, the owner, a retired orchardist from Florida said, "I could replace this for about $20,000 in construction costs, but it's almost impossible to find another lot in this neighborhood. So I figure $35,000 would be a fair price." Another nice-looking neighborhood is near the local sports stadium, with prices even lower. All have nice landscaping, some with wrought iron fences.

Housing costs in Alajuela seem to be exceptional bargains, considering the quality of the area. Other places available during my last visit: a two-bedroom, two-bath home for $17,000 and a four-bedroom place for $30,000. An interesting aspect of Alajuela's housing market is that $200 a month can rent a satisfactory home, one that would sell for between $25,000 and $30,000. This raises the question: is it better to rent or to buy? Some local people are convinced that property will continue going up here, so they advise buying. Who knows?

Heredia

When I first started visiting Costa Rica, Heredia seemed to be located way out in the country—a small town with a scattering of nice homes with acreage on the outskirts. Today, the town has expanded toward the sprawl of San José, Alajuela and other nearby communities. The outskirts are still rural and countrified, but smaller homes have intruded between the large estates, somewhat filling in the openness of yesterday.

The center of Heredia, like its sister city of Alajuela, features a large, friendly central park complete with weekly band concerts. This park is shaded by stands of enormous mango trees and has the usual park benches for informal meetings and gossiping. Heredia doesn't attract as many foreign retirees and residents as does Alajuela, at least not in the central part of the city. The foreign community seems to be scattered in and around the city.

Heredia's famous market is quite large, with quality meats and exceptionally fresh vegetables, fruits and greens of all descriptions. Much of the market's exotic produce is grown by local residents in their back yards. Saturday is market day and selections are bountiful as well as fresh-picked. People from all over the valley come here for Saturday shopping. The market is near the Parque Central as is the old church, dating from the late 1700s.

From Heredia's northern edge, hills and mountains rise steadily toward the Poas volcano. All along these foothills are winding roads that travel past beautifully maintained homes, alternating with evergreen forests, small farms and verdant pastures. This is one of my favorite parts of the Meseta Central (I almost bought a coffee farm here a few years ago). As the roads climb higher into the mountains, temperatures become progressively cooler, thus allowing prospective home buyers and renters a precise adjustment in their environment. Some foreign residents live on small coffee farms here, with excellent views of the valley, and with orchards of citrus, avocados and tropical fruit supplementing truck gardens for home use and income. At the time I write these words in mid-1992, coffee prices are extremely depressed and unlikely to rise in the near future. This means that coffee-producing property should be somewhat lower in price; this is the time for serious bargaining. Incidentally, those foreigners who spend half the year in Costa Rica and the rest of their time in their home country are often anxious to rent their rural property in their absence to insure that someone will keep an eye on their place and protect it from vandalism. Some attractive rental deals can be worked out in these instances.

Other Towns and Villages

To the north, west and south of Heredia and Alajuela are several smaller towns and open stretches of countryside with small farms and beautiful homes set on several acres of grounds. Grecia, Atenas and La Garita are pleasant places which are gaining in popularity, particularly with foreigners who prefer cooler weather. Some folks are hard to please!

The road from Heredia to Turrucares is particularly striking, with lovely, high-quality homes interspersed with small, neatly kept farms and residences. Our taxi driver, who was renting his cab and services by the day, drove us there and proudly pointed out some of the prettiest homes along the way. "I was born in this area," he said proudly. And then, with a hint of sadness in his voice, said, "Of course it is too expensive for me to live here now."

For those who like to be near the big city, but who are so fussy that even Escazú temperatures are too warm, there is a cooler alternative where living is pleasant and heavy exhaust fumes from diesel buses seldom foul the air. This is the Poas area, up on the side of the mountain and volcanic crater of the same name.

To get to Poas, a winding, scenic road takes you past fields of strawberries and coffee, past comfortable houses with spectacular views. Along the way are roadside stands vending the specialties of the mountainside farms. Strawberries, enormous and sugar-sweet, are year-round treats here, displayed on stands along with homemade cheeses, candies and fresh veggies from back yard gardens. As you gain altitude, the air becomes cooler and slightly crisp. The panorama of the valley in the distance looks impressive indeed. The vegetation becomes even more lush; enormous plants with leaves six feet across hang over the roadside and flowering trees filter the sunshine overhead.

Finally the road tops a grade and enters the town of Poas. This is a quiet, middle-class town of workers, farmers and lately, an influx of North American *pensionados* and *rentistas*. Its unimposing, no-nonsense business center lacks spiffy boutiques and gourmet restaurants yet maintains a folksy, neighborly atmosphere with adequate commercial conveniences.

The Poas area isn't for everyone, only those who view temperatures over 70 degrees as beastly hot. If any place in the Meseta Central can be described as "the place of eternal spring," it would have to be the area around Poas. I've been told that temperatures almost never rise above 75 degrees, neither do they ever drop below 60, day or night, summer or winter.

Escazú

Only eight kilometers from San José, and 15 minutes or less driving time, depending upon traffic, the town of Escazú seems to be as far from the hustle and bustle of San José as one could imagine. Nestled at the base of a magnificent backdrop of mountains, Escazú has always drawn the affluent and those seeking peace away from the city. Somehow this area managed to preserve the peace and beauty of its agricultural past, yet provide a modern backdrop for suburban living. As one hotel advertises: "Close to the capital, but worlds away." Of all the suburbs where foreigners choose to live, Escazú is the most popular and well-stocked with English-speaking expatriates.

Three magnificent mountains tower over the town, the tallest, Cerro Rabo de Mico at 7,770 feet, and the most spectacular, Pico Blanco at 7,250 feet with a dramatic, sheer rock face which challenges the skill of many a mountain climber. Residential streets on the edge of town ascend the mountainside bravely, with each gain in altitude presenting an even better view.

The total population of the Escazú area is said to be 40,000, but it doesn't look nearly that large. It looks more like a sprawling village, with its cobblestone streets and quaint adobe buildings painted in a traditional two-color motif. Incidentally, the three-foot, colored stripe you'll see painted along the bottom of a house is believed to ward off evil spirits and witches. It must work, because I encountered few evil spirits or witches during any of my visits.

Escazú is effectively divided into three separate towns: San Miguel de Escazú, San Rafael de Escazú and San Antonio de

Escazú, each having its own church and patron saint. The red-domed church in San Miguel de Escazú was constructed in 1799 and has survived numerous earthquakes since. As San José grew and spread out, artists and those in search of serenity, began moving to Escazú. It is still the peaceful retreat of yesterday, retaining its reputation as an artists' colony as well as a retirement center. Escazú's higher elevation is ideally suited for those who think that San José's climate is too warm. It is also high enough that the occasional smog that touches the city remains far below. For this reason, an exceptionally large number of North Americans choose Escazú and the surrounding towns as their place of residence. Here is where the United States ambassador's home is located. Two famous country clubs provide the area with golf, tennis and a focal point for the country club set. Escazú is the center of much of Costa Rica's social life.

An odd-sounding place for newcomers to go for orientation and assistance, is Escazú's very active American Legion Post. This is the largest such entity outside of the United States, and is combined with VFW Post 11207, making it even larger. More than just a veterans' organization, this group reaches out to *all* foreigners and Costa Ricans, offering "a socially active, bilingual fellowship of warm, interesting, international people." You needn't be a Legion member or even a veteran to be welcome. A Lions Club, Rotary Club and several other service organizations also make their headquarters in this charming and picturesque setting. All of these organizations welcome visitors; the clubhouse is a must stop for newcomers seeking a welcome and introduction to the community of Escazú and neighboring town of Santa Ana. Clubs and charity associations are valuable windows of opportunity for making friends and building a network of social contacts.

Escazú (and its environs) has a sophistication that makes it stand out among San José's suburbs as a prestige address. Although it is admittedly one of the more expensive places to live, modestly priced homes and apartments are available throughout the community. Those who choose to live here say they wouldn't think of settling anywhere else. "We have the best of all worlds," explained a couple who owns a small house on the slope of Pico Blanco. "We live in the country, with a gorgeous view of the city below, yet we are just five minutes away from a supermarket, a good restaurant or whatever we need." They pointed out that although they are close to San José, they rarely go there on other than essential business. There are well-stocked supermarkets, fancy boutiques, doctors, dentists and a first class health clinic. Gourmet restaurants of all descriptions abound, including European, Barbecue, Chinese and even a Cajun restaurant for the yuppie trade.

Although new subdivisions seem to be continually underway on the fringes of town, the municipality requires that construction near the town's center conform to colonial or traditional style. Most buildings are one story, two story at most, fulfilling a sense of rural, Costa Rican countryside living.

"Property here is probably the most expensive of anywhere in the valley," explained one of Escazú's many real estate agents. "Everyone wants to live here. You can pay $80,000 and more for a nice three-bedroom home that you could buy for $45,000 elsewhere, but this is a quality area." He pointed out that there is no real "foreign colony" in Escazú where Gringos tend to gather together. Although there are several "sealed-in" developments—compounds with high walls and 24-hour guards—more folks live in ordinary homes or townhouses. A two- or three-bedroom condo in one of the exclusive compounds might start at around $80,000 and go up from there (way up), whereas a similar place in an ordinary building might start at $50,000. Those who choose to pay more for the security feel it is worth it, since they can comfortably leave their places unoccupied for months at a time while they return home for visits. Others rely on neighbors and friends to take care of things while they are gone.

Escazú is a great place to make your headquarters while exploring the Meseta Central. There are several nice hotels here, some as inexpensive as you can hope to find. We stayed a couple of times at a lovely inn high on the slopes of Pico Blanco, at a rate of $35, with a breathtaking view of the valley from each room. Several bed and breakfasts in Escazú are priced at $25 to $30 a night. Getting into San José and environs is easy, since bus service is frequent. The only problem could be getting home from the bus stop should your hotel, bed and breakfast or apartment sit high on the mountain (as ours did). Our solution is to walk downhill to catch the bus to San José and on the return trip, take the bus to the center of Escazú and then a taxi ride up to the hotel—at a cost of about a dollar for both of us.

Santa Ana

Another part of the Meseta Central that attracts North Americans residents is Santa Ana, a sunny mountain valley just another six kilometers to the west of Escazú. The altitude here is lower than either Escazú or San José, making it warmer and dryer. A number of small rivers cross the rolling valley and several mountains provide a scenic backdrop. Santa Ana's setting is also more rural than Escazú, with crops such as sugar cane, rice, beans and coffee growing all around this town of 20,000 residents. Roadside stands sell braids of garlic and onions, garden-fresh vegetables and jars of rich local honey. (Despite the killer bees' reputations, they produce high-quality honey and more of it than ordinary bees.) All roads converge upon a central area, giving Santa Ana the feeling of a downtown center, rural, yet sophisticated. High above the town on the mountain Cerro Pacacua is a 20,000-acre forest preserve and bird sanctuary, keeping nature ever-present in the ambience.

A few generations ago—before it became an easy thing to drive to the beach for vacations—San José's wealthy families maintained summer homes in Santa Ana. This was the place to spend weekends and school vacations, a place for the social upper crust to host parties and entertain lavishly. This old tradition left its traces on today's community, with an air of excellence readily apparent. Some of the most luxurious developments, complete with swimming pools, gardens and 24-hour guard security, are found here. This is the place for polo matches and international equestrian competitions.

Like its neighbor, Escazú, Santa Ana has its resident writers and artists. The town is particularly famous for ceramics, with production of excellent pieces a major industry with almost 30 workshops and 150 local people engaged in the art. Excellent restaurants, a first-class supermarket, and shopping of all description is at hand, eliminating the need to go to that outside world of downtown San José for odds and ends. Yet, when necessary, it's but an easy 10-mile drive.

Of all the Meseta Central retirement locations, this probably has the most potential for rapid development. The reason I believe this is that a planned extension of the road from the capital will soon hook up with Highway 34, which is the only route to two very popular beach communities: Jaco and Quepos. This will make Pacific beaches just an hour's drive from Santa Ana. The convenience will make the area even more attractive as a place to live, and real estate possibly a good investment.

San Isidro de General

At first glance, this town would seem to be a rather ordinary place for North Americans to choose as a place for residence or retirement. There is nothing spectacular about San Isidro de General; it is an ordinary Costa Rican town, neat, orderly, with the ubiquitous mountain views common to most of the country. Few vacationers ever visit San Isidro, and those who have passed through the town may get it mixed up with one of the other half-dozen San Isidros in the mountains. But those North Americans who have discovered San Isidro's secrets love living here. The climate is considerably warmer than San José, which suits some folks just fine, and the pace far slower. Being located on a wide ridge, and not far from the high peak of Cerro Chirripó, a continual breeze keeps the air clear and aromatic with flower blossom perfume. Daytime temperatures are pleasantly warm for my tastes (maybe hot for some folks), and evenings are tempered by cool air flowing down from Chirribó Peak. Although not as peaceful and idyllic as some other Costa Rican towns, once you are away from the main square—and the inevitable cars, motorcycles and trucks circling the square in search of a parking space—the pace slackens to a very peaceful stride.

Like most older Costa Rican towns, San Isidro features a main square in its center, the usual, well-kept park. Since the park is the social gathering place for local residents, it isn't surprising that the North American community uses it as their social focal point as well. The open-air restaurant of Hotel Chirripó faces the park, and at any given time, you can count on at least some of the tables being occupied by English-speaking patrons.

Real estate and rentals are exceptionally inexpensive here. I talked with one man who had just completed building a small, two-bedroom home, and was having trouble finding a tenant. He was offering to rent it for just $100 a month. Surprised at such a low rent, I asked, "Is this an average price?" The reply was, "No, if I waited a while, I might get $150, but I'm anxious to get someone in there to take care of it." Several North Americans have taken advantage of the climate and low-cost real estate, living on small farms on the outskirts of town, or along the highway toward the beach at Dominical. The views along this road are absolutely spectacular, with neat, prosperous-looking farms and picturesque homes in the mountain valleys below looking like toys along a model train set. At the time of my last visit, one American from Texas, who was married to a Tica lady, operated a motel, restaurant and bar on the highway, midway between San Isidro and the ocean.

Lake Arenal

The northern portion of the mountain chain, until recently ignored by North Americans, has one of the best potentials for growth of any place in Costa Rica. Certainly that's my opinion and one shared by many other 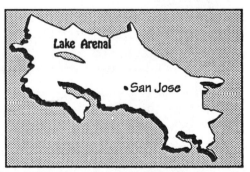 North Americans who are buying property around Lake Arenal as quickly (and quietly) as they can. Those who know about Lake Arenal would love to keep it a secret, but truth will out! The character of this region is so different from other parts of Costa Rica that it's difficult to believe you are in the same country.

The Lake Arenal district is in the upper end of the same mountain chain, but that's as far as the similarity with other highland areas goes. As I understand it, the mountains dip lower at this position in the chain to form a low break or window in the Cordillera. This interruption in the mountain ridges permits a reversal of wind patterns, allowing strong *easterly* winds to bring moist air off the Caribbean with an abundance of rain. There is no such thing as a *dry season* in the Arenal area; it's a year-round wonderland of greenness and lush vegetation. When I asked one long-time resident how much it rained, she replied, "On the average, about 14 months out of the year."

Before the government started to work to build a dam to create the wonderfully scenic lake, very few people lived here. The project required several thousand workers and support people and 16 years to complete. Roads were cut into the area, opening it up to Costa Rican settlers who started farms and small villages. After the lake was created, many workers elected to stay on in the company housing that was built during the construction stages. The population here is still very scanty, but it is growing daily, particularly in the numbers of foreigners who have "discovered" Lake Arenal.

To get there via paved road, the quickest way is by turning off the Pan American Highway at Cañas, an extremely hot, dry and dusty place during the dry summer season. Were it not for the ample irrigation water coming from Lake Arenal, Cañas would be more like a desert than a rich agricultural region. An air conditioned auto and lightweight clothing are necessities here. Yet just 18 kilometers away by a tortuously winding road, the air conditioner is shut off and car windows roll down to take advantage of the delightful fresh air.

By the time you reach the little town of Tilarán, only 23 kilometers from Cañas, a sweater might feel comfortable when the sky happens to be overcast. The countryside changes from pool table-flat to steep-sided hills, from dusty-dry to bright green. The road climbs gently now, as the fields seem to become greener with every curve, past fat cattle grazing fetlock-deep in richly grassed pastures and—where land hasn't been cleared for cattle or agriculture—some astonishingly heavy stands of tropical forest. Just about every imaginable kind of tropical tree or crop thrives here, from bananas to macadamia nuts.

Suddenly, the view of Lake Arenal bursts upon you, one of the prettiest lakes in the world. The fact that it is artificial is something that fades in importance when the total beauty is considered. Windsurfers claim this is the second-best place in all the world to enjoy their sport. What the first place is for windsurfers, I don't know, but it surely can't be any more beautiful than Lake Arenal.

Almost all residents in this area live on or near the drive that skirts Lake Arenal. The paved portion of the road has a scattering of European-type homes, chalets and an occasional commercial unit such as a *pulpería*, those community store-tavern combinations so common in rural Costa Rica. Most homes are obviously recently constructed, giving evidence of their newness in a developing land. This somehow doesn't seem like Costa Rica. Were it not for the colorful bougainvilleas, flowering oaks and luscious yellow Cortez trees, this countryside would look like an exaggerated version of the Tennessee or Kentucky hill country, or perhaps the lower elevations of Switzerland in the summer. Of course, the banana plants and broad-leaved philodendrons quickly dispel this notion.

A few neat, prosperous-looking villages are spaced along the highway, which has a surprisingly good paved surface. However, once you drive past the town of Arenal, the road turns into graded clay and occasional pavement—slow, with astonishing potholes the size of bathtubs rather than pots—but entirely passable in an ordinary rental car. If and when the government gets around to paving this stretch of road, the Arenal district will be quickly accessed from the Meseta Central, and should grow at an even faster rate. For those living or working in San José, this could be a wonderful site for a weekend getaway.

Arenal itself is a surprisingly prosperous-looking place, with neat little houses interspersed with expensive-looking ones. The town sits high on the sloping bank of Lake Arenal, with most homes and businesses situated with a lake view in mind. Streets are well-paved, and more are in the process of being paved in anticipation of a population explosion. Parts of town have an oddly unfinished look, with newly paved streets, vacant lots with neatly trimmed lawns, but just an occasional house. The center of town has the inevitable soccer field, but with spectator benches curiously pointed towards the street, away from the soccer field, as if the soccer team is so bad that locals would rather watch the traffic, scarce as it is.

Arenal obviously was a development planned by the government during the dam's construction phase. Many of today's homes here are left over from that era. Unlike the traditional Latin American residential style—built close together and against the sidewalk to allocate space for interior patios—Arenal homes have real *lawns*, ample and neatly mowed, looking much like a typical, affluent U.S. suburb! This adds greatly to Arenal's strange, non-Latin American look.

Because of the area's beauty, the temperate-tropical combination climate, and because of the low cost of real estate, Lake Arenal is undergoing a buying frenzy. Buyers from Canada, the United States and Europe are furtively looking at property and investing. Germans, Swiss and Italians appear to be the biggest sharks biting off chunks of the land as quickly as they can. They try not to appear eager as they snap up bargains, and they try their best to keep this place a secret, lest hordes of other foreigners descend upon paradise and ruin their scheme of being the only ones there.

Prices were astonishing at the time of my 1992 visit. A livable three-bedroom place, built of reinforced cement and stuccoed, looking very much like a California ranch house, could be bought for as little as one million colónes; that's just 7,300 U.S. dollars! A hectare of bare land with a view of the lake was going for about the same price. (A hectare is about two-and-a-half acres.) We looked at one place, one hectare with a small house for sale at two million colónes. It included an orchard with citrus and macadamia trees plus a productive truck garden. "You could keep a horse or a cow on this property," said the lady who had it for sale, "or you could do nothing but enjoy living there." The price was less than $30,000.

When asked if there were many North Americans living in Arenal, the lady indicated that yes, there were. When asked what they do here, she shrugged her shoulders and said, "They are here buying property, of course!"

Another example: I looked at a 6.5 hectare *finca* (about 16 acres) with two houses—one a four-bedroom cement home and the other a one-bedroom wooden place, suitable for a caretaker's cottage—and a chicken house-barn plus a lovely view of Lake Arenal. Half of the property was in coffee, with string beans planted between the rows of coffee trees. The other half was in pasture with six cows which each gave 25 bottles of milk per day. How the cows got the milk into the bottles was never explained, but they did seem very healthy and contented, standing knee-deep in rich green grass munching away. The asking price? $43,000!

I have the feeling that it's only a matter of time until prices will be bid up by foreigners as has happened along the Pacific coast from Nicaragua to Panama. But in the meantime, this is one of the few places where inexpensive waterfront property is still available. Another favorable circumstance: since this is lake front property, it doesn't fall under the complicated and restrictive laws that regulate ownership and construction by the ocean. You can build pretty much what you like and wherever you care to without fear that someday in the future the government will begin enforcing the coastal building laws more rigorously.

Windsurfing

Something sure to increase the development of tourism, business and residential growth is the lake's world-famous windsurfing. The best is on the western end of the lake, near the town of Tilarán. Aficionados from all over the world come here to brave the steady winds, choppy waves and icy water. "This is the cleanest water in the world," said one sportsman from Montreal. "You can drink it right out of the lake with no worries."

Because of the lake's growing fame, a large number of surfers come here in search of adventure, but find accommodations scarce. This creates a good climate for business opportunities and investment. Several North Americans operate windsurfing rental enterprises and I understand others are planning on constructing a hotel catering specially to windsurfers.

Chapter Four

Tropical Costa Rica

The same mountain chain that creates the delightful weather in Costa Rica's highlands further separates the country into eastern and western tropical zones. Because of this separation, the Caribbean and the Pacific zones have distinct personalities. Each side has its own boosters, those who wouldn't dream of living on the other side. The differences are not only in weather patterns, animals, plants and sea creatures, but marked cultural differences as well. The Caribbean is Jamaican, the Pacific is European.

These two tropical zones, combined with the temperate central plateau, define Costa Rica as a unique, exciting country. Tropics mean long stretches of deserted beaches with thick jungle hovering at the edge of the sand. It means monkeys jostling branches in the strangler fig trees while parrots, macaws and a thousand other birds screech, twitter and sing lyrically in the sunset. Costa Rica's tropics have all of this, and much more.

Caribbean Coast

The Caribbean coast has two distinct regions. Its southern portion, which is moderately populated, displays Jamaican and African influences blending with Costa Rican culture. The northern half of the coast

is almost uninhabited, visited mostly by fishing fanatics and ecology students. (Incidentally, Costa Ricans often refer to this coast as the "Atlantic" rather than the "Caribbean.")

The northern inland lagoons and waterways are famous for world-class fishing of all kinds. Record size tarpon and snook are routinely hooked in these scenic jungle rivers and inlets. Best snook angling is usually from the shore, around river mouths with 20 to 30 pounders not uncommon. Fishermen also bring in jacks, mackerel, barracuda, snapper and other species when fishing the Caribbean coast. While waiting for exciting action, you are treated to sights of monkeys frolicking in the trees, parrots, toucans, and sometimes an alligator or even a crocodile lurking along the shoreline. Tortuguero is known as an important nesting place of the endangered green sea turtle.

No roads enter this northern region; the only way you can get there is by airplane or motor launch. My belief is that it is far too isolated and the climate is too humid for much development other than ecotourism projects.

Limón Coast

This southern Caribbean coast attracts surfers, snorkelers and reggae enthusiasts as well as ordinary tourists and ecology buffs who want to savor the unique tropical environment. Weather patterns here are unpredictable, with no sharp distinction between winter and summer. Rain can fall at any time, and usually does. Winds often blow down from the north, sometimes causing the Caribbean coast to duplicate Miami's weather. I recall one time in Puerto Viejo, when Miami was suffering from one of those rare, orange-freezing winter storms. The frosty winds didn't linger in Miami, they blustered on down to Costa Rica's Caribbean coast. Unprepared for cold, I pulled on every piece of clothing I had with me, and shivered the night away huddled under a flimsy blanket. I had to keep reminding myself that I was in the Caribbean tropics and not in St. Paul, Minnesota. All the while, San José's weather was normal.

The plus side of the Caribbean weather is that things stay green and lush year round, unlike the Pacific coast. The down side is that it is always more humid and insects grow healthy and robust on this side of the continent.

The city of Limón, a two-and-a-half hour drive from San José, is where Columbus sighted the American mainland for the first time, back in 1502. Apparently he thought it was another island and didn't bother going ashore himself. (If Limón was as depressing back then as it is today, I understand why.) At best, Limón has always been a ramshackle affair—a tropical banana port, too large to have the charm of a village, yet too small to offer the amenities of a real city. To make matters worse, Limón still hasn't completely recovered from the big earthquake of 1991. Several damaged buildings are simply being ignored, and probably never will be repaired. Many other buildings look as if they are waiting for the next earthquake to come along so they can throw in the towel as well. To be truthful, most of Limón's buildings look ready to fall if someone should slam the door too hard.

Cahuita and Puerto Viejo

To find real charm along this shore, you must travel farther south along the paved highway that heads for the Panamanian border at Sixaola. As is the case all along the Caribbean shores, from Belize to Panama, many inhabitants are descendants of ex-slaves from the island of Jamaica. In Costa Rica, their ancestors came as construction workers on the railroad from Limón to San José in the late 1800s. Isolated from the European culture of the Meseta Central—partly because of the difficulty in traveling between the areas, and partly because of malaria and yellow fever quarantines—the coastal black people developed a unique Afro-Caribe culture, a combination of British Jamaica, Spanish Costa Rica and deepest Africa. Because English is the area's first language (spoken with a delightful British-Jamaican lilt), this area is favored by tourists and visitors who don't want to bother learning another language during their stay.

From San José, three-and-a-half hours of scenic driving brings you to the village of Cahuita. (It's about four hours by bus.) The village has a picture-book quality in its tropical Afro-Caribbean setting. Many houses stand on stilts to discourage insects, some buildings are painted bright colors similar to the style in Jamaica. Women and girls carry bundles on their heads with grace and enviable posture. The main road follows the shore, past black sand beaches and coral reefs to the north, and past more coral and beaches of yellow sand to the south. Along the yellow sand beach is Cahuita National Park, a 13-kilometer stretch of jungle complete with howler monkeys (which the locals call *congos*), feisty parrots and wildlife of all description. A foot trail parallels the beach through a thick tangle of tropical trees, vines and orchids. Butterflies, huge land crabs and iguanas keep you company on the hike. A trip to Costa Rica isn't complete until you have walked this trail.

Several North Americans live here year round, some operating successful businesses. Others regularly arrive in November and head home by April. I had the good fortune to meet a young California couple who invited me to visit their winter quarters in Cahuita. They lived in a picturesque, thatch-roofed cabin perched next to a coral reef and shaded by graceful coconut trees. Their house was very rustic and the furniture minimal, but they obviously enjoyed their winter home immensely. The surf washed at their front door, spilling into a small depression of smooth black rocks where children played as if in their own private swimming pool.

The Limón coast is particularly attractive for the younger set. A special emphasis is placed on youthful activities, with reggae music thumping loudly from tropical bars, with surfboards, snorkel gear and brief swimsuits the order of the day. People who love Cahuita or Puerto Viejo—Cahuita's sister village a few miles south—will tell you that the rest of Costa Rica is too tame for them; they prefer this movie-set tropical setting—romantic, picturesque and inexpensive. A bar in the very center of Cahuita features extraordinarily powerful loudspeakers on the front porch which blare Jamaican rock music day and night. The volume is such that it rattles windows a block away and peels the paint off of passing automobiles. I love to visit here, but for long-term living in the tropics, I much prefer the Pacific coast.

Pacific Coast

The Pacific coast is characterized by dryer winters, higher ocean surf from the open ocean and a much larger population of foreigners. Although most come from North America, a surprising number of Europeans are moving into the area. Many operate successful hotels and other tourist-oriented ventures which the business-friendly Costa Rican government makes possible.

This coast can be divided into three basic geographical sections: the Guanacaste-Nicoya Peninsula area in the north, the beaches from Jacó to Uvita in the middle, and the Golfo Dulce-Osa Peninsula area to the south. Each area has its boosters and aficionados who will assure you that there is no place in all of Central America as nice as their favorite location. I've seen them all and I can say that all are correct in believing as they do. Making a choice between them would be difficult indeed.

A nice feature of all these tropical beach areas is that they are accessible from the Meseta Central, within a day's drive by bus or automobile, and a few minutes away by airplane. Some locations require longer driving times than others, but as pavement replaces gravel roads, travel time will decrease.

Certain areas are highly developed, focusing on tourism, with discos, restaurants and boutiques as well as expensive hotels and homes. Other places are oriented toward permanent and semi-permanent residents, including many retirees. Still other locations are almost totally deserted with no facilities other than what you carry with you. Bring camping equipment if you care to; camping is permitted on all of Costa Rica's beaches except for parks and residential areas. The law considers the first 50 meters of beach land public property. Costa Ricans take full advantage of camping, and during the traditional summer vacation period (January and February) you'll see a multitude of tents lining the beaches as families enjoy economical vacations.

Eastward from the ocean's surf, rolling hills of forest and farmlands spread inland and up the mountain slopes, becoming steeper and more picturesque with each kilometer. Much of this land is wilderness, traversed by occasional dirt roads that become quagmires in the rainy season. Despite the isolation and transportation difficulties, foreigners find these rustic sections to be exceptionally desirable places to live. As the government gradually paves the roads along the coast and into the interior, more and more settlers will surely swell the ranks of North Americans and Europeans who live here and operate businesses. With easy access, property values ought to increase dramatically.

Guanacaste's Pacific Coast

A number of important beach locations on the northern coast attract Costa Ricans and foreigners alike for vacations, retirement or business opportunities. These beaches are easily reached from San José in about four hours of driving. The highway is paved and in generally good condition (if you discount the ever-present potholes), but can be agonizingly slow when you are stacked up behind a string of slow trucks. Relax, go with the flow and enjoy the sights and the ever-changing scenery from the Meseta Central to the Guanacaste coast. Rainfall is lower here than anywhere else in the country. Unlike most of Costa Rica, the dry season here is truly dry, with almost no rain falling during the months of December, January or February. Grass turns parched and yellow; most trees lose their leaves replacing them with blossoms. Around homes or along inhabited beaches, you'll see more evergreen, leafy trees because they've been deliberately planted.

Playas del Coco

A quickly developing complex of *playas* (beaches) begins at Playa Panama, and stretches south through Playa Hermosa, Playas del Coco and ending at Playa Ocotal. The prettiest beach in this complex, and the one with the most potential (from my viewpoint) is Playa Hermosa. (*Hermosa* means "beautiful" in Spanish and Playa Hermosa lives up to its name.) This is a lovely place, with a curving shoreline of clean sand and a peninsula which shields

it from the open ocean and dangerous riptides. Development lags way behind nearby Playas del Coco, the most commercially developed of all the beach communities. Since the pavement ends in the center of El Coco, tourists tend to stay here rather than braving annoying stretches of washboard gravel roads to get to nearby beaches. In contrast with neighboring communities, which are sleepy and tranquil, Playas del Coco restaurants, bars and discos stay open all night on weekends, with happy people singing and shouting in exuberance all night long. (It seemed that way to me one weekend when I was trying to catch up on my sleep!)

Playas del Coco is a fun place to be, and a possibility for business opportunities. At least 30 North Americans live here. But for retirement or quiet, long term vacations, I might choose one of the other places. A number of North Americans have houses along the fringes of the quieter beaches. I understand that several North American families live in Hermosa Beach and more are in the planning stages of building. Italians and Germans seem to like it here, as well.

One resident, a retired air force sergeant, related his reasons for settling here. First of all, he bought ten acres (by mail) before he retired from the military. Then, before he had the chance to visit the property, he received a letter offering to trade the ten acres for one-and-one-half acres of jojoba bean property. This seemed to be a good deal, so he signed the papers for a trade; again, all by mail. When he finally retired and arrived in Costa Rica to claim his jojoba bean plantation, he discovered that jojoba beans don't grow in that area, and furthermore, the property was not only inaccessible by automobile, it had a Nicaraguan family living on it who were not inclined to move simply because the owner wanted them to. While he was looking for a way to visit his jojoba bean farm, he fell in love with a Costa Rican lady and got married. He forgot about his jojoba bean fiasco and settled down in his wife's village. "Now I have a seven year-old daughter, a house in a village where I am the only Gringo, and I have a good life. My army pension is only $855 a month, but I live like a king." He has a part-time job at a Canadian-operated hotel as night watchman to supplement his pension. "The only thing I don't like about being a night watchman," he said plaintively, "is weekends when party people make so much noise I can't sleep." He was right; they kept me awake too.

There can be no question about Coco's potential for business, retirement or long-term living. Several very successful, American-owned enterprises operate here, and more are on the way. But if I don't sound particularly enthusiastic about the place, it's probably because here is where I locked my keys in my rental car and struggled for two hours in the hot sun before figuring out a way to get inside without breaking a window. A good car thief could have done it in less than 20 seconds. One of the most horrible sights in the world is a set of ignition keys hanging in a locked rental car.

A few kilometers to the south is Playa Ocotal, a place that maintains a true village atmosphere despite also having a deluxe tourist resort. The accommodations are tastefully done to blend in with the natural surroundings. The village is on the shore of Bahía Pez Vela (Sailfish Bay), and the fishing is said to live up to the bay's name.

Flamingo Beach

The next beach complex is just a few kilometers south as the crow flies. But since there is no connecting road, unless you can fly like a crow, you must return to the paved road and make a wide loop on paved and dirt roads—a 65 or 70-kilometer drive. This array of beaches starts with Playa Pan de Azucar, and continues south to Playa Tamarindo, including the beaches of La Penca, Potrero, Flamingo, Brasilito, Conchal, Playa Grande, Tamarindo and Langosta, in that order.

By far, the prettiest is Playa Flamingo. A wide, curving beach of white sand, with startling blue waves turning to white-capped rollers before crashing loudly against the shore, creates one of the prettiest beaches imaginable. Hotels here cater to affluent tourists who can afford to fly in from San José and spend $120 a day for rooms. Ordinary budget tourists will find few (if any) reasonably priced rooms.

As you might guess, North Americans have taken over this beach, and have built some very nice homes. Some private homes offer rooms for rent, and probably do well, for there were absolutely no vacancies in town when I visited here last. Most of the non-developed beachfront is also owned by foreigners. However, local authorities have done well in keeping the first 50 meters open, with unlimited public access.

The beach adjacent to Flamingo is Brasilito. At this time, it is mostly an inexpensive place for Ticos to come and enjoy themselves. It's also a place to look for an inexpensive cabina or a room, although very few foreigners seem to do so. The beach isn't bad at all; I'm surprised there isn't more commercial development. The next village is at Playa Conchal. The Spanish word *Conchal* refers to the shells on the beach. In fact, the entire beach is composed of tiny, water-worn shells instead of sand. Although very undeveloped today, a planned 5,000-room resort could change all of that, should it really happen!

Turtles and Tourists

An excellent example of how tourism and conservation can work hand in hand is found to the south of the Flamingo beach complex. Starting at Playa Grande and continuing south past Playa Tamarindo, a broad, sandy beach serves as nesting grounds for endangered Leatherback turtles. It used to be that local residents awaited the arrival of these huge, prehistoric survivors, and collected the eggs in buckets as they were being deposited, and sold the harvest to bars and restaurants all over the country.

Alarmed by the possibility of the turtles' extinction, the Costa Rican government instituted a model conservation program. Local people were enlisted to help protect the nesting grounds. Jobs for guards and guides to direct tourists through the nesting grounds put local people to work. Hotels and restaurants opened to take care of the growing number of tourists. Even more local residents found jobs. This boom has only begun; future development seems inevitable.

Some conservationists have mixed feelings about this program. While they praise the protection of the nesting grounds, they point out that the extra tourist foot traffic causes damage by visitors inadvertently stepping on the hatchlings. On the other hand, the number of baby turtles killed in this manner is nothing when compared with the ones which used to end up as a tasty *boca* in some San José bar.

Playa Grande

Turtles need a wide, sandy beach with ample portions not touched by high tide; Playa Grande fills these requirements admirably. It's long, unpopulated, with few human footprints to disturb the solitude. A few homes and one or two small hotels have sprung up along the northern part, but nothing like the construction underway on other west coast beaches. As a part of Tamarindo Refuge, the area will always be somewhat restricted in tourist development, even though the natural beauty and wildness of the area is bound to attract more people in the future.

I looked at a small development (about a half-dozen luxury homes) on beachfront lots which are supposedly "grandfathered," or titled before restrictions were placed on the beach. One place was for sale, a large, tastefully constructed home with a neatly manicured lawn ending at a beach wall marking the 50-meter boundary. Priced at $235,000, it would seem high for Costa Rica, yet the gorgeous location made it worth every dollar. The owner half-apologized for the home's isolation and lack of anything to do, adding, "The hope of this little community is that things *won't* change. What we offer here is location, nothing else." He indicated the broad expanse of beach visible through a stand of coconut trees, and said, "The whole idea here is to fit into the ecology without disturbing things, particularly not the nesting turtles and their life cycle." The house's window frames were made of wood instead of the more practical aluminum, "because metal frames reflect moonlight and confuse the hatchling Leatherbacks. We don't allow any lights from our homes to escape at night. For bright lights and nightlife you have to go to Tamarindo."

Playa Tamarindo

Tamarindo Beach begins where Playa Grande ends, with a picturesque estuary separating the two. Tamarindo is where most turtle-watchers find hotels. Launches begin ferrying passengers across the estuary about midnight. Tourists tiptoe quietly along the beach and pause to observe the huge turtles as they awkwardly pull themselves up on the beach to bury their eggs six feet deep in the sand. This is an unforgettable sight; some of these turtles are more than 12 feet long and weigh up to 1,500 pounds! The one I watched laying eggs must have been a pygmy; she was barely eight feet across. Our guide claimed that during the peak of the season as many as 350 turtles can be on the beach in a single night.

The village of Tamarindo is a perfect example of foreign development. Almost every business—restaurants, hotels, boutiques, bars and so forth—appear to be owned by Canadians, Americans, Italians, or Swiss. The influx of foreign money and the resulting buying frenzy has pushed the price of most properties into the range of the ridiculous. According to local Ticos, the asking price for a lot (not a hectare, but a lot) can top $50,000! There seems to be no end to the buying and selling, constantly jacking up prices.

The emphasis here in Tamarindo is strictly on foreign tourism. I find this a little disturbing; native Costa Ricans are being left out of the picture. Few Tico families can afford to pay the $60 or more that hotels demand, and the price of real estate makes property ownership impossible. Several local people expressed a concern over this trend, saying, "We keep selling our land and moving farther back into the hills. We end up working for foreigners on land we once owned. Before long, we won't be able to afford to live in our own village any more!"

Several real estate developments are either underway or completed in this area, plus some private houses for sale. Personally, I wouldn't be interested in them for a number of reasons. But you need to visit, see for yourself and make your own decisions on this.

Beaches of Nosara

About 35 kilometers south of the Tamarindo-Flamingo area is an area with a different developmental emphasis: the beaches of Nosara. Starting at Playa Ostional—a turtle-nesting beach and wildlife refuge for Ridley turtles—a string of lovely beaches and wildlife reserves extends south to Playa Guiones. Property owners here are attempting to keep this portion of the coast residential as they shun commercial development as much as possible.

It all began about 25 years ago when an American investor purchased a huge tract of forest and beach and decided to develop the property in such a way as to preserve its natural beauty and wildlife resources. He developed a plan to market about 500 lots, each set into its own part of the wilderness. Almost all buyers were from the United States or Canada; they loved the isolation and the idea of preserving beaches, forest and animals.

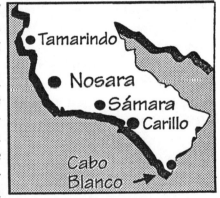

Things were going well until a few years ago, when the original developer unexpectedly dropped out of the picture (an income tax problem in the States, as I understand it). Residents feared the area could turn commercial like Sámara Beach farther to the south. They formed a property owners organization, totally committed to protecting their surroundings. They've convinced the government to dedicate portions of the land to wildlife and nature reserves and are offering to donate even more land. Together, property owners work diligently to keep commercial development to a minimum.

Michael Landweg, a Tico from San José, was hired to manage the association, and in turn he hired a staff of guards and caretakers. He said, "Can you imagine what this place would look like if we cut down all these trees to put up cabinas, bars and cheap restaurants?" The association has spent over $10,000 in legal fees, even taking a case to the Supreme Court, in an effort to keep Nosara natural.

"One major problem we have is that newcomers aren't as ecologically conscious as the original owners, " Michael said. "Over the past 20 years many of the original owners have died, grown old or lost interest. So we try to educate newcomers about the treasures we have here, about the importance of not cutting down the trees or destroying our animals' habitat." He explained how the monkeys have regular "trails" through the treetops that they use daily to go from one feeding area to another. When the trail is broken by clearing some of the trees, the monkeys are forced to move away.

I was invited to sit in on a property owners meeting. It was interesting to listen to the kind of problems they considered relevant. Their largest concern, second only to taking care of Nosara's natural beauty, was maintaining good relations with the Tico community. For example, members voiced a fear that outsiders from the United States or Canada might open stores in competition with the local businesses, which could make things difficult for the Tico, family-operated places. About 200 members belong to the association, accounting for 30 percent of the foreign residents in the area.

Conservation Pays Off

It's interesting to compare this area with the resort area of Sámara, just 25 kilometers to the south. There, the natural vegetation has been stripped away to make room for commercial projects. What is left is burned off every dry season to make room for new plant cover the following rainy season. Native plants, those specially adapted to this climate, no longer exist; they've been crowded out by plants whose natural winter state is to lie dormant or by those whose seeds resist fire.

But in Nosara, tall native trees and shrubbery shade the ground, conserving water during the dry season. This keeps vegetation green the year around. Unlike dusty Sámara Beach, Nosara's landscape is covered with native grasses, bushes and vines, all uniquely adapted and suited to this environment.

Nosara Real Estate

Because commercial development in Nosara is still in its infancy, property prices haven't skyrocketed as they have in Tamarindo Beach and other places along the coast. I discussed this with Paulina Anderson, who manages property for the Association and helps people sell their real estate when they move away. She said that at any given time, about 50 lots are up for resale as well as a few houses. Prices ranged from $8,000 to $25,000 for a lot of one or two acres. Actually, I was tempted to buy when I looked at two one-acre parcels at a price of $35,000 for both. They sat on a hill overlooking the ocean with the rear half of the property descending into a ravine that was populated with parrots, howler monkeys and coatis. Construction costs for a reinforced cement, two-bedroom home would have been between $20,000 and $35,000, depending on the extra amenities. I next looked at a completed home, a lovely place with a gorgeous view of ocean surf about 400 meters away with neatly landscaped grounds, for $115,000.

A surprising find is an Italian-owned beach resort which occupies a beautiful little bay at Punta Garza. Called the Villagio, it is elegant to the nth degree, with a tremendous amount of money invested. Complete with gourmet restaurants, swimming pools and even a gambling casino, it seems absurdly incongruent in such a lonely and rustic setting.

Cabo Blanco

South of the Nosara area is a long string of beaches with tremendous potential. It runs from the middle of the peninsula to Cabo Blanco at the very tip of the peninsula and then around the blunt end. A friend claims that, "Puerto Carrillo has the best and safest beach "between Los Angeles and Tierra del Fuego." Most investors agree that the developmental potential between Cabo Velas and Cabo Blanco is among the best in the country.

Getting to this area by land has always been a problem. The paved highway abruptly ends at the little town of Carmona, presenting about a 30-kilometer stretch of dirt road to the coast.

The road paralleling the coast dwindles to a trail from time to time and you have to ford several good-size streams. An easier way is to take a ferry from Puntarenas to Playa Naranjo which shortens the drive somewhat, but the roads are still bad.

But conditions are changing. For better or worse, progress is coming to the Cabo Blanco area in the form of a huge construction project at Playa Tambor, funded by a Spanish corporation. They plan on constructing up to 1,500 rooms. To encourage the development, the Costa Rican government has agreed to construct a new ferry terminal to bring tourists from Puntarena, to pave the road to the hotel and to construct housing for workers who will be working on the project and later will be employees of the resort.

I say for better or worse, because the Spanish construction crews immediately began filling in the mangrove wildlife preserves and leveling a mountaintop. According to some ecologists, they are destroying the natural wonderland that they came to exploit. At the time of writing this book, legal proceedings are underway against the project, and complaints have been lodged against local authorities for not enforcing regulations more strictly.

Regardless of whether the Cabo Blanco project is successful, the rest of the area is ready for less ambitious development. Costa Rica doesn't have more enthusiastic or optimistic supporters than those property owners on this part of the Nicoya Peninsula.

Costa Rica's Gold Coast

If there is any place in Costa Rica deserving of the title "Gold Coast," it would have to be that stretch of beachfront from Jacó to Quepos, and even beyond to Dominical. This is not to say that this area in any way resembles Mexico's famous resort-studded Gold Coast (from Mazatlán to Acapulco) or Florida's Gold Coast of spiffy hotels and first-class resorts. Except for a few elegant developments, this beach front area would seem rather ordinary to anyone who has seen the *real* gold coasts of the world.

This coast is just now undergoing an evolution that some day could place it in competition as a world-class resort area. Although pretty beaches line both sides of Costa Rica, these particular ones are most convenient for residents of the populous Meseta Central. Just a short drive or bus ride makes this coast very accessible for a short weekend trip. A weekend place here is convenient and usable by family and friends, whereas one that requires a five-hour drive over bad roads will sit vacant most of the year. When the main route has been paved and time-saving shortcuts completed, a drive from Escazú or other suburbs will take but an hour or less.

Playa Jacó and Playa Herradura

Because they are the easiest to reach from the Meseta Central, the most popular places for ocean swimming and weekends at the beach are at Jacó or Herradura. It's possible to drive down in the morning, enjoy the surf and return home for supper.

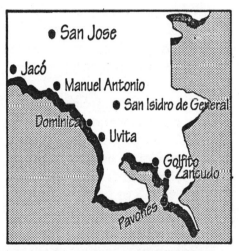

Playa Herradura is smaller than Jacó, enjoys gentler surf and has more shade trees. Five minutes farther down the coast highway, Jacó offers more amenities and places to stay than Herradura, but with rather dangerous surf. Unless you are used to handling riptides, you should be cautious here. Neither of these places are loaded with glamour or elegance, but I'm predicting that in the future they will be. In the meantime, Jacó and Herradura offer economical hotels and weekend homes for highland residents. Many lots within walking distance of the beach are for sale, and construction is booming.

Manuel Antonio

It was the middle of February, and I was sitting with a group of friends in a restaurant overlooking the Pacific. A long, palm-fringed beach stretched out into the distance as far as we could see. Behind us loomed mountains covered with virgin rain forest, sweeping down to accent the beach with its azure-blue water and sparkling surf. The sun was at its zenith and beating directly down with dazzling strength. Two members of our group were complaining about the heat. We consulted a thermometer and found that the temperature was 85 degrees. Suddenly they broke into laughter as they realized that Baltimore, their home town, was buried under four inches of sleet and snow. Two weeks of Costa Rica's idyllic weather had turned them into indignant complainers over an ordinary 85-degree day at the beach! We all ordered a cold beer served over ice cubes (a summer tradition here) and looked out over the panorama with renewed appreciation for where we were: Costa Rica's famous Playa Manuel Antonio.

Doesn't that seem to be an odd name for a beach? According to legend, a husband, worried about his pregnant wife, placed her in a dugout canoe and headed north for Puntarenas, hoping to find a doctor to help her. But before they could go very far, the wife went into labor and they paddled ashore to camp in the shelter of the protected beach. She gave birth to a healthy child whom they named Manuel Antonio, and the beach has been called that ever since.

Travelers who have visited beaches all over the world swear that Manuel Antonio is the most beautiful of all. The coastline north of Manuel Antonio is a long beach of golden sand that catches the full force of the Pacific's waves as they roll in from China. Then at Manuel Antonio park, a narrow peninsula juts out into the ocean, curving about to form two protected coves on either side of the land. The waves suddenly become gentle. You'll usually find a sailboat or two anchored here, gently swaying, resting on the way to the Panama Canal or for the big voyage north to Acapulco.

Originally United Fruit Company banana property, the area was made into a national park in 1972 with almost 700 hectares of land, partially expropriated, partially donated. The park contains three beaches, each with its own character. The first is Playa Espadilla Norte which is famous for its riptides—although many people swim here anyway. Next is Playa Espadilla Sur and then Playa Manuel Antonio, both quite safe for swimming and snorkeling. From the beginning, the emphasis has been on preserving the natural beauty and protection of wildlife. A band of red monkeys used to frequent the treetops along the peninsula, often coming here to bed down for the evening. I haven't seen them during my past two trips, but some say the monkeys are still here.

One of the earlier tourist developments, Manuel Antonio soon became a popular place for retirement and vacation homes, hotels and restaurants. Nowadays, new construction must be connected with tourism in some manner, cannot be over three stories high and must provide a minimum of three times the square footage of green space for each foot of building. To satisfy the requirement that development is tourist-related, several North Americans have built places with rooms or apartments which can be rented out to tourists; they keep an especially nice apartment as their living quarters.

Since Manuel Antonio's fame makes it an almost obligatory part of a tourist's itinerary, a bed and breakfast or room rentals can be a very viable business. Rooms will likely be rented solidly through the summer (December, January and February) and have low vacancy rates during the rest of the year. On my last trip, we rented an apartment from a lady who came from Florida 18 years ago, to build a small house for herself. She added a couple of rooms for extra income during the tourist season. As the volume of tourism during the off season increased, she added more rooms, until she now has a pleasant 10-room hotel plus two apartments across the road, all with a splendid view of the ocean. "I hadn't considered becoming a hotel owner when I came here," she explained, "it just happened to work out that way."

Although many people love this area and wouldn't live else-where, I have to admit that Manuel Antonio doesn't hold my fascination as it once did. With more and more commercial development, it loses some of its charm and pristine quality. During my first visit, I would often be the only person on the beach. But I keep telling myself: Manuel Antonio was created for everyone, not just for me alone. It doesn't seem fair, but the real world is seldom fair.

South of Manuel Antonio, the road is badly in need of pavement. When paving happens, you can be sure development will zoom. As with most of the coast, few bargains are to be found right on the beach, since North Americans and other foreigners have long ago bought up the land, yet something always is for sale as previous owners decide to take their profits and run.

Dominical

South of Quepos and Manuel Antonio—over another 40 miles of gravel surface—is another of those "undiscovered" places I feel has great potential for retirement and/or investment. First of all, plans are in the works to complete the pavement from Jacó Beach all the way to Palmar Norte, thus opening this section to traffic from three directions. Buses travel this route now, and it's possible to drive it in a rental car, but it is slow going and hard on equipment. Once paved roads are in place, you are going to see a steady stream of traffic cruising along the beach—tourists looking for rooms and retirees buying property. The village of Dominical and its surrounding communities can't help but flourish. However, many residents prefer it the way it is today; they dread the thought of resorts and hotels that will destroy the peace and tranquility that has been theirs for so long. But the road crews are already at work; it is too late for anything but anguish. As one man said, "It will seem funny to think that in a few years we'll be looking back fondly to the time when there were no traffic lights here."

Dominical is best reached by traveling south on the Pan American Highway and turning toward the Pacific at San Isidro General; just follow the signs through town. Because of San Isidro's system of one-way streets, you may have to ask directions by pointing in whichever direction you are going and asking "Dominical?" Someone will steer you right.

This road is one of the most scenic in all of Costa Rica. The narrow, paved highway traverses rich farming country, up somewhat steep grades and runs along ridges with breathtaking views on both sides of the road, looking into deep valleys where the farm houses are so distant they seem like toys. Even during the dry season, the countryside here is lushly green with trees heavy with foliage and banana trees shading the roadside. Although the drive is less than 25 miles, it takes about 45 minutes. That's the way it should be, because the scenery is so spectacular that you might miss something if you could whiz along at 100 kph. Also, the pavement has a way of disappearing from time to time, turning into stretches of gravel road where construction crews are still at work. The problem is not serious, just slow down and relax.

The paved highway ends at the gravel and cobblestone coastal road at the Barú River, a picturesque mountain stream which empties into a lagoon at this point. A turn to the left, over the river's new cement bridge and you are at Playa Dominical. Take the first right turn past the bridge. This is not a town—even though it may appear as such on the map; it's a collection of cabinas, private homes and a handful of restaurants, sometimes almost hidden behind tropical vegetation.

Dominical's main street (there are only a couple of streets here) follows the river, past several rental cabins and businesses, then ends at the beach where another road follows the beach down to Punta Banda. Camping beneath a grove of shade trees is free and your tent is just feet from the broad, sandy beach of Playa Dominical. Restrooms and showers are strategically spaced along the beach. The surf is spectacular, booming in on the sand but swimming is dangerous here, with riptides to harass those not used to handling them. "You usually don't realize what is happening," said Richard Dale, the owner of Auberge Willdale, a set of cabinas where we were staying. "It seems as if you are staying still in the water, but the beach is moving away from you. We lose a couple of tourists every year to these tides, and it isn't necessary. Instead of frantically trying to swim against the current, the best thing to do is to relax and wait until the beach stops moving away, and then leisurely begin swimming parallel to the beach, stopping to float once in a while to rest, and then begin working your way back to shore. The water is so warm and so salty that you can float all day long and never get tired. There is no reason for anyone to drown in a riptide."

Serenity and calm at Playa Dominical and Playa Barú make this a great place to spend the winter, away from the ice and snow of northern climes. Many people do just that. Prices are particularly affordable if one doesn't need an ocean view. A visitor from the Yukon, a man who has been coming here for several years, was very excited as he described the house he was buying in a nearby village for $18,000. It was a brand new, two-bedroom place on three hectares of land. "To make sure everything is all right, I agreed to rent it for two months. At the end of that time, if the house is satisfactory, I'll go ahead and buy it."

A couple from New York invited me to look at their rental home for which they paid $300 a month rent. "If we took a one-year lease, the owner said we could have it for $200." An American oil worker, who has worked and traveled all over the world, decided Dominical is the place to settle down. He was in the process of constructing a bakery and was learning how to handle Costa Rican workers. "I have good employees and they work very hard, but sometimes they drive me wild. The other day, I had to go out of town and when I returned, the workers had built a wall where there wasn't supposed to be a wall." They were busily dismantling cement blocks from the wall as we talked.

Every night a couple of the restaurants break the tranquility with loud stereo music as they try to attract customers. Since surfing is said to be the second best in Costa Rica, there are always a few sunburned, salt-soaked revelers to join the more sedate patrons of these "night clubs" in hoisting a cold *cerveza Imperial*. The music doesn't last long, however, since early-to-bed is the norm here.

Unusual Climate

Dominical and surrounding villages sit right on the water's edge, and rainfall is about the same as in other coastal towns to the north or the south. Logically, Dominical's climate should also be similar: hot days and warm evenings. But this is not the case. Mornings and evenings are much cooler, and even during the middle of the day pleasant breezes come in from across the ocean.

At night temperatures drop into a delightful range, making it possible to sleep without an air conditioner.

Don't misunderstand, the climate here isn't like the Meseta Central, but it is considerably cooler than most parts of the coast. This is due to an odd juxtaposition of geographical features. Not far from the beach, mountain slopes start climbing sharply from the flat shelf of land that borders the ocean. They swoop higher and higher until they reach Costa Rica's highest point: Chirripó peak. During daylight hours, the sun beats down on that narrow strip of land between the ocean and the mountain slopes, heating the air, causing it to rise. As the warm air flows upward along the mountain's face, cooler air is continually pulled in from the ocean. Then in the evening, when the sun's heating action stops, cool air from the high peaks descends (cool being heavier than warm), reversing the direction of the breeze, pushing the humid, muggy air out to sea.

Points South

South of Dominical, as far as the village of Uvita, numerous beaches flank the shore, some with houses or tiny farms, places which will someday become villages. One of the prettiest on this part of the coast is called Punta Dominical. A high point juts out into the ocean with cliffs and surf reminiscent of California's Big Sur or Spain's Costa Brava. Below a small hotel, cliffs and rocks catch the full force of the ocean's strength as waves crash and send cascades of white foam flying high in the air. This is worth a visit if only to dine on pan-fried red snapper as you gaze out on the scene. The hotel only has six cabins, and the owners can't obtain permission to construct any more. The cabins are rustic, with fabulous views, but are worth the effort to book them far in advance.

All along this coast, as far south as Uvita (18 kilometers south of Dominical) the land seems to be owned exclusively by North Americans, and they don't appear to be particularly anxious to sell. Occasionally a beachfront property can be found, but at highly inflated prices. Affordable property is found away from the beach where Ticos have land for sale. I looked at one parcel in Uvita, about a kilometer from the beach, five hectares of land (12 acres) with a nice house (comfortable but not luxurious) for only $15,000. There were many fruit trees and enough pasture for keeping a horse or two. (By the way, horses are very practical form of transportation here, with the roads in their present condition.)

Uvita is not as nice as Dominical by any means, but the folks living here are very friendly. They see very few tourists; most of the North Americans they encounter are residents who are happy to fit in as neighbors. From here south, the road gets worse until it connects with paved roads at Palmar, on the Pan American Highway. When the road is paved all the way, more property will become available for development.

Medical Care

One problem with isolated areas like Dominical, is the lack of sophisticated medical care. Usually, a resident doctor in the village can handle emergencies, but for serious problems the nearest emergency clinic is in Barú, about ten kilometers from Dominical, or the hospital in San Isidro, some 45 kilometers distant. An ambulance is stationed in Dominical, which can get a patient there fairly quickly, but it is a distance. This problem was brought home to me on my last trip. As I was driving from Dominical to San Isidro, a *campesino* ran out into the road and flagged me down. His hand was bleeding from an accident, and he needed to get to the hospital. I had to act as an ambulance driver, not knowing whether to go top speed and risk killing us both or to slow down while my patient bled to death. He was the only calm one, as he insisted on trying to show me his wound and describing in minute detail what had happened. Fortunately, we both lived.

Golfito Area

For years, I had heard people speak of Golfito and the Osa Peninsula. The area sounded like a place of adventure—panning for gold in forest streams, fishing for trophy sailfish or hiking rain forest trails. In order to complete research for this book, I resolved to spend some time around Golfito to collect information. But when I asked folks around San José, who either owned property or regularly visited here, I found their answers short and vague, always skirting the subject as if trying to draw my attention elsewhere. When I spoke with a man who owned property on Zancudo Beach, his face burned angrily as he said, "Zancudo is my special place, and I don't want any damned travel writers drawing attention to it! It would destroy things for all of us!"

Obviously, our interview was over, but now I *knew* I had to go! I rented a car and was soon on my way to Golfito, the jumping off place for the Pavones-Zancudo Beach areas. The drive south on the Pan American Highway is gorgeous. One unbelievable view after another invites a pause wherever the car can be parked safely off the pavement. Ordinarily, the trip takes six hours, but by the time I stopped several times to sample pork *chicharones*, to marvel over the views and take a nap in the shade of a banana tree, the trip stretched into an eight hour day.

Golfito is an often-neglected part of Costa Rica, with scanty information provided by most tourist guides. The only complete description I found was in *The New Key to Costa Rica*. The town began its existence as a banana port for United Fruit Company, but was abandoned when the company decided that the operation had became unprofitable. As a banana port, there was no incentive to develop it as a tourist attraction, although today it is trying hard to do so.

Sitting on the water's edge of Golfo Dulce (Sweet Gulf), Golfito's water scene is absolutely gorgeous, reminiscent of the San Juan Islands in Puget Sound. The coastline and islands jut steeply from the water, green and matted with trees, vines and thick brush. The water is so calm at times that it is hard to realize that this is not a lake, but a protected little bay of the Pacific Ocean. From the slope, a rain forest watches over the town as fishing boats ply the calm waters of the Golfo Dulce. During the heyday of the town's banana shipping days, the company wisely kept these mountain slopes as a wildlife preserve and watershed, assuring Golfito a relatively pure water supply.

The town itself can hardly be described as anything but picturesque. It looks like a cliché movie set of a banana shipping port. Just a few blocks wide, the town follows the water's edge, with some houses actually standing over the water on stilts, others clinging to edges of the hills and hanging out into empty space. A couple of excellent hotels on the edge of town accommodate the growing number of curious tourists, but most accommodations are rather rustic.

A surprising number of North Americans live in or around Golfito. One place to meet them is at the Hotel Costa Rica Surf, a place that advertises itself as a "Gringo Aid Station." Operated by an American and his Tica wife, the large upstairs bar-restaurant is the unofficial meeting place for residents and also the official place for monthly American Legion meetings. The hotel is located on the main commercial street that climbs up the hill, parallel with the road that runs along the water. Other little open-air restaurants are also patronized by North Americans along this movie-set street, along with hardware stores, shops selling tackle and boating supplies and several red-light bars.

Bargain Property

Because of special circumstances, some of Costa Rica's better property bargains can be found around Golfito. A local resident explained why by saying: "When the United Fruit Company pulled out it left us without our biggest employer. Workers started moving away, selling property for what they could. Next, a disease called the Panamanian Blight hit the cacao crop, which was the second line of defense for farmers here. Property became a drug on the market. There were plenty of sellers but few buyers, and you know what that does to the market." In the immediate vicinity of Golfito, partially wooded land was selling for as little as $5,000 for a hectare; add another $5,000 for one with a house on it.

The government is working hard to find a solution, trying to attract new businesses to fill the niche that United Fruit left when it abandoned the economy. New types of agriculture is not a good option because chemicals and pesticides used to grow bananas make it difficult to grow anything else. One project that helps local commerce is a Free Trade Zone, a special place for manufacturing and exporting by Costa Rican and foreign businesses. Those operating within the zone's coverage are exempt from all taxes and customs on importation of raw materials, components and parts. This should attract investors who would like to take advantage of the tax breaks and the availability of good local workers.

Buses from San José take seven hours to Golfito and charge about $6.00, leaving San José from Calle 4 at Avenida 18. The lovely scenery makes the time well spent. For the impatient, a SANSA plane flies twice a day and costs about $40 for a round trip.

Playa Zancudo

Although Golfito is the central focus of the area, most North Americans do not actually live here, their homes and business interests are in nearby communities or on isolated bays around the Golfo Dulce. Zancudo is one of the communities that has attracted many foreigners, particularly those from the United States or Canada. Those who live here are convinced it is the best place on the whole coast.

A long, black sand beach with widely spaced homes, small hotels and cabin rentals, Playa Zancudo promises someday to be the largest traditional tourist development of the Golfito area. Unlike Pavones, the famous surfing beach just to the south, Zancudo's beaches are very swimmable and its land ownership free of the legal nightmares that plague Pavones.

Property isn't cheap here, not by any means, but not exorbitant either. In 1992, the going rate for Zancudo ocean front property was between $20,000 and $25,000 for a one-hectare plot (2.44 acres). In the case of one property I inspected, this included a generous stretch of beach front, with perhaps 150 feet of land between the road and the high tide level, and the land on the other side of the road, ending at a small river which parallels the road. Along the beach the usual coconut and strangler fig trees concealed the property from view of swimmers and surfers. The rest of the property was in varied tropical trees, shrubs and flowers. A continual breeze made this a suitable location for a residence.

Several bars and restaurants serve as social centers, with some featuring dances on the weekends. A stop at any restaurant will usually find a table or so of North Americans or Europeans discussing the local news and making plans for the development of their property. Paving the road is one common topic. Those who own homes along the beach shudder in horror at the image of the throngs of tourists, property-buyers and developers the paved highway will surely bring. They feel that since they have discovered this part of Costa Rica, it is rightly theirs and it would downright rude for others to crowd them. Those who have businesses, who depend on tourists and new residents to make their enterprises grow, eagerly look forward to the road and the increased prosperity it will bring.

Several folks I spoke with routinely come here for three months and longer every year. A cabin with a small kitchen, right on the beach can often be found for as little as $250 a month. During the off season, there is no problem finding such a place. Bob and Monica Hara, who moved here from San Francisco some years ago, recently completed a pleasant and comfortable facility, the *Cabinas Sol y Mar*. The restaurant, as all of the other buildings, is absolutely immaculate, with an employee constantly cleaning, sweeping and mopping. This may be the only restaurant in Costa Rica where you must take off your shoes before entering; no sand on those polished floors, please! Boats to Golfito can often be taken from the Sol y Mar.

"Everyone wants to come here in the winter months," Bob remarked, referring to winter and summer in their North American sense. "People seem to think that summer is a total monsoon. But the weather is wonderful then. It's actually a little cooler during June, July and August. Every day is sunny in the morning, and at least part of the afternoon. Often it doesn't rain at all."

Another Zancudo booster is Susan, an artist who lives nearby and who is also building rental cabins. Originally from England, Susan fell in love with this part of the country several years back and decided to become a permanent resident. When speaking about Zancudo's potential as a tourist development, she said, "Something people overlook is that our waves are excellent for surfing. When the surf is right, our beach is almost as good as Pavones. The waves aren't as long, of course, but fine surf just the same."

Buses and stake-bed trucks, loaded with people from Golfito, make the 45-kilometer drive on Sundays to allow the kids a romp on the beach. The waves are gentle, the water is warm, and kids are in no danger of anything worse than sunburn. It's not an easy drive, but because this is the only place of its kind within a two-hour drive from Golfito, it is very popular with the townspeople. The easiest way to get here is by boat from Golfito; a one-way trip costs between $2 and $4, depending on who takes you.

I chose to drive, however, and bounced along a dirt and boulder trail for two-and-a-half hours. This is the same trail which goes to Zancudo's sister beach to the south, Pavones. The trails split apart near the half-way point, with the turnoffs clearly marked. Maps don't seem to be of much help in finding either Zancudo or Pavones. I had three different maps, and for all practical purposes, they might as well have been of three different countries. Local residents, when looking at the maps, scratched their heads and made comments like, "This road doesn't go like this, and this town isn't here at all!" It's best to stop when you see someone walking along the road and make inquiries. The road is paved from Golfito until you come to a interesting little ferry which chugs across the Coto River using an old automobile engine for power. The river is quite wide at this point. To cross, you honk your horn and the operator, usually a teenager, comes running, starts up the old engine, and away you go.

Pavones

Located in the most southern region of Costa Rica, near the mouth of the Golfo Dulce, the last bit of Costa Rica before the coast becomes Panama, Pavones at one time was attracting attention as a possible place for investment and/or residency. Reputed to be the beach with the longest and best surf in the world, Pavones is well-known among surfboard enthusiasts who pilgrimage here from all corners of the world.

However, in 1991, some unfavorable publicity cooled the public's interest, at least for the time being. Squabbling over property rights escalated into armed conflict between foreigners and local Ticos. A tense, anti-Gringo atmosphere prevailed for a while, forcing the government to intervene to keep the peace.

The problems originated a few years ago when a United States citizen bought up about 15 miles of beach and began selling parcels to other Americans, who then established homes and small farms on their properties. Unfortunately, the original owner-developer was accused of narcotics dealings (which had nothing to do with the land) and ended up in jail in the United States. Suddenly, the status of his property was in question. Who is authorized to sell it? Who can guarantee title? To further complicate matters, a group of *paracaidistas,* or squatters, moved in, attempting to establish their right to the land. Their position was that the original owner didn't legally own anything in the first place because he was a criminal. In a sort of wild west showdown between land owners and squatters, one of the intruders was killed by a guard protecting an American's property. The government, in an attempt to bring peace and order here, established a police outpost to keep the quarreling factions separate. The situation is so complicated that most people are leery of investing here, at least until the situation clarifies.

Perhaps a dozen foreign families still live along the beach front road, mostly North Americans, mostly young (if you consider anyone under 55 young, as I do). Of course surfers continue to visit here, their numbers unabated, blissfully unmindful of any worldly problem that doesn't involve the height and angle of today's waves. In the local cantina, waves seem to dominate most conversations. A road parallels the beach for several miles just north of Pavones, with only an occasional ranch house or cabin observable from the road or the beach. Farm clearings alternate with tracts of virgin forest, with lovely stands of native trees, tangles of vines and a profusion of birds and animals. Until the government establishes just who owns what and whether the squatters have any rights, things will remain confused.

Pavones isn't much of a village; it's basically a scattering of homes, with a few small enterprises such as a *pulpería,* a restaurant with four rustic rooms upstairs, and of course, a soccer field. A couple of kilometers south is a lodge with a few rooms and some cabinas for rent, and a little farther on is another place which offers cabinas with three meals a day.

Chapter Five

Touring Costa Rica

Every nook and cranny of Costa Rica has something special to offer, something to dazzle the eyes or gratify the senses. Newcomers are never satisfied until they have seen it all; long-time residents tend to repeat their travels, to see everything again and again. Fortunately, getting around the country is easy; within a few hours, you can visit just about any section of Costa Rica you choose, and you usually have several modes of transportation available to you.

Air Transportation

The quickest way to travel about the country is by SANSA, the national airline serving Quepos, Golfito, Palmar Sur, Barra del Colorado Nosara, Tamarindo and Sámara. Tickets are affordable, ranging from about $12 for a San José-Quepos flight to about $25 to Tamarindo Beach. The plane will probably be an old reliable DC-3, or else one of those small foreign jobs that you have to stoop over in order to get to your seat. But, when was the last time you bought an airplane ticket for $12?

Because these flights are popular, they are frequently booked solid. It's essential to reconfirm your reservations, even though you have tickets. Someone else could have your boarding pass if you just show up at the airport without reconfirming 48 hours in advance. Furthermore, reservations do not mean a thing unless you actually have tickets clutched in your hand. So don't trust a travel agent to take care of things for you. My recommendation is to go to the SANSA offices in person to make your reservations and walk away with your tickets. It's cheaper that way, too, since the airline doesn't give discounts to travel agencies and the agency tacks on an additional 10 percent to the price of the ticket. The airline's office is in downtown San José, easy to get to, and you will be sure your reservations have been made.

Another air option is an "air taxi" which will take you just about anywhere a bush pilot can set down a small plane. The cost is about $300 an hour for a twin-engine plane and five passengers. For a single-engine job, the price drops to $220 an hour for the same five passengers. A $440 an hour, seven-passenger plane can also be rented. When you consider that the country is small and flying times short, an air taxi isn't as expensive as it might appear. You'll find several companies in the phone book classified pages under the listing *Taxis Aereos*.

You are a pilot and would like to rent a plane and fly yourself? Not so easy. Even if you are a certified pilot with a license from another country, you cannot rent a Costa Rican plane until you've earned a Costa Rican license. You need to show proof of your total air hours logged in your country as well as log a certain amount of time in Costa Rica.

Buses and Trains

Guidebooks often rave about the scenic wonders of the country's train system. Especially tempting are descriptions of a spectacular railroad trip from San José to Limón. However, when you read about train trips in Costa Rica, you know the book is a bit out of date. Since the earthquake of 1991, there are no passenger trains in operation. Sad, but true. Some roadbeds and a few ancient bridges slipped downhill—common occurrences in Costa Rica earthquakes—but this time the government decided not to rebuild. The lines were losing money anyway. It's possible that some time in the future, service to the Pacific port of Puntarenas could be resumed, but there are no plans in the air at the moment.

Buses are another story. In addition to excellent city bus service, eight inter-city bus companies provide frequent service. Unlike the United States, where monopolistic inter-city bus fares border on extortion, tickets on Costa Rican buses are downright cheap. A four-hour ride from San José to Limón, for example is less than $4.00. San José has no central bus station; each line departs from its own terminal, sometimes just a curbside parking place in front of a small ticket office. For example, to go to Quepos and Manuel Antonio, you take the buses that leave from the "Coca Cola" terminal.* Buses for Limón leave from the eastern side of the National Park on Avenida 11, but buses for Cahuita, just a few miles farther south of Limón leave from a location a dozen blocks away. Most tourist publications list the bus terminals, destinations and travel times. The *New Key to Costa Rica* has a comprehensive and up-to-date schedule.

A number of smaller bus companies carry passengers to all imaginable sectors of the country. Very few places lack public transportation. Several times, while negotiating impossible back country roads, bouncing through deep potholes, skirting boulders in the trail—wondering whether my rental car would ever make it back in one piece—a passenger-laden bus would appear from out of nowhere, sound its horn impatiently to move me aside, and then rumble past as it hurried on its way. These country buses tend to be of an older rattle-trap variety. Often they are secondhand school buses bought at surplus in the United States. Sometimes the owner-drivers don't bother to change the paint, and the bus finishes its transportation career bouncing along dusty trails in Costa Rica, with the legend "Maplewood Unified School District" still painted on its side.

Since the distance between San José and any destination in the country is not very great, bus travel is very practical. From San José to Quepos, a very popular tourist destination, bus travel time is less than four hours. By air it is only 20 minutes or so, but by the time you get out to the airport an hour early, wait for the plane to leave (always a half-hour to an hour late) and then wait for a bus to take you from the air strip to town, you haven't saved all that much time. Plus you've missed a lot of interesting scenery.

* The Coca Cola terminal gains its name in a typical Tico fashion: there *used to be* a Coca-Cola bottling plant in the neighborhood.

However, be aware that different bus lines have varying schedules. For example, travel from San José to Puntarenas takes two hours by one bus line but four hours on another line.

I knew Costa Rica has a lot of competing bus companies, but for a while I was astounded at how *many* city bus lines there appeared to be in San José. And, it seemed that the names of the bus lines were very creative. Then I discovered that the name painted on a bus's side or on the back wasn't the name of a bus company, but rather an imaginative name given to the bus by its driver as an expression of his individuality. The *Tico Times* (3/6/92) ran a feature article on these names, at which point I realized that the *Papa Lolo* bus that passed by my house every morning as I waited for my ride, was not owned by the "Papa Lolo Bus Lines" but was driven by a driver with the nickname "Papa Lolo." Some buses are named after family members, other names are exercises in imagination. Other names listed by the *Tico Times* were: Desert Storm, Krakatoa, El Principe Azul (the blue prince), Mil Amores (thousand loves), the Dancing Queen and El Guerrero del Camino (the road warrior).

Rental Cars in Costa Rica

This is by far the most convenient way of touring the country. When you get serious about looking for a place to live for a few months or for the rest of your life, renting a car for a week or two allows you travel about freely in search of your dream location. You don't have to bother with bus schedules; you can check out side streets or country lanes, and you can stop whenever you find a particularly interesting view. With a car, you needn't worry about hotel reservations; chances are if one hotel is full, another will have room. You can drive about, checking out for sale or for rent signs. You can investigate for yourself instead of being under control of a salesman, a rental agent or someone with a vested interest in showing you only their own properties.

Although your rental car is insured—it's mandatory—the deductible is a hefty $300 to $700. Small fender-benders seldom exceed the amount of the deductible, so unless you practically total the car, the repairs will be on you. Check with the rental company as to their deductibles; at least one imposes a $1,000 floor on their liability! At the time of writing, three agencies allow American Express card limited insurance coverage. (Adobe, Budget and National. The companies with the lowest deductibles at this point in time are: Miki, $250; National, $320; American, $325 and Budget, Discovery, El Indio and Global—$500 each.

Be aware that accessories such as antennas, radios, tires, mirrors aren't covered; if they are stolen, you are liable. The answer to the insurance problem is to keep your car in a guarded parking lot overnight. Auto accessory theft is not a big problem in the smaller towns but in San José and some of the bigger cities, you need to be aware.

Before you start driving a rental, always check the car for dents, scratches and other problems, and make sure the rental car employee notes them on your contract. If damage is there, but not duly noted, you have no recourse but pay for it. Make sure you have good tires because you will probably be driving on gravel roads. A sharp rock can penetrate a tire if the tread is thin and the sidewalls weak. Insist on another car if the tires are not new, or practically so.

On the Road

Your regular driver's license is perfectly legal in Costa Rica for 90 days from the time you enter the country. After that you will need a Costa Rican license. For residents, or for those awaiting *residente* status, a license is relatively easy to get, simply apply at the proper office and present several passport-sized photos. The license is issued while you wait. I know of one man, who walked away with a fresh, valid Costa Rican license even though his U.S. license had been suspended for drunk driving. I only hope he doesn't drive on the same streets as I do.

The first rule of driving in Costa Rica is one that should be followed in most foreign countries: do not leave anything stealable in the car—even out of sight. A favorite trick of thieves is to monitor the car rental desks at the airport, watch who rents a car and fills the trunk with interesting luggage. They then follow the car to the hotel and while the passengers are inside at the registration desks, the thieves open the trunk and help themselves to the luggage, extra money, cameras and whatever other loot lady luck provides. If at all possible, leave someone in the car during that crucial first stop. This method of stealing isn't unique with the Ticos, it has been imported from Europe, probably originating in Italy or Spain. Once outside of San José, the chances of something like this happening is much less, but why take chances? By the way, it is easy for thieves to tell which are rental cars because of the documents pasted prominently on the inside of the windshield.

Driving through the Costa Rican countryside isn't difficult, it's just slower. With all that gorgeous scenery, who wants to travel fast? Be especially careful when passing. Make sure you have time to get around safely and be cautious near hills and curves; drive as though you expect trouble. That's just good common sense in any country, but particularly in Costa Rica; too many drivers have a daring, gambling attitude that urges them to pass on hills and curves. For this reason, accident rates in Costa Rica are unusually high. Drive defensively. Watch for oncoming drivers who flash their headlights off and on. That means trouble ahead, usually in the form of a radar speed trap!

Don't worry about a traffic ticket if you're caught speeding. This isn't as serious a matter as it is back home. Just smile, accept the ticket and pay later at any bank at your convenience. If you are driving a rental car, save up the tickets and hand them to the clerk when you return the car; the rental company pays them for you. Never, never pay a cop money! He might tell you that the ticket can be paid at a bank, 30 kilometers in the opposite direction from which you are traveling. And then he hints that it would be easier to pay him. He is telling the truth, hoping you will offer him money to pay the ticket for you thus avoiding a long drive. But the *whole* truth is, you can pay the ticket at *any* bank in the country! Costa Ricans usually save up their tickets and pay them once a year. As of spring of 1992, a speeding ticket cost only 750 colónes—less than $6.00—a tiny fraction of what a similar ticket would cost at home. What's the point of paying a thousand-colón bribe when the ticket is only 750 colónes? A ticket for eight hours of illegal parking costs less than two hours of legal parking in a commercial lot. Frankly, it would be a good idea if fines were stiffer; it might encourage Costa Ricans to drive more carefully!

Driving in city traffic anywhere around San Jose can be frustrating. As you get the knack of it and learn the system, it gets easier. Theoretically, finding your way around San José should be easy because the city streets are logically organized on a north-south, east-west grid. *Calles,* or streets, run north to south and *avenidas,* avenues, east to west. However, it isn't as simple as it sounds. For one thing, about half the streets are missing street signs which are normally placed on the corners of buildings. Furthermore, most streets are one-way, yet often without signs to indicate *which* way! Perhaps you know that *avenida nueve* is a one-way street going west, but how do you know the street you are looking at is *avenida nueve* if there are neither street signs nor one-way signs? All you can do is wait to see which way traffic is flowing. If no cars are coming either way, you don't dare take a chance.

In the surrounding towns of the Meseta Central, traffic is lighter than in San José, but the problem of missing street signs becomes even worse. Some streets are one-way and others two-way, but too often there aren't any signs to clue you in. Sometimes an arrow painted on the pavement indicates which directions you can turn, sometimes not. It's especially disconcerting to be driving along what you believe to be a two-way street and suddenly notice that all cars parked on both sides of the street are pointing in your direction. Since parking on either side of the street is okay in Costa Rica, you have no way of knowing if they just *happen* to be facing your direction or if you are traveling the wrong way again. When in doubt, park and wait for a car to drive past, then follow suit.

Away from the cities and major highways you find gravel roads that require very slow driving. Going too fast over the rocks can cut tires, marooning you several kilometers from a tire repair place. You may have to change it yourself! When this happened to me, I stood around looking perplexed until two men passing by stopped to changed the spare. They refused to accept any money. Next, I drove to a sort of auto repair place where two kids fixed my tire in a jiffy using strips of an old inner tube, some kind of glue and what appeared to be a steel crochet needle. They didn't even have to take the tire off the rim, as I had expected. They charged about $1.50, and that included putting the repaired wheel back on the car and placing the spare away in the trunk.

Taxis

Costa Rica enjoys an excellent system of taxis, with about 2,500 of them zipping about the streets of San José—double what there were in 1990. Almost all cabs are late model Japanese imports, usually Toyota or Datsun. Occasionally you'll see a Volkswagen or a Volvo. By law, taxicabs are painted bright red. You can't miss them.

Not only is taxi equipment in good shape, but fares are inexpensive. It costs 60 colónes (about 43 cents U.S.) to go the first half-dozen blocks or so, and 25 colónes for every kilometer after that—an absolute bargain! In San José, you can go practically anyplace in the city for two bucks or less. After 10 p.m. drivers are permitted to charge an additional 20 percent.

All cabs are supposed to have meters, and most do. For some reason, the meters are called *marías*. Avoid those cabs parked outside the more expensive hotels or discos. They will tell you that they don't have to use meters because they pay more insurance, or some other bull like that. The truth is they will charge from two to four times the normal rate. When in doubt, ask, ¿*Hay una maría*? If the driver claims the meter isn't working, don't enter the cab until you've established a price.

Although the law says that taxicabs must use meters, bear in mind that any trip over 12 kilometers is exempt; bargaining is the only way. A trip from the airport to downtown San José, for example can cost between $8 to $14, depending on how good you are at bargaining and how badly the cabby wants the fare. If you gather fellow passengers to share the cost of the trip, that's okay, but by law the driver cannot take you to different hotels or locations because he is only supposed to have one set of passengers at a time.

Why are all the cabs new? Because one of the side benefits of owning a taxi is that it is bought free of import duties, as long as it is kept for three years before selling it as a used car. This means that after three years of generating income, the vehicle may be sold for more than it cost in the first place.

It used to be, a few years ago, almost all cabs were either Mercedes-Benz or expensive U.S. models. The cab owners figured that as long as they were buying something duty-free, why not buy the most expensive and make even more money on the resale? But today, everything is Japanese. I asked several drivers why, and was told, "Because only Japanese companies sell on easy time payments." Some U.S. residents are a bit miffed at the thought of their government giving Costa Rica a hundred million dollars a year in aid, yet seeing almost no U.S. cars on the road.

Taxi-Chauffeurs

Driving a car around San José or through the narrow roads in the countryside isn't exactly a relaxing pastime. I sometimes find myself so involved with traffic and confusion that I see very little. My passengers see even less since they spend a great deal of their time praying, cursing or shouting, "Watch where you're *going*, you dummy!"

There is a better way of doing things: *rent a cab*! It turns out that some taxi drivers like the idea of driving one fare a day, for the entire day, instead of wandering all over town waiting for someone to flag them down. It isn't nearly as hard on the cab either, since most passengers want to stop, get out and spend time looking around, giving the old car a deserved rest.

It is not only convenient to let someone else drive (someone who knows where he is going), but it actually costs less than renting a car for the day. A competent, English-speaking cab driver chauffeured us around the Meseta Central all day for only $43. A rental car and gasoline would have cost $60. In other words, after you buy the driver's lunch and give a tip, you'll still save money.

The taxicab rental idea is great for any sightseeing trips around the Meseta Central. Instead of four people paying $25 to $45 per person for a five-hour commercial tour, a cab driver will show you the same sights for $43 plus tip. Some drivers will even take you on longer trips, to just about anyplace in the country you care to go—Monte Verde or Manuel Antonio, for example—as long as you also take care of their hotel and meal expenses.

Not all drivers are willing to rent by the day; not all can speak English well enough to explain what you are seeing. To find one who does, you may phone Ramón Benavides at 85-05-28. He can put you in contact with a reliable driver at a guaranteed price. (His wife, who usually answers the phone, does not speak English; ask your hotel desk clerk to call and leave a message.)

Used Cars versus New Cars

One of the coveted benefits of residency *used* to be the right to buy a new car without paying the horrendous duty. However, it appears that foreign residents are losing this benefit due to an action of the legislature. Local pensionados and rentistas are bemoaning this development and some are threatening to return home should this benefit definitely be taken from them. Heretofore, saving more than half the value of a car permitted handsome profit-taking every five years when the used car was sold for more than it cost new. As you might imagine, this privilege didn't sit well with the ordinary Costa Rican citizen, who has to pay full taxes on all his purchases.

As explained elsewhere in this book, this loss of tax exemptions isn't as tragic as some make it out to be. At the same time lawmakers decided to eliminate benefits, they also set a schedule for reducing the import duties on *all* cars—from the present 125% to 225% all the way down to a mere 20% of the value of the new vehicle. This places Costa Ricans and pensionados on a level playing field. Automobiles will be far more reasonable for all.

A practical way to deal with this situation is to simply buy a used car. Because autos are expensive, their owners tend to take good care of them, so used cars are usually in excellent shape and their resale values are excellent. One couple told of their experience when they arrived in Costa Rica in 1981. They paid $2,000 for a 1972 VW with a recently overhauled engine. Over the years, they did little more than ordinary maintenance, plus seat covers and a paint job. Ten years later, because of inflation, their car is now worth $2,500.

Used cars can be driven into the country or shipped in from Miami ($400 to $600 shipping fee). Taxes are based on year and make, so it makes sense to bring in an older model at the lowest custom duties. The import rules on used cars are rather complicated, so it pays to investigate the differences for various types of cars and the tax liabilities. You might consult a lawyer for information on this. For instance, a pickup or commercial vehicle is taxed at a much lower rate than a passenger or a luxury car. One Costa Rican explained why he bought a pickup with dual seats rather than a regular van. "As a pickup, it's considered a work vehicle and therefore taxed very low. But a van with front and back seats is a passenger car, even though it won't carry any more passengers than my pickup truck." Another man told of buying a luxury van in Miami and driving it to Costa Rica. "When I got to Nicaragua, I had a garage take the body off of the car and put a platform on the back. That made it into a cargo truck. After I registered it, I went back to Managua and had them replace the van's body." (I'm not recommending that you do this; I'm merely reporting what one person did. Who knows, he may be fined later on.)

Hotels and Lodging

The tourist boom over the last five years has made the hotel situation somewhat tight at times. To compensate, new hotels are opening their doors up and private homes are being converted into bed and breakfasts as quickly as they can. In smaller communities, new hotels and ecotourism facilities are popping up to accommodate demand. You can often find a room in places where camping was the only choice before.

The tightest housing market is during Christmas-through-Easter season. Not impossible, just tight. Making reservations before you leave for Costa Rica, even if for only a couple of nights is a good insurance policy. This is where the *Tico Times* comes in handy; almost all tourist hotels advertise prices and have fax numbers. Once you arrive, you can check around and locate something more suitable to your taste or to the size of your pocketbook. If you want one of the middle-priced hotel rooms, from $35 to $60 a night during the tourist season, you had better make the reservation far in advance so you will have time for your check for the first night's rent to arrive, be deposited and returned to your bank, so you know you've made contact.

Around San José, hotels come in all sizes and flavors, with expensive rooms considered anything over $100 a night, and cheap rooms under $10. I looked at one for under $5 on my last trip, but shivers ran down my spine when I peered into the gloomy-looking room with dirty linen on the bed. For my personal tastes, a $14 room would be my bottom choice, yet many of the younger set and the backpacker brigades believe that anything over $5 is far too expensive. My wife's preferences fall into the $35 range or above.

Away from the Meseta Central, there are not only fewer hotels to choose from, but the rooms are often more expensive. This will change as competition grows tighter. Nevertheless, I've found satisfactory places for as little as $24 even in such out-of-the-way places as Nosara or Cahuita. Understand, what may be satisfactory for me could be terrible for someone else!

If you are traveling on a budget—as long-term travelers usually do—you will sometimes find yourself in strange room situations. You may pay a good price for a room with a private bath, only to discover that the shower puts out cold water only. When there is supposed to be hot water, you'll often find one of those rinky-dink electric heaters attached to the shower head. This contraption has a lever that can be set to one of three positions, none of which does anything but output cold water. The position that says "off" is the only one that works *all* the time. At best these electric water heaters give a slight warming effect to the spray of water, barely taking the chill off the water. This encourages short but exhilarating showers.

Inexpensive hotels habitually use low-wattage light bulbs, so weak you have trouble reading in bed. The solution is to carry a 60-watt bulb in your luggage and substitute it whenever you feel like reading. Other items you might keep in your bag is a drinking cup, a roll of toilet paper and some nylon string and clothespins so you can wash out things. Very important is a set of earplugs. I've suffered through several nights, made impossible by inconsiderate people partying all night, or standing outside my door making plans for the next day's trip—at two in the morning! One additional item is one of those spiral insect repellent things, called *spirulas* which perch on a metal stand and burn like incense. Light one up an hour before bedtime to discourage mosquitoes.

Should you be stranded out in the country, unable to find a place to stay, your ace in the hole is to inquire at the local pulpería. This is the Costa Rican equivalent of a country "general store" and it also serves as the social center of the community. Sometimes drinks and sandwiches are sold, and neighbors come to exchange news and gossip tidbits as well as purchase necessary items ranging from matches to machetes. The proprietor of the pulpería can almost always find you a room with a local family. This is a unique opportunity to see how country folk live in Costa Rica, but don't expect luxury. A pulpería is also an excellent place to inquire about real estate. If anything is for sale or rent in the neighborhood, the proprietor will know, and probably knows the bottom-line price as well as the asking price.

Chapter Six

Living in Costa Rica

While having breakfast in a picturesque village on the Caribbean coast, a Canadian couple at the next table learned that I was writing a book on Costa Rica and we began discussing the idea of retirement in Costa Rica.

"I don't know," the husband said, "I don't think prices are all that great here. Some hotels where we've stayed charge as much as they do back home. And good restaurant meals aren't all that inexpensive, either. I simply don't see the point in retiring here."

"Well, if rock bottom expenses are your priority," I replied, "you are correct. Many places in the world offer cheaper living than Costa Rica, but is the quality of life the same? Is the weather as nice? Are the people as friendly? Besides, it isn't fair to judge retirement potential by the cost of luxury hotels or restaurant meals."

The hotel where we were staying charged $40 a night for a couple in a *cabina*, including breakfast. It wasn't a luxury hotel, but clearly offered much more than any budget hotel in the U.S. or Canada for that price. Yes, some Costa Rican hotels charge from $80 to $120, but similar hotels in many parts of the U.S.A. or Canada will cost far more than that. Restaurant meals? Go to just about any good restaurant in Costa Rica and check the menu. Very few entrees will cost more than $6. A juicy steak goes for about $8 and for over $10 you are probably ordering lobster.

Cost Comparisons

Let's forget about hotel prices and restaurant costs; they don't figure heavily in most long-term residents' budgets. More important is comparing the style of everyday living here with the lifestyle the same amount of money provides elsewhere. You would be hard pressed to find a place with so much to offer, for such reasonable prices.

In many foreign countries North American residents feel they must live in certain "safe" areas, for which they must pay premium costs. Because Costa Rica is not a stratified society, North Americans feel comfortable living in just about any neighborhood. This means a wide selection of rents and housing prices. While you can pay $1,200-a-month rent in a luxury section of Escazú, you can also find a nice place for $200 in a very livable area like Alajuela. Both places are just a few minutes away from San José; both offer quality living with superb climates.

Utilities, a most important part of most budgets, seem almost free in Costa Rica when compared with the United States or Canada. Homes here have no furnaces or air conditioners to drain money from budgets. One couple from Kansas City pointed out that their utility bills in Heredia run no more than $35 a month, less than a fifth what they paid back home. "We used to spend as much heating and cooling our home as most Costa Ricans *earn* every month!" According to folks living in the San José area, electricty runs $10 to $14, water $8 and a telephone with unlimited local calls is $10 a month. Compare these bills with those in your own home town.

Food is wonderfully affordable too, with tropical fruits and veggies not only at giveaway prices, but also deliciously fresh. Costa Rica produces some of the best-tasting, grass-fed beef in the world; a fillet mignon in a San José market costs about the same as ground beef in a San Diego market. Some new residents here report spending half as much on their food budget as they did at home.

Property taxes are almost nothing, at least not for North Americans accustomed to forking out big money for taxes. According to people we interviewed for this book, an average middle-class home—with three bedrooms and two baths—is taxed at the rate of $50 to $60 a year. (Many folks pay three times that much every *month* on their average homes in the United States.) A mansion in the $300,000 range may go as high as $130 a year—never more than $150.

Besides affordable housing, utilities, taxes and food costs, what other bargains does Costa Rica offer? Oh yes, servants. A housekeeper-cook will clean your house, wash and iron clothes for $7 to $8.50 a day and your gardener works eight hours a day for $110 a month.

Is everything inexpensive in Costa Rica? No, of course not. Clothing prices will probably be the same as where you came from. Gasoline costs about the same as in Hawaii or Canada, about $1.80 a gallon. Also, since the bulk of Costa Rica's governmental income comes from import taxes, anything imported will be quite pricey. Cameras, TVs, electrical goods and many other imported items will cost two and a half times as much because of the high tariffs. Since tropical countries aren't suited for wine production, drinkable wines must be imported from Chile, Europe or California. Almost anything that comes from Europe or North America is expensive. Local consumers solve this problem simply by making do with goods made in Costa Rica or other Central American countries.

Automobiles are expensive, too. New-car sticker-shock will knock your socks off with import duties of 125 percent to 225 percent (plus sales tax). The cost of a Japanese import with a small engine is about $35,000. The same car sells for $12,000 in Cleveland! Something with a larger engine—say a Mercedes that would sell for $35,000 back home—will set you back over $100,000 in Costa Rica. However, don't let these prices frighten you; the import duties, as I've noted previously, are scheduled to be slashed dramatically. By 1993, taxes should be a small fraction of today's horrors.

Fortunately, as discussed in Chapter Five, public transportation is excellent and inexpensive. A car is really unnecessary. Buses travel all over the Meseta Central, at frequent intervals, for as little as a dime, or 35 cents for longer distances. Taxis are plentiful and inexpensive.

Money Matters

Costa Rica's currency is the colón which, until the spring of 1992, had an official value of 138 to the dollar. However, government controls were removed and the value was allowed to float freely with the market. It was expected that the value of the colón would drop in relation to the dollar because of a high demand for dollars. To everyone's surprise, the opposite happened; the dollar plummeted to a ratio of 125 to one. This was not the intended outcome, so the government began taking steps to shore up the dollar. The eventual value of the colón is anybody's guess, of course, but my guess is that it will remain somewhere between 125 and 140 for some time to come.

A big business in Costa Rica is buying and selling dollars. As you walk along the streets, especially in San José, money-changers will approach you, offering to buy your dollars. When the value of the colón is going down, you can usually get a little more than the current rate. When it's going up, you break even. A word of caution: street currency exchange is supposed to be illegal—although the police seldom enforce the law—but some of these money-changers are also con men who can shortchange you before you know what's happening. You might also end up with a handful of excellent-quality Colombian counterfeit bills.

In early 1992, a nice rate of interest was being paid on time deposits of colónes. The rate was around 21 percent for CDs of three-month duration and 24 percent for one year. (By the middle of the year the rates had dropped to 14 or 15 percent.) While this sounds like a terrific return on your investment, you must consider that over the past years, the value of the colón has dropped at a steady rate. That is why interest rates are as high as they are. You are gambling that the colón will either devaluate less than expected or that it will actually increase in value, in which case you come out ahead. Should it go otherwise, obviously you could lose money. My guess (and it's only a guess) is that deflation of the colón may be coming to an end. The reason I say this is that Costa Rica seems to have plenty of foreign reserves for the first time in a long time, and the government is in a much better position to control currency fluctuations.

Banking

Although in many ways Costa Rica is a modern and efficient country, for some inexplicable reason, a visit to the bank is an Alice in Wonderland experience. It takes forever to do a simple transaction such as changing dollars or travelers' checks into colónes. Each bank handles things a little differently, but it always involves standing in one line while a clerk examines each person's passport, examines the bills or checks, fills out some forms and pounds everything in sight with a rubber stamp. Then you go to another line and wait until a second clerk fills more forms in quadruplicate and does more rubber stamping. The money is counted at least three times, then counted again as the clerk hands the money over.

Since banks are also used to pay traffic tickets, utility bills and Social Security payments for your maid and gardener, and since each transaction requires a flurry of forms, rubber stamps and calculations, you can count on spending a lot of your time in Costa Rican banks. At least one bank has an organized system of waiting your turn—one only possible in Costa Rica. Customers sit patiently in rows of chairs, arranged theater-style. When a clerk is free, the customer in the first right-hand seat goes to the window, and the other customers all shift over one seat or move to the next row, as appropriate.

Because of the time-consuming process of dealing with banks and government bureaucracy, some Ticos make their living by standing in line for you, by knowing who to contact and when. They are called *tramitadores* (from the verb *tramitar* to transact, to take legal steps). Your friends and neighbors can recommend a reliable tramitador to make your life easier.

Bank accounts can be in either colónes or dollars. But an unpleasant side of bank practice is the habit of holding dollar checks from foreign banks for 30 days before crediting them to your account. Another quirk is that they often do not have the actual dollars on hand to cash a very large check. You have to take a cashier's check instead. This is okay if you are making a local purchase with the money, since the party to whom you are giving the cash will probably deposit it in his account anyway. But when you need cash for a trip home, better plan ahead.

The Post Office

Although Costa Rican mail service is excellent compared to most Latin American countries, international delivery requires time. Air mail going to or coming from the U.S.A. or Canada involves ten days each way. To avoid this 20-day turnaround, many people use a Miami delivery service, which guarantees same-day delivery by air courier to and from Costa Rica. Information can be obtained from one of these services by writing: Costa Rican Mail Service, P.O. Box 025216, Miami, FL 33102-5216. My understanding is that the service is $25 a month, and that there may be other rates, depending upon mail volume.

In a country where streets often don't have names, and where most houses lack street numbers, you can imagine that home mail delivery can't exactly be termed reliable. Most folks rely on post office boxes, known as *apartados*. This means a trip to the post office every couple of days, but at least you are fairly certain your mail will be waiting for you. During 1991 and the early part of 1992, many people reported mail being stolen by employees within the post office system. Postal officials assure us that they are working on this problem and that it will be cleared up before long.

Telephone Service

Generally, when a government tries to handle the telephone system, you'll find absolute chaos. In some countries you expect to be on a waiting list for a new phone for several years. When you finally get one, it may not work, and you get on another waiting list for repair. But Costa Rica must be doing something right, because the system actually works, and works well! The number of telephones per 100 inhabitants is the highest in Latin America, and 99.6 percent fully automatic. Yes, there is a waiting list for a new phone installation but it's measured in weeks, or a couple of months at worst, not years, as in most Latin American countries. Should you need a new phone installation and are impatient, you can look at classified ads in *La Nación* for people who want to sell their phone lines.

Making a telephone call in many foreign countries can be difficult and frustrating. You don't know how many coins to use, what kind to use, or when to drop in the coins. The apparatus often makes strange noises: whoops, wails and whistles, all having meaning to someone who knows the system, but a total mystery to those of us who don't. Sometimes, after you finally get through to your party, the call terminates before you can begin talking.

Costa Rica's phone system isn't at all difficult to use, and is surprisingly efficient even though it does send out mysterious signals at times. Phone calls to anywhere in the country go through very quickly. Even when dialing from a tiny village from one end of Costa Rica to the other, connections are as clear as if it were just across the street. And the tolls are surprisingly low. A five-colón piece (less than four cents) will place a call anywhere in the country. The length of time allowed for a five-colón coin depends upon the distance, but the time allocated per coin is generous; you can speak for about a minute from as far away from San José as you can get and still be in Costa Rica.

Public pay phones operate differently from those we are used to. Hotel phones usually only take a five-colón coin, whereas the public phones located on the streets or public squares accept five, ten or 20-colón pieces. The way hotel pay phones work: you dial the number *before* dropping in the coin. You wait until the tone indicates that the phone on the other end is ringing and then deposit the coin. You must be ready to drop in another five-colón piece when you hear a funny noise or beeping sound on the line, a sound that indicates the call will be terminated unless you quickly drop in another coin. Public pay phones have a kind of rack at the top where coins go. To make a call you line some coins in this rack—more if you are making a long call or a long-distance call—and then start punching in your number as soon as you receive a high-pitched tone that indicates the phone is ready. The coins can be any combination of five, ten or 20-colón denominations. When the connection is made, the phone automatically swallows a coin, permitting the others to roll down and be in position to be eaten as you stay on the line and go over the limit for that particular coin.

Placing a call to a foreign country is incredibly simple. You dial 114—no coin necessary—and wait for an international operator. An English-speaking operator will accept your credit card number or place the call collect. Compared to other countries, where it takes hours of waiting around a telephone office to get a call through, this is a miracle. Direct dialing is not only easy but it's the most inexpensive way to make an international call. The telephone directory lists codes for each country. You dial the country code, wait for the connection and then dial the number you wish to reach.

Costa Rican Food Treats

Guidebooks and travel articles almost always will tell you about *bocas* or free appetizers that you snack on every time you order a drink in a bar—usually fried shrimp, a chicken dish or some barbecued specialty. I suspect that the writers of guidebooks and travel articles don't frequent bars often, because the days of tasty bocas are almost a thing of the past. Very few places serve them nowadays, and then only to regular customers or to those who specifically request one. So, when you see someone else being served a treat, don't hesitate to ask. You may be in luck and have the opportunity to try a turtle egg; bars are just about the only place where you can legally get them, and only rarely then.

One time I found a bar-restaurant that was still serving bocas with drinks, and they were exceptionally good. I told the owner that next time, I was going to bring my wife to sample them. He was so delighted when I brought her in that he presented us with the delicacy of the house: a raw turtle egg apiece. Not wishing to hurt the restaurant-owner's feelings, I managed to down mine in one gulp. But my wife's expression told me that I would have to somehow dispose of *her* raw egg as well. When owner turned his head momentarily, I grabbed the other turtle egg, closed my eyes, performed the heroic deed, and quickly replaced the empty dish in front of my wife. The owner was so pleased that we enjoyed his treats he set us up with two more! As I recall, my appetite never returned that evening.

Dining Out

It's difficult to look at any particular restaurant menu and point out many dishes that could be described as "typically Costa Rican." Curiously, for a country with so many unusual ingredients available, restaurant cuisine tends to be rather ordinary. Steaks, fried chicken or shrimp seem to be almost obligatory on every menu; they taste fine, but after while one gets very tired of fried chicken or steak. One of the most common complaints tourists have about Costa Rica is the large number of boring restaurants.

On my last trip, I stumbled across a new restaurant, one which advertised "good old-fashioned American cooking." Since it was operated by an American, I anticipated a good meal. I ordered the featured dish of the evening: a specially prepared beef tenderloin. The owner assured me this was not at all like the normal Costa Rican fare. It wasn't. It turned out to be an over-cooked slab of dry sirloin, topped with a slice of Velveeta cheese and doused with canned mushroom sauce. (Yes, I said Velveeta cheese.) The veggies were canned string beans and carrots. So much for good old-fashioned American cooking.

Not that there aren't some wonderful dining establishments around. It's just that there are many more less-than-ordinary places. Around the San José area you can find a variety of interesting places, ranging from elegant French restaurants to superb pizzerias. Several excellent Chinese restaurants will surprise you with dishes that are quite different from the oriental cuisine you are used to back home. Their style of cooking is a cross between traditional oriental and tropical American.

One very common Costa Rican food—served everywhere, sometimes for every meal—is *gallo pinto*, which inexplicably translates: "spotted rooster." This is a mixture of cooked rice and black beans which are fried together until the rice turns a purple color. Mixed with eggs and topped with *salsa Inglesa* or *salsa*

Lizano, it makes a very filling breakfast, nutritious, but boring when served at *every* meal.

In small restaurants away from the city, a typical menu item is a *casado*—a kind of lunch plate with beans, rice, fried *plátano* (a green cooking banana) with some sort of meat, chicken or egg. *Olla de carne* is a tasty meat stew with vegetables such as chayote, squash, yuca or plátano. *Arroz con pollo*, chicken with rice, is one of my favorites when properly done and not too dry. *Sopa negra* is a soup made of puréed black beans with an egg poached in it, topped with green onions and a little cheese or sour cream. Another favorite is *empanadas*: fried dumplings filled with meat or cheese, often sold by children who carry them around in galvanized buckets. A *tortilla* in Costa Rica is properly defined as an omelet made with chopped potatoes or yuca root. Lately, Mexican-style tortillas have become popular in the country and are also called tortillas.

Great Coffee!

A big plus for Costa Rican cuisine is the coffee. Some of the best coffee in the world grows on shaded mountain slopes in Costa Rica. These exceptionally rich-tasting beans are used by coffee merchants around the world to add flavor to otherwise bland Brazilian or African varieties. In Costa Rica, you can brew your coffee from 100 percent flavorful beans. I prefer to purchase coffee beans direct from the roaster, and take them home while they are still hot. The use of instant coffee (a barbarous practice) hasn't caught on here. A *café con leche* with just a dash of sugar makes a wonderful starter for breakfast and something to wash down mouthfuls of gallo pinto.

Costa Ricans have an interesting way of making coffee here which gives characteristically rich flavor to the brew. Instead of using a percolator or an automatic coffee maker, Ticos use a wire or wooden stand holding a cloth strainer bag which hangs over a waiting cup. They place two teaspoons of coffee into the bag and pour boiling water over the grounds letting it drain into the coffee cup below. Then, for each cup of coffee, another teaspoon of ground coffee is added. The result is a flavorful, velvety drink that grows richer with each cup made. The grounds aren't discarded until the sack is full of grounds or until end of the day—whichever happens first. "The aroma and essence of the coffee is much better if it isn't boiled," explained a Tico. "We call our coffee-making system a *chorreador*. It brings out the flavor without acid bitterness. This method requires more coffee grounds, but since coffee is inexpensive here, we use nothing but the best."

Cooking at Home

For those staying for longer than a vacation, an apartment or house with a kitchen is a wonderful way of enjoying Costa Rican cooking and experimenting with the unusual tropical ingredients available in the markets. Around the San José area, every neighborhood has at least one supermarket, supplemented by weekend *ferias* or open air markets, and every neighborhood has its little *pulpería* or convenience store where you can buy items you forgot at the other markets.

Major supermarket chains are: Auto Mercado, Periféricos, Pali and Mas X Menos. The 'X' in the latter market is pronounced *por*, which means "for" in Spanish, making the store's literal name: "More for Less" markets. Open-air markets are held on weekends, the major ones being: Saturday in Escazú, on the south side of the main square; Saturday in Pavas, about five blocks from the main shopping center; and Sunday in Zapote, next to the Bull Ring. Heredia's farmers' market, also on Saturday, is perhaps the best known of all, with local families selling produce raised in their back yards. Heredia's main market, open every day of the week, is a wonderful place to browse for food, clothing, tools, furniture, whatever you can imagine.

Costa Rica's selection of fruits and vegetables are sometimes bewildering for us North Americans. In addition to delicious pineapples, strawberries, melons and other things we are used to, you'll find *chayotes, pejibayes, palmitos, plátanos* and other strange-looking items which will soon become standard parts of your menu. A common substitute for potatoes, the yuca root, in my opinion, tastes much better than ordinary spuds. Exotic tropical fruits such as guayabas, tamarindo or carambolas are exciting to experiment with, and make delicious drinks, called *refrescos*. One of my favorite refrescos is made by blending fresh cacao nuts (the source of chocolate) with horchata (a rice flour and sugar drink). My wife prefers a *batida* of fresh papaya, milk and ice, whipped to a milkshake-like consistency. Some fruits are so exotic they border on fantastic—with shells, spines and barbs—looking like something from a science fiction book cover. Especially interesting is the *marañón* fruit, the source of the common cashew nut. The nut itself grows at the end of a edible orange or yellow fruit that can be eaten raw or, more often, made into a *refresco* by blending with sugar and ice cubes. But the cashew nut itself is encased in a rubbery shell which is primed with cyanide, making it bitter and extremely poisonous. I have to marvel over the wonderful way nature designed this fruit as a way to disperse its seeds. In the wild, monkeys, parrots and other creatures pluck the fruit and carry it away to be consumed. When they finish eating the sweet fruit, the bitter-tasting seed is discarded, dropped on the ground to produce another tree.

Since Costa Rica is a cattle-growing country, steaks and roasts are as good as you might expect, with the flavor that only grass-fed beef can have—and it's inexpensive. But you might be surprised to discover that pork and chicken are higher priced than filet mignon. One reason is that pigs and chickens require large amounts of protein in their diets, which isn't available in bananas or other cheap tropical foods, so imported protein supplements bring prices up. The quality of pork and chicken is very good. Eggs are delicious, having a brighter-colored yolk, and a better flavor than we're used to up north with our mass-produced egg farms.

With an ocean on both sides, of course Costa Rica enjoys a wide selection of seafood. And since shipping distances from either ocean involve just a few short hours, the seafood arrives fresh. Almost any kind of fish and shellfish you can imagine is available, plus some you can't imagine. You might want to try some of the shellfish and conch that only thrives around the Costa Rican shores.

Imported foods are expensive. Partly because of shipping costs and partly because of foreign exchange differentials, most

North American and European products are prohibitive. Central American substitutes are often as good, and locally grown—fresh foods are always much better than something canned or packaged.

Furnishing Your Home

It used to be, when foreign residents received their papers they had the right to import household goods duty-free. This was a valuable consideration, since electrical appliances, televisions, video recorders and the like are incredibly expensive in Costa Rica because of high import duties. The rules were, after the goods had been in your possession for three years, you could legally sell them, probably make a profit and then buy new ones.

Unfortunately, this benefit was repealed in April of 1992. The anguish and wailing over the loss of these privileges rocked the North Americans residente community to its heels. A series of appeals are underway in an effort to reverse this action, and there is always a possibility of this happening. Apologetic government officials claim that they are searching for ways to make up for this lost benefit to foreign residents, possibly through other rebates.

Even if these tax breaks are a thing of the past, we should be aware that duty-free imports on household goods aren't nearly as important as they once were. At one time, demand for furniture outstripped the capacity to produce it. It was cheaper and more convenient to ship your used stuff from Miami than wait several months for the factory to fill your order at exorbitant prices.

Today, supply has caught up with demand; stores and markets offer a wide variety of furniture at reasonable prices. The amount of money you'd have to pay to have that bedroom suite and living room furniture shipped from Des Moines, Detroit, Denver—or wherever—would go a long way towards furnishing your new home in Costa Rica. While browsing in the Heredia public market (a great place to shop), I jotted down some furniture prices. These pieces seemed to be of acceptable quality, at least to my untrained eye. A bedroom set—bed, dresser and night stands—was priced at $160; a dining room set with six chairs, $102; and a living room suite—sofa, two easy chairs and a coffee table, $250. Granted, my taste for furniture may be dull, and I may not know quality workmanship when I see it, but everything looked serviceable.

Household appliances such as refrigerators, washing machines or TVs can be purchased from a local dealer without waiting for months, as it used to be. It's true that customs duties will boost prices for foreign residents, but local folks have been paying full price for years. The good news is that prices should be dropping as the government cuts the import taxes to a more reasonable level. In the meantime, what is so bad about having to pay the same prices for goods as your Costa Rican neighbors? You can be sure that this special treatment was a source of irritation and resentment among the Costa Rican community. Perhaps they couldn't blame foreigners for paying less, but they did fault their government for taxing them *more*. This will remove a bone of contention with our friends and neighbors.

Household Servants

The notion of housemaids and gardeners seem a bit wild for most of us who live in the United States. (The last time we hired a cleaning lady, she charged $14 an hour and wouldn't do windows or dishes.) But in Costa Rica, servants are affordable. With the minimum wage for domestic servants at 11,796 colónes a month ($84.25 at the present exchange rate), it makes sense to hire a housemaid and a gardener—at least on a part-time basis. Ticos are generally hard working and honest, and if you can afford it, you can have someone working around the house, who won't complain about doing windows and dishes.

However, be aware that fringe benefits added to the basic minimum wage raise the true cost of hiring servants. By law, you are responsible for things like vacations, Christmas bonus, social security and severance pay. Yet even with all of these things added, a housemaid in Costa Rica costs an employer about $115 a month, at today's minimum wage rate. (Wages are indexed twice a year, according to inflation.) Many people report that they pay more than minimum wage; it makes their employees happier and loyal. Servants are affordable, but you must be aware of the laws covering their benefits. You are responsible for knowing about them and paying them on time. These rules are discussed thoroughly in Chapter Eleven of this book. Don't hire a servant until you've read the rules!

Television and Other Media

Costa Rica has a modern television system, with six local channels. One of them is a governmental operated cultural channel. Several TV systems transmit in English; these are Channel 19, Cable Color, Super Canal and Grupo Master TV. These channels present some of the best programming direct from the United States. Video rental stores routinely stock big-game sports events, such as the Super Bowl or World Series games which are taped in the U.S. and sent to Costa Rica by air express the following day.

In San José and most of the surrounding cities, you'll find English-language paperback books and magazines. In addition to the essential *Tico Times*, you can buy a daily edition of the *Miami Herald Latin American Edition*, the *New York Times*, *Washington Post*, and the *Wall Street Journal*. These papers are a bit expensive—they have to come in by air—but there are times when North Americans become absolutely starved for a big-city daily newspaper. You'll find yourself devouring it from front to back, including the advertisements.

Movie Theaters: In San José, 11 cinema theaters show first-run and recent English-speaking films—mostly from Hollywood. Tickets cost about $1.75. Because the dialogue is almost exclusively in English, Spanish subtitles are printed over the lower part of the screen, giving one the opportunity of improving Spanish skills by reading while listening to the meaning. In many countries where almost no one understands English, the sound is turned down to a whisper, and the audience chatters away, making comments about the movie or whatever. But in Costa Rican theaters the soundtrack runs at a normal volume so the many Ticos who know English can listen. They enjoy sharpening their English by listening and using the subtitles to clarify the meaning. The end result is that Tico audiences are as polite as you could hope for and everyone can enjoy the movies.

Besides the regular cinema theaters there are usually some film festivals of special interest. For example, at the time of writing, there is a Chinese film festival sponsored by the Republic of China Embassy and a series called "The Mafia in the Movies," at the University of Costa Rica.

Live Theater: There are nine legitimate theaters, mostly in Spanish, offering entertainment for those who are well along in their study of the language. One ongoing production is about the history of coffee in Costa Rica, tracing its arrival from Arabia, plus legends and beliefs about the wondrous substance. It is half in English and half in Spanish, with discounts for Costa Rican citizens and pensionados. Two little theater groups produce plays in English.

Two *folklorico* groups regularly present traditions from various parts of the republic, one at the Herradura Hotel and another at the Melico Salazar Theater. Also there are regular concerts by the National Symphony Orchestra. Sponsored by the government Ministry of Culture, Youth and Sports, many visiting musicians from other countries add to the quality of the presentations.

Latin Lovers

Single women visitors find that many Costa Rican men fancy themselves prototypes of the "Latin lover." It's as a Latin friend once explained, "When I was a young man, my father one day took me aside to tell me the facts of life. He said, 'My son, in this world you must understand one thing: you *cannot* go to bed with every woman you meet. But, you must at least *try*!'"

Mostly trying comes in the form of *priopos*, or flirtatious, double-entendre remarks as ladies walk past a group of "Latin lovers" on the street corner. The remarks are intended to be humorous asides to draw laughs and approval from the man's companions. Unlike in some countries, the remarks here are rarely blatantly obscene, so a lady can safely smile as she continues on her way. Costa Rican ladies take it all in stride, either pretending they heard nothing, or smiling if the priopo was particularly flattering. But American women, unused to this unwanted attention, often take offense. Showing anger is a mistake, because your indignation simply amuses the offender and the bystanders. Although you may disapprove of this cultural absurdity, priopos are a fact of life in Costa Rica. When you, as an outsider, try to change things, you end up making a fool of yourself. If you absolutely cannot ignore the remark, a simple curling of the lip as an expression of disgust, as you continue on your way, is ample. You've put him down as repugnant instead of clever enough to get under your skin.

It's perfectly acceptable for single women to enter bars, restaurants or nightclubs, and they won't likely be bothered by priopos because most bartenders won't stand for it. But since the bar will be full of "Latin lovers" you can be sure that before too long some feisty man will be testing his luck and charm by professing his undying love. Curiously, according to the foreign ladies I've talked to, every one of the men who tried to date them in bars was either "single" or "divorced." Now, isn't that convenient? The fact is, divorce in Costa Rica is not common, yet married men trying to pretend they are divorced is extremely common!

What About Single Men?

"After the divorce, the first thing I thought about was coming here to get away for a while. There's something romantic about the name *Costa Rica,* and I needed something to cheer me up after all my problems. I just knew it would be a great adventure." This is a typical reply when I would ask a single man why he was visiting here. A common follow-up statement was, "Actually, I only planned to stay for one month, but before I knew it, I met this pretty young lady, and now I'm married again!"

My research was conducted in San José's famous "Gringo Gulch" area. I've met a dozen or more fellow countrymen who married Costa Rican women, yet only one American woman who married a Costa Rican man. Why? I asked an ex-New Jersyite who married a Tica lady almost five ago. "Why? Because Costa Rica women are different in many ways. It's not just that they are pretty and young. That's not what it's all about. We come here looking for something we think we lost somewhere back through the years. What we find is a pretty young thing who treats us as if we were special and 20 years younger. They don't complain, they don't bitch, they do whatever they can to make us feel at home and wanted. It turns out to be a pretty fair arrangement; she agrees to treat me like a king until I kick off, in the meantime, she and her kids from her first marriage have financial security plus my pension after I'm gone."

What's the downside of this kind of relationship? "When you marry a Costa Rican, you marry her whole damned family! I'm expected to buy a new refrigerator for Mamá when it goes out, and new false teeth for Papá whether he needs them or not. When cousin Raúl needs a transmission for his car, guess who he 'borrows' the money from? I have to attend every family function from birthdays of third cousins to funerals of great-aunts-once-removed. And I can't understand a thing anybody's saying!"

Gringo Gulch, by the way, is an area around the odd-numbered avenidas and odd-numbered calles, on the edge of the downtown area where a number of inexpensive hotels and singles bars attract a large number of male fugitives from the northern climes. From the spacious, romantic Key Largo bar—which features a drove of glamorous, $50-a-night hookers—to the tiny New York bar where $15 will rent a lovely for the evening, most patrons are either divorced, widowed or confirmed bachelors. (Prostitution is legal in Costa Rica, with women undergoing mandatory testing on a regular basis.) The majority of the Gringos are of Social Security age, looking for that one last go-round. Surprisingly enough, some actually find it. Many of the ladies in these bars are "amateurs," who are really looking for some foreigner to marry and to take them away from all of this. An older one with a pension will do just fine.

One word of caution to would-be Don Juans: after dark, stay away from the *zona roja* (red-light zone) in the opposite corner of town. The street girls here are professionals, teamed with their boyfriends to make a living by stealing wallets. In any part of downtown, particularly near the Gringo bars, beware of girls working in groups of three. Their scam is pretending to be overwhelmed by a man's sex appeal and two of them distract him by attempting to unzip his fly while the third goes through his pockets.

Gambling Casinos

For those addicted to the sound of a roulette ball bouncing along the wheel, or to the riffling sound of cards being shuffled, you'll find no lack of action in Costa Rica. There are numerous gambling casinos scattered about the country. Many large hotels have casinos, sometimes in the lobby as if this were a miniature Las Vegas. Some gambling casinos are found upstairs over night clubs or restaurants.

While I like to gamble, I also like to have a chance of winning. I have the distinct feeling that gaming in the average Costa Rican casino is not really gambling, merely donating to the profitability of the establishment. House rules make it highly unlikely that you will break even, much less win. The games aren't standard ones which can be easily understood—games like poker or blackjack. Play is similar to Las Vegas or Reno, but the rules and payoffs are different, sometimes confusing, stacking the odds in favor of the house.

Another disquieting thing about gambling in Costa Rica is that there is almost no government regulation. Although the house doesn't have to cheat you, since the odds are so much in their favor, there is little or nothing to prevent them from doing so.

Latin American Time

A most difficult thing to get used to is the way Costa Ricans view time. When invited to a social event in the United States or Canada, it's considered ill-mannered to arrive late. Not in Costa Rica. Should you receive an invitation for dinner, say at 8 p.m., and you actually arrive at that time, you are likely to embarrass the hosts; she is probably in the shower and he is still at the office. Typically guests arrive from one-half hour to two hours late. It doesn't matter, because the 8 o'clock dinner isn't served until midnight anyway, with guests going home about 1 or 2 a.m. Even after several decades of exposure to Latin American time, I've never understood it nor will I ever. When invited for a social gathering at 8 p.m., I always ask, "Is that 8 o'clock *Tico* time, or 8 o'clock *gringo* time?" The reply is usually a grin and, "Better make that 9 o'clock."

Gratuities

Restaurants, by law, add a 10 percent service charge to the bill. Then it's up to the customers if they care to leave something extra. I find that a 5 percent tip is greatly appreciated and leads to extra special service the next time. Barber shops and beauty salons expect a 15-20 percent tip. At Christmas time it's customary to give something to the newsboy, supermarket attendants, garbage collectors, and of course you give a yearly Christmas bonus to the maid, gardener and any other employees. As you will read in Chapter Eleven, this Christmas bonus is not a gift or a tip, but is required by law.

If you are a guest at someone's home where there are servants, it isn't necessary to tip them, not unless they've done something special for you, such as laundry, ironing or running errands. If a friend lends you the services of her maid, it's customary to tip and to pay for her taxi or bus fare home. Hotel chambermaids like to be tipped just as they do back home. I carry a few solar-powered calculators with me which I hand out as special gifts for someone who goes out of their way for me. Although these can be purchased for a couple of dollars back home, in Costa Rica they are rather expensive because of import duties.

Courtesy and Custom

Costa Rican social behavior is a curious mixture of old-world, Spanish formality and a special Tico-style of relaxed interactions. You always shake hands politely when being introduced or when meeting an acquaintance on the street, women as well as men. Women also may greet other women friends with a kiss on the cheek; with close friends a man may receive a light kiss, but only if they know each other well. The exaggerated hugging and kissing which is often common in the U.S. is not approved here.

Men, when greeting truly close friends, will often give an *abrazo*—a quick hug and pat on the back—or perhaps lightly clasp the friend's wrist or forearm instead of shaking hands.

"Getting down to business," as we North Americans are apt to do, without any preliminary greeting and small talk is considered somewhat rude in Costa Rica, yet not as rude as in some other Latin American societies. Costa Ricans know how we North Americans are, so they never make a big deal out of it; they realize that "business" is the custom in our countries. To be polite, you might spend a few moments inquiring about someone's children, or spouse, or perhaps give a compliment about their clothing or anything else you might think to say before talking business. It gets things off to a smoother start.

Costa Ricans have a delightful habit of issuing off-the-cuff invitations to visit them at their homes, for dinner or for cocktails, but you should always wait for the invitation and not just drop in. An exception to this is when someone moves into the neighborhood, or when you move into a new home. Then it's considered polite to knock on the door and introduce yourselves. When invited to someone's house for the first time, it's customary to bring flowers or some small gift.

Bringing Your Pets

Those who cannot stand the thought of going anywhere without their pets will be happy to know there is no legal problem in bringing them to Costa Rica. It does, however, require a bit of paperwork. To get a doggie passport, you must write to: Jefe del Departamento de Zoonosis, Ministerio de Salud, Apartado 10123, San José, and request a *permiso de importación* (import permit). Complete the form, send it to the ministry with the fee and documents.

You will need a health certificate signed by a registered veterinarian, which must be certified by a Costa Rican consul. Your hometown veterinarian should be able to handle all the paperwork, which must state that the animal is parasite-free, has all current vaccinations against rabies, distemper, hepatitis, parvovirus and leptosporosis. The rabies shots must be at least three months old, but less than three years. Doggie or kitty fingerprints are not necessary. Your pet then becomes a legal *residente* with full rights of litterbox use or guard duty; however, without voting privileges.

To leave the country, your pet needs an exit permit, just like human residentes. You need a health certificate from a Costa Rican veterinarian, complete with vaccination records. You take this document to the Ministry of Health to obtain a stamp, then to the Banco Central for a *permiso de exportación* and more stamps. Unlike a human residente, your pet doesn't need a certificate of good conduct to leave, so that time Fifi took a chunk out of the mailman's leg doesn't count.

Costa Ricans love their pets but they tend to keep them on leashes or in their yards more than do some North Americans. Your free-wandering pooch or kitty could be at the not-so-tender mercy of the many big watchdogs lounging about the neighborhood, always ready to bully. Contrary to some Latin American countries, pet food is readily available at most Costa Rican supermarkets, and sometimes in the local pulpería. Veterinarians are numerous, at least half a dozen practicing in the San José area.

Miscellaneous Information

Electric current is the same as in the United States or Canada: 110 volts alternating current.

Time: Costa Rica is on Central Standard Time, but because the length of the days is virtually unchanged over the seasons, Daylight Savings Time is not observed.

Tipping: Hotels, restaurants and night clubs are required to add 23 percent to the bill; 13 percent sales tax (IVA) plus 10 percent service charge. Altough the 10 percent is considered a tip, the usual custom is to add an extra 5 percent to 10 percent to the bill for good service. The 13 percent IVA is added to all bills.

Drugs: The law provides a jail sentence of eight to 20 years for anyone involved in drug dealing. Drug use is considered rather serious, and mere possession of drugs can be interpreted as evidence of drug dealing.

Chapter Seven

A Healthy Country

In many third world countries you play a game of Russian roulette when choosing a restaurant. A dining room can look wonderful, with white tablecloths, gleaming silverware and tuxedo-attired waiters, but the kitchen can be a virtual cesspool. Not so in Costa Rica. If a restaurant looks good, then its kitchen will be just as nice. I've found very few places where I would hesitate to eat, and I've never been served bad food. I can't say that about some United States restaurants.

The level of cleanliness of Costa Rican restaurants is remarkable indeed. This is partly due to government regulation, but more because the Ticos have a natural inclination toward neatness and cleanliness. Another factor in restaurant safety is the relative scarcity of houseflies in Costa Rica. Since this is the tropics, you might expect to see more insects than you would in the more temperate zones of North America, and you do, but in balance. Yet, you'll see remarkably few houseflies, the true villains in spreading disease. In San José and other towns on the Central Plateau, you can eat outside at a sidewalk cafe without sharing your lunch with flies. This seems strange to visitors from North America's Midwest, where fly population blooms in the summer to a plague. Yes, an occasional fly might drift past, curious as to what you are having for lunch, but this is rare. The same thing goes for mosquitoes; in the dry season, they are as scarce as houseflies, and even in the wet season they aren't so plentiful as to require screens on the windows in many areas.

You Can Drink the Water!

As a part of its commitment to serving the public, the Costa Rican government has spent large sums of money on water and sewage treatment. Unlike in most Mexican and Central American cities, you can drink the water in San José and other major towns around the country. Many smaller towns have excellent quality water, as do most hotels, where drinking water comes from safe wells. The government strictly monitors these water systems, even those private ones used by a handful of people. Every two months, at a minimum, tests are made for purity.

There are, however, a few places with questionable water supplies, where ordinary precautions should be observed. Amoebas and giardia are not unknown. Local people know about this and will warn you. Escazú, a ritzy suburb of San José, is an example of a place where drinking water can be unsatisfactory. The problem is intermittent, so if you are renting a place here, check with neighbors and follow their example.

By and large, you don't have to worry about drinking water or brushing your teeth in the Meseta Central. However, should you come down with something resembling "travelers' disease," with symptoms of diarrhea and nausea, you should take a stool sample to a local laboratory and have it analyzed for a small fee. The lab doctor or a pharmacist can tell you what kind of medicine you'll need; prescriptions are unnecessary in Costa Rica except for addictive or dangerous drugs.

Medical Care

The United State's irrational health-care system, with its exclusion of about 37 million citizens from the ranks of medically insured, is yet another reason people think favorably about living in a country where health care is not only available, but affordable. In a United States hospital, patients with Medicare coverage usually pay far more just for their *deductible* share than the total operation and hospital bill would cost in Costa Rica!

In the United States, should you visit the emergency room, the first thing they ask for is your hospitalization plan or credit card. If you have neither, you could be told to get lost. In Costa Rica, when going to an emergency room in any government hospital, there is no charge for resident, visitor, or even someone in the country illegally! This affordable medical system is another of the benefits Costa Rica enjoys because there is no military to absorb resources. Statistics show that the general level of care is equal to or superior to the United States. In fact, the United Nations recently noted that Costa Rica is in first place in Latin America for development of preventive and curative medicine, ranking with the United States and Canada among the 20 best in the world. Infant mortality is lower in Costa Rica than in the United States. The average life expectancy is 74 years for men, about the same as in the United States, but far above other Latin American countries.

Why is quality health care inexpensive in Costa Rica? A prominent physician (in private practice in San José) explained it this way: "Here, our government considers medical care as a public service and obligation, just as it considers education and highways a public responsibility. The government builds hospitals and trains medical specialists to serve the people, not as a business. But in the United States, medical care is a profit-making industry, a big business where profits are maximized to the highest point people can pay. Here, a doctor working for a government clinic earns between $500 and $1,000 a month. In your country, where doctors work for profit, $20,000 a month is more common. Some heart surgeons in the United States will schedule five heart-bypass operations the same day. At $50,000 from each patient, this assembly-line practice brings in $250,000 for one day's work!"

The doctor went on to say, "Where there is no competition, medical specialists can charge what they like. But here in Costa Rica, we have competition between our free, public hospitals and private clinics and private doctors such as myself. We private doctors must keep our fees in line, or patients will go to free clinics."

Medical Costs

In San José, a visit to a private physician's office costs about $15 to $20. As of spring 1992, a day in a modern, first-class private hospital came to $72.68! The food is excellent, by the way, not the skimpy, tasteless food we're used to in U.S. hospitals, but delicious, and usually more than you can eat. The $72.68 rate is the *most expensive*—for a private room, private bath, color television, plus an extra bed and meals for an *acompañate* or companion. (It's customary for a family member or friend to spend the night in your room after an operation or when you are in serious condition, at no extra charge.) If you are willing to put up with sharing a bath with the room next door and can do without your own private phone, the cost drops to $42.76 per day. And for a shared room and shared bath, you pay only $36.50 a day! Compare these prices to those in your community. You'd have a difficult time renting a motel room at these rates. In many places in the United States, if you can get out of a hospital for less than $1,500 a day, just for the room, you can feel lucky.

Choosing a Doctor

Foreign residents can "buy into" the Social Security system (Caja, as it's called in Costa Rica) by paying a fee from $40 to $50 a month, and then going to government hospitals for treatment. However, since medical care is free, it isn't surprising to find that the system is crowded, well-used by the people. When people don't feel quite up to snuff, they traipse off to the hospital to see a doctor. For emergency treatment, there is no problem—you are seen immediately—but for an ordinary office visit with a government doctor, you could find yourself standing in line or sitting in the waiting room for a long while. For elective surgery, you can expect a wait of several months for your turn. However, there is a better way; you choose a family doctor who is in both public and private practice, and then use the same doctor in both systems. Most doctors commonly work in both systems.

A resident of Heredia told of his strategy for choosing a family doctor. He said, "I joined the Social Security plan by paying approximately $40 a month. Then I visited a free clinic a few times until I found a doctor I liked. Then I made an appointment to see him in his private practice. Now, as my regular doctor, I can see him any time simply by making an appointment and paying $20 for an office visit. But if something expensive ever comes up, such as a major operation, I'll make an arrangement to go into the government hospital for free treatment by the same doctor!"

Even if a patient chooses a private doctor and uses a private hospital, costs are ridiculously low compared to the United States. For example: In San José, the typical bill for a gall bladder operation is $2,000, and for an appendectomy $1,200 to $1,800. The total cost of a heart bypass operation is currently $15,000—that's "out the door," for everything—as opposed to $50,000 in the United States, *plus* hospital room, anesthesiologist, medication and all of the medical team's fringe benefits.

For those with Medicare, be aware that it is not valid outside of the United States. However, for those under 70 years of age, there is a Costa Rican government insurance company, the National Insurance Institute (INS), which offers a policy for $170 a year for adults and $110 for dependents under 24. This policy pays 80 percent of hospitalization (private room), post-operative care, medicines, lab tests, X-rays, CAT scans, cardiograms, therapy, home care and support systems. For surgical fees, the policy pays 100 percent up to a maximum which is based on a surgical table. Doctor visits are also covered to the limit of the schedule. The limits of the policy are said to be generous, taking into account the low medical costs in Costa Rica.

All retirees we interviewed swear by the quality of Costa Rican medical care. I can tell you my personal experience: I went to a doctor with a bad case of the flu, severe back and neck pains, and a fear that I had pneumonia. The doctor decided that I was going to be okay, but he suggested that I go to the hospital for a checkup and a rest. I asked for a shared room, but since the hospital wasn't full, they didn't put another patient in with me; essentially it was a private room for a two-bed ward rate. After three days of tests, medication and tender loving care (plus great meals) I was presented a bill which made me feel even better. The entire cost of three days in the hospital, including electrocardiogram, blood tests and X-rays, was less than if I had stayed in a moderately-priced hotel and dined in ordinary restaurants for those three days!

Dual System

Many Costa Rican doctors, after graduating from medical school, go to universities in the United States for further study and to do residencies. This is particularly true for specialists; since Costa Rica is such a small country, there aren't enough patients with the same problem to allow a doctor the opportunity of seeing the wide variety of patients needed to get the experience in his specialty.

I asked a physician from Ohio who had retired in Costa Rica some years ago, "Why would a Costa Rican doctor, who does a residency in the United States or Canada, return here to work for only $1,000 a month?"

"You have to understand," he replied, "most doctors only work half time for the government, and half time for themselves," the doctor explained. "Take the case of a cardiologist who charges $35 an office visit. If he sees five patients a day on his own, that's $175 a day or about $45,000 a year, plus his $12,000 salary from the government. When you consider that most doctors manage to pay little or no income taxes here in Costa Rica, and that the cost of living is far less here, a huge percentage of the doctor's earnings is available for savings or investment. Even though Costa Rican doctors earn a fraction of what U.S. doctors do, they live here just as well or better, *and* they are living in Costa Rica instead of Cleveland!"

Hospitals in San José

There are three large Social Security system hospitals in San José, with round-the-clock emergency care—regular hours for laboratories, X-rays, pharmacies and doctor's appointments. These are the Calderón Guardia, San Juan de Dios and Mexico. Private hospitals are the Clinica Biblica and Clinica Catolica, both excellent hospitals—the Clinica Biblica being the newest and

Street Market in San José

Ecotourists in the Mud

Comfortable Lodgings in the Countryside

Photographs by the author and by Michael Medill of Rainbow Adventures

Tropical Harvest

Jungle Waterfall

Parrots

Banana Tree

Cabin at Rainbow Adventures

Beach at Selva Alegre

GUATEMALA

Lake Atitlán

Indian Weavers

Ruins at Antigua

more modern—offering the same services as the government hospitals, but with no waiting for elective medical care. Next to the Clinica Biblica is the Clinica Americana, an office complex with a group of English-speaking doctors, most of whom did residency in U.S. hospitals. The KOP Medical Clinic in Escazú specializes in treating foreigners, with a staff that speaks English, French, Spanish and Japanese. They offer a wide range of services, including obstetrics and gynecology, pediatrics and dermatology.

Note that *clinica* usually indicates private hospitals or clinics, available to anyone, including foreigners. The government facilities will treat tourists and foreign residents in their emergency clinics at no charge. Some emergency rooms specialize; for example Hospital Mexico specializes in heart attacks and San Juan de Dios has a burn center. Most other towns of any size will have a hospital and those that are too tiny will have a doctor with emergency equipment to handle problems.

Rest Homes

Care for infirm elderly patients is excellent in Costa Rica, with the cost paid for by the government. However, I believe that this is something available only to long-term residents who become infirm *after* becoming pensionados or rentistas. In order to receive residency permission, one needs to pass a health examination, and I cannot imagine a doctor giving an Alzheimer's patient a clean bill of health. However, if you contract Alzheimer's or some other condition that requires long-term care after you have been living in Costa Rica as a resident, that's a different story.

A government facility may not be suitable for a foreigner because of language and communication problems. But there are several private full-care facilities, at least one offering specialized care for Alzheimer's patients: Golden Valley Hacienda in Alajuela. Also in Alajuela is the Villa Confort Geriatric Hotel which specializes in folks who are not bedridden but who need care in everyday living. The cost is about $1,500 a month for round-the-clock care. A facility in Los Yoses, the Hogar Retiro San Pedro, has been given high praise recently by an American lady for the care there. The third facility is the Hogar para Ancianos Alfredo y Delia González in Heredia. This one is in the process of starting something new in Costa Rica: a senior citizen residence-development of individual cottages for folks who do not require full care. Housekeeping services and meals will be provided plus recreational facilities and physical therapy services. In addition to medical care it will have recreational, hobby, arts and travel programs for its people. Residents must be over 65 and able to purchase a cottage. A catalog can be obtained by writing to Apdo 138 in Heredia.

Dentists

The University of Costa Rica trains medical specialists of all kinds, including highly skilled dentists, periodontists and or-thodontic surgeons. Like medical care, dental care in Costa Rica is also affordable. To learn what the current costs are, I asked friends to recommend an English-speaking dentist in Alajuela. I made an appointment for an examination and peridontal clean-ing. Back home, I pay my regular periodontist $51 to have this work done. In Costa Rica, I paid $26.

When asked about Costa Rican dental prices compared to the United States, the dentist, Dr. John Pinchanski, said, "Depending upon where you live in the United States, dental care can be three to six times as expensive. For example, in Costa Rica the standard price for a porcelain cap is $125. In Los Angeles the same work costs from $600 to $700. A bridge typically costs $375 here, but a similar job in Los Angeles would cost at least $1,800. I've had patients who fly here, pay for their hotel, food and airfare, and still save money."

What about quality? "Dental work in Costa Rica is equal to that done in the U.S.A.," he replied. "There is absolutely no difference in the competency of the dentists. However, the quality of dental laboratory work is usually better here in Costa Rica. I happen to have my own dental lab, but all of our dental tech-nicians are excellent, equal to those in the United States. Don't misunderstand, the U.S.A. also has excellent dental labs, but because they can get the work done cheaper in the Philippines, dentists are sending the bridgework and dental caps overseas, to low-cost laboratories. The quality just isn't up to the standards of Costa Rica or American labs. If I were to have caps or bridgework done in the U.S.A., I'd certainly insist that my dentist use an American dental laboratory."

Plastic Surgery

Costa Rica has gained worldwide recognition for another of its medical services: reconstructive surgery, commonly known as plastic surgery. San José is becoming known as "Beverly Hills South" because of the number of people going there for body renewal. Several excellent surgeons specialize in face lifts, liposuction, breast reconstruction and other corrections of nature's mistakes. Not only are Costa Rican plastic surgeons ranked among the best in the world, their fees are based on Costa Rican medical standards. In a word, inexpensive.

Why would Costa Rica be so popular with those wanting to rid themselves of wrinkles? Besides affordable costs and quality surgery, it turns out that San José is a perfect place to slip away to have an operation because of its climate—never hot, never cold—which makes recuperation faster, safer and more comfortable. Since the healing process takes three or four weeks, many patients find this a great time to learn Spanish in one of the many "total immersion" schools around the city. These schools provide for home-stays with a Costa Rican family and have small classes or even individual instruction if you prefer.

Another attractive thing about Costa Rica as a base for facial or other cosmetic surgery is that many folks feel embarrassed about having their friends and family know they are going to have it done. Therefore, a growing number of them vacation in Costa Rica—where they are unlikely to run into acquaintances—have the operation and return home a month later when all traces of the surgeon's handiwork have disappeared.

San José's leading plastic surgeon is Dr. Arnoldo Fournier, who did his residency in reconstructive surgery at New York's Columbia University and who has the oldest established plastic surgery practice in Costa Rica. He says, "Since I started my practice back in 1973, there have been several important developments in reconstructive surgery. Just a few years ago, the common face lift procedure was merely to stretch the facial skin to the sides of the neck and cheeks. This procedure was often unsatisfactory because of a stretched appearance of the face and because the operation had to be repeated when the skin sagged and wrinkles returned after a few years.

"Today, a face lift should be called 'face remodeling' because it involves far more than simply stretching the skin. The excess layer of fat is trimmed away from the neck and fat sacks are carefully removed from the cheeks or jowls by liposuction. Then the facial muscles are moved to the facial center and stitched together under the chin. As a result, the neck has been tightened from both sides and from below. This repositioning of facial tissues produces a lasting, youthful and smooth appearance, with a natural touch instead of looking tightly stretched."

Eyelid surgery completes the face lift, and it can be done at the same time although many people opt to have them separately. Dr. Fournier explains, "Puffy eyelids and bags under the eyes, whether congenital or a result of aging, give the appearance of tiredness or sadness, and make a patient look old beyond his or her years. This can be effectively corrected through a surgical procedure called *blefaroplasty*, and is the operation most frequently requested by men. The procedure involves removing the excess fat that produces the bulging and trimming away the loose skin that makes the under-eye bags. The fine scars are concealed in the upper eyelid crease and in the lower eyelid, just below the eyelashes. They are invisible after three or four weeks. Since the removed fat will never return, the results are more or less permanent."

What does all of this cost? Happily, the cost of a face lift, a breast job or a tummy tuck with liposuction—including surgery, postoperative care and hospital stay—is less than one might pay just for three days in a hospital in the United States! For example, a complete face lift is less than $4,000, including three days in the hospital. To have the same operation in New York or Los Angeles, the bill would be $22,000, possibly more, depending upon the cost of the hospital room. Dr. Fournier charges $800 for the eye operation when done separately. Nose surgery or liposuction to abdomen and thighs costs about $2,000 to $3,000, compared to U.S. rates of about $10,000 for the same procedures.

How safe is it? Costa Rican hospitals are excellent, with all modern equipment. Personnel are highly trained. Dr. Fournier points out, "Most of my surgery is done under local anesthetic and sedation. The patient is given some pills a couple of hours prior to the operation, and intravenous medication is given by an anesthesiologist during surgery. This is much safer than using a general anesthetic. Some patients just stay one night in the hospital and then check into a bed and breakfast for a few days. Others prefer to stay a while, since hospital rooms don't cost any more than a first-class hotel."

For more information, you may write to Dr. Fournier and ask for his free booklet, *A Brief Introduction to Plastic Surgery*. The address is P.O. Box 117-1002, Paseo de los Estudiantes, San José, Costa Rica, Central America. The FAX number is (506) 55-43-70. This publication explains thoroughly what to expect, illustrates the procedures with detailed drawings and gives preoperative and postoperative advice.

Chapter Eight

Renting or Buying

Because North Americans in Costa Rica don't feel the need to group together—living in compounds or sealed-off neighborhoods as they do in some other countries—housing selection is far more open. Costa Ricans and North Americans are so similar that most of us feel comfortable living just about anywhere in the country. Even though Spanish is the dominant language, almost everyone has been exposed to English in Costa Rica's excellent school system. Since juvenile delinquency isn't out of control, and because neighborhood kids are generally well-behaved, we North Americans don't feel threatened as we might in some lower-economic areas back home. Except for a few condominiums and special developments in the more expensive areas, you'll find North Americans spread out all over the Meseta Central, and in fact, all over the country.

Renting

For an idea of what you might have to pay to rent a house or an apartment, check the *Tico Times* classifieds for a wide range of rents. Houses and apartments are offered at rents ranging from $200-a-month to $1,500 a month. While the $1,500 home will be spacious and luxurious, chances are the $200-a-month place is perfectly livable, and just as nice as similar places back home that rent for twice that amount.

But for many Costa Rican families, the idea of paying even $200 a month seems expensive. So, if you are looking for the rock bottom in rents, check the classifieds in the Spanish-language newspaper, *La Nación*. The ads in that paper are read by local people who do not have the ability to pay higher rents.

Apartments and Rooms by the Week

Most people, when trying out Costa Rica for livability, don't enter into long-term rentals or sign leases until they are sure about their situation. An ideal way to savor living in one part of the country or another is to rent an apartment for one month or even one week. Short-term rentals are particularly useful when determining which neighborhood you'd like to settle in.

San José has several "apartotels," small apartments complete with cable TV, telephone, cooking utensils—in short, everything you need for a trial of Costa Rica living. One apartment complex regularly advertises rates of $22 a day or $480 a month for a three-bedroom apartment, another for $360 monthly or $160 weekly for a one-bedroom place, with telephone, TV and washing machines. You can pay a lot more, but these apartments seemed okay by my standards. (Realize that I am easily satisfied in accommodations.)

Another excellent way of discovering whether you like a neighborhood or a city is to rent a room in a Costa Rican home. Because of pressure on hotels for tourist rooms, many private families are converting spare bedrooms into rentals. They are happy to host North Americans on their visits, to take them into their homes and treat them as part of the family. A bonus to living with a family is the opportunity to perfect your Spanish by total immersion in the language. Most language schools encourage students to stay in private homes, and make arrangements for the students. Typically, a family will charge from $80 to $120 a week for a room, which includes two meals a day (breakfast and supper), and your laundry.

Don't confuse the private home setup with the traditional bed and breakfast. There are several of these in the Meseta Central, which are actually small hotels that include breakfast with the room. These are nice too, but offer neither the economy nor the family atmosphere of the private family home. Bed and breakfasts range from $10 a day, single, near downtown San José on up to

$175, single, on a coffee plantation near Heredia. Most are around $35, double.

Buying a House

Many, if not most countries in the world severely restrict the rights of foreigners to buy property. Some absolutely prohibit it. Not Costa Rica; this is one country where you needn't be a citizen or go through all kinds of legal gymnastics in order to own property. If you're big enough to buy it, it's yours.

The standard recommendation to visitors is always to wait at least six months before buying property. However, many catch real estate fever within the first few days of their initial visit, and end up buying something anyway. At this particular time, there seems to be a buying frenzy in Costa Rica, with people from all over the world plunking down money to buy something—anything—before it's all gone.

Although buying property in Costa Rica should be rather straightforward, it can be tricky if not handled right. One rule is: never count on a verbal contract for anything. A handshake means nothing. You may think that you have a deal, and when you return with the cash, someone else owns the place and is moving in furniture.

A second rule: find a competent, English-speaking attorney to handle the deal for you. This can be a challenge in itself. Since qualifying as a lawyer in Costa Rica isn't as complicated as in other countries, so you'll find many people who *call* themselves attorneys, but actually practice law as a sideline or specialize in a particular line of business, and know nothing about real estate. A poor attorney isn't necessarily crooked; he could be inefficient and incompetent, which is just as bad. You need to be sure the person who is selling you the property actually owns it. You must be positive that liens, mortgages and second deeds aren't attached to the property like lamprey eels on a shark's belly.

Since Costa Rica is so small, the government is able to keep all land records in one place, at a central title registry called the *Registro de la Propiedad* in Zapote in southeastern San José. All liens and attachments must be registered here and are open to the public. Even though the process of checking out a deed takes but a few minutes, your attorney needs to know how to go about it. If you find nothing against the piece of real estate, you can safely transfer it to your name, and any outstanding debts or obligations not registered are null and void. But don't feel smug until you make sure that your lawyer actually registers your new property and the documents are stashed away in your safe-deposit box. Inquire around the North American community for recommendations for an attorney. Some claim that an attorney from one of the "old families" are best, because they know a lot of people in the bureaucracy who can make things easier.

Do not trust the seller or agent just because he is a fellow North American! There's something about a foreign country that seems to bring out latent tendencies toward larceny in some of our compatriots. If you follow the *Tico Times* crime news, as I do, you'll read about an astounding number of inherent confidence men who come out of the closet the moment they arrive in Costa Rica. Mostly they are rank amateurs, but since they are dealing with people like me—also rank amateurs in business deals—they can cause much damage before they are finally caught. Make sure you are dealing with someone who is competent and honest; ask around town.

In Costa Rica, installment sales are not the norm; you need to plop cash on the barrel head for most property transactions. Real estate agents take a commission of between five and ten percent, and closing costs amount to another five to seven percent—usually split between buyer and seller. Prices are usually quoted in dollars, even though I understand that's illegal.

Above all, do not become so overcome with the beauty and tranquility of Costa Rica that you accept the first price asked. Ticos sometimes have an irrational streak when valuing their houses or farms. North Americans, who are bloodthirsty for profit can be even worse. The selling prices of comparable properties often have no effect on logic when it comes to asking price or bargaining. Keep looking around until you find the exact property you want for a fair price. Vigorous bargaining will pay off here.

Beach Front Property

Prices are booming all along the Pacific coast. Prices in some areas are going wild, although other places have bargains going begging. The situation is somewhat murky, because much of the land that is being bought and sold has tough building and owner-ship restrictions—even though you might not be told about them until after you've bought. Foreigners are supposedly limited as to the amount of ocean front property they can own, and everyone is restricted as to how close to the beach they can build.

Although laws protecting beach front properties are on the books, in some areas they don't appear to be rigidly enforced. In fact, in many localities the laws are all but ignored. When buying beach front property, it is important to know the rules and be prepared for the government to someday step in and begin enfor-cement. It may never happen, then again, if there is enough public outcry, there could be problems.

Generally, the laws go like this: The first 200 meters ashore, from a mark halfway between low tide and high tide lines, is the Maritime Zone. The first 50 meters, the "public zone," belongs absolutely to the public, and is strictly off-limits to construction of any kind. The next 150 meters is called the "restricted zone." Any construction within this zone must be with permission from the municipality. Construction permits are intended for the development of tourist projects. It's also my understanding that permission can be, and often is, withheld from non-citizens until they have five years residency.

People have been dodging these laws by buying the property under the name of a Costa Rican corporation (owned by the foreigner). Theoretically, the owner is an anonymous corporation, not a foreigner (see explanation below). This sounds like subter-fuge to me, but attorneys claim that it is perfectly legal, and that everyone is doing it. Clearly, they seem to be getting by with it. As a matter of fact, it appears that almost all desirable beach property was long ago bought by foreigners (mostly Americans and Canadians). Now they are trading back and forth, boosting the price on each transaction and selling to Europeans who are getting in on the act. The Germans and Swiss, in particular, seem to be buying everything they can get their hands on.

A hidden problem is that much Maritime Zone beach front property belongs to the government and can only be leased from the government for a 99-year period. Thus, you might assume that your bargain $25,000 two-and-a-half acre lot on the beach is an outright purchase, whereas you actually paid that money merely for the right to renew a lease every five years—providing you have done everything right, paid the lease money and taxes on time and obeyed all the rules. Should you miss a move, you could see your lease evaporate. I repeat, make absolutely certain that you own the property, or at least you know what it is you are buying—the property or the right to lease the property.

Another problem: Many sellers believe that their buildings, which fall within the 200-meter mark, are legal because they've been "grandfathered." The actual fact could be that someone in the past ignored the rules, and the bureacuracy hasn't gotten around to enforcing the laws. The government can force you to dismantle the buildings and restore the property to its original state, should it choose to do so.

Problems with Parachutists

Anyone who has followed the battles between North Americans and squatters in the *Tico Times* is aware of hair-raising stories concerning squatters and legitimate property owners. The popular name for a squatter is a *paracaidista* or "parachutist," that is, a person who "drops in" on your property and claims it as his own, in short, a "squatter." (Local people often drop the *d*, spelling it *paracaista*.). If you're thinking of buying a piece of property, you need to be aware of the squatter problem.

If the property you are interested in has an extra house and family on one corner, *beware!* Don't let the seller pass this off as the "caretaker's home." It could be a paracaidista's home! Make sure you see documents proving that this is indeed a caretaker employee, not a squatter. In order to be a caretaker, a person must receive minimum wages of at least $110 a month, social security payments made for him each month, plus all other legal benefits.

The papers proving all of this *must be up to date.* Have your lawyer examine the proof.

To most of us, the idea of someone simply moving in on your property is outrageous; it is trespassing; it smacks of the old wild-west battles between cattlemen and sheepherders. Can something like this really happen in a law-abiding country like Costa Rica? Aren't property owners protected by the law? Isn't all of this illegal?

Well, it turns out that it *is* legal, to an extent. There are laws to the effect that unowned or abandoned property is open for homesteading, just as it was in the early days of the United States and still is in some Western states. These Costa Rican laws were intended to prevent a few wealthy people from hogging land they don't use and don't need. This is precisely what's happened in all other Central American countries; two or three percent of the people own up to 90 percent of the land, while the majority goes hungry. One reason Costa Rica is so much better off than her neighbors is that citizens have access to land. The laws are well-intentioned and fair. The problem comes when interpreting these laws.

Just when is a piece of land abandoned? This is the problem. One law, which seems clear, states that when property goes unattended for ten years, whoever has been using the land for that period may apply for a title. And they will be successful, unless the original owner has some pretty good lawyers and valid excuses. Even shorter periods of occupancy can cause problems. The longer the occupancy, the more serious the problems become.

We've heard stories of North Americans who purchased lovely tracts of forested land with the intention of building a home someday, then when they returned a few years later, were surprised to find the land cleared and someone farming it.

Typically what happens is that someone's unattended property becomes a tempting target for paracaidistas. They'll set up a cabin and plant a crop, in hopes they won't be discovered for a year, after which time they have certain rights. Before this year passes, they can easily be tossed off the property and charged with trespassing. After a year, the owner has the option of paying the squatter for his expenses (often greatly exaggerated) or else going to court. If the property owner hasn't shown any interest for as long as ten years, the squatter has a very strong argument for abandonment. At that point, the owner has the option of paying the squatter the money he has put into it, or walking away from the property. When the bill is too high (you can be sure it will be padded), it's sometimes cheaper to walk away. Understand, these problems seldom occur anywhere but on agricultural land. Land zoned residential doesn't fall into the category of this law.

The solution to this problem is simply a matter of prevention. While you are out of the country, have a friend or a management agent drop by the property once every three months. At this point, a simple complaint to the police is usually enough. Be sure to keep records of all your expenses and improvements to the property; this constitutes proof that you haven't abandoned the property. Having a friend plant a tree or clip some hedges once in a while covers this.

Occasionally a problem arises when someone returns home for an extended stay and decides to lay off his employees. If he isn't familiar with the laws, and neglects to pay workers' benefits such as severance pay, accrued vacation and year-end bonuses, the employees could feel justified in taking over the land as compensation. Chapter Eleven covers this in detail.

However repugnant the idea of squatting may be to you, it is important to operate within the law. After all, paracaidistas have rights as well. One lady, who had just purchased some property, told me that she was informed that "the only way to deal with squatters is to burn down their houses," and that is what she intended to do if she ever found any on her property. I was horrified to think of someone on a tourist visa, a guest in the country, taking the law into her own hands by setting fire to someone's home!

Property and Corporations

When buying property, one of the first things you'll probably want to do is form a corporation. This may sound strange, but there are several advantages to this. The section on tax havens in the next chapter explains how corporations are used for tax purposes, hiding assets and certain questionable activities, but there is nothing at all questionable about using corporations for real estate.

The procedure is this: Your attorney sets up a corporation with you owning all of the stock. Then, the property is registered in the name of the corporation, not in the name of the purchaser. Under Costa Rican law, whoever has possession of the firm's stock certificates owns the corporation and all of its assets. Therefore, since you own the corporation, you also have control of the house. A big tax advantage here is that should you decide to take a profit on the property, you sell the corporation's stock, not the house itself. From what I understand, you are not liable for capital gains taxes on the property, since the real estate was never sold, only the majority stock. Presumably, you would owe taxes on the profit from the sale of the stock, but this would fall under a different category of taxation, and I suspect that many never bother to report it since the stock ownership is untraceable. All of this sounds great, but do check with a qualified attorney before listening to my highly unqualified opinions. The next chapter gives more information about Costa Rican corporations.

Chapter Nine

Business Opportunities

Many countries severely restrict foreign business investment. Anxious to develop their own industry, these governments grant special considerations to local businessmen to the detriment of foreign investors. The rationale behind this practice is that foreign investors only want to take advantage of low wages and slack government controls to generate high profits, which are then spent in the foreigner's home country.

Costa Rica takes a different view of foreign investment, looking upon it as a way to spur needed development. Any investment that promotes tourism, creates jobs and doesn't harm the environment is considered desirable. Instead of discouraging investment, Costa Rica offers generous incentives and tax breaks. Depending on the type of business, there can be a 12-year exemption from income taxes as well as waivers on import duties. If ecology is concerned—particularly projects involving reforestation—the tax exemptions can be forever!

Therefore it is not surprising that during the past few years more and more businessmen and investors have demonstrated that Costa Rica, in addition to being a wonderful place for a vacation, also has a pleasant business climate. Among the things Costa Rica has going for it are political stability, a strategic location, an inexpensive labor force and an up-to-date infrastructure. Governmental incentives, in addition to tax breaks, include lines of financing for specific industries, elimination of customs duties on importation of primary materials and equipment and a Free Zone program. Since 1990, about $40 million U.S. dollars have been invested in Free Zones, of which approximately 65 percent is of U.S. origin.

The Free Trade Zone program was developed for foreign-owned firms for the operation of exporting enterprises and related industries. Generous tax exemptions are granted on all types of equipment, machinery, merchandise and goods needed for operation. Depending upon where the enterprise is located, up to ten years' tax exemptions are granted on property, real estate transfers, net capital and assets. Up to 100 percent exemptions on profits or other taxable income is granted for the first eight years of operation, and at a lower rate for the next four years. Firms operating in Free Zones can also sell up to 40 percent of their production in Costa Rica, with approval of the Ministry of Economy, Industry and Commerce. (Regular customs duty must be paid on these sales.)

The goverment-sponsored National Center for the Promotion of Exports (CENPRO) offers training programs and statistical information on products and markets. The goal is a central clearing house for fulfilling all requirements and paperwork involved with export-import commerce. Another organization dedicated to integration and representation of exporters is the Chamber of Costa Rican Exporters (CADEXCO).

Investments of $50,000 or more in specially approved projects qualify the investor for residency and eventually, a Costa Rican passport (after five years, as best I can tell). Because of these regulations, an unusual twist on Costa Rican investment is being played out in Hong Kong. Residents there fear what might happen when the People's Republic of China takes over the British Crown Colony in a few years. Therefore, by becoming legal residents of another country, such as Costa Rica, Chinese businessmen feel more secure in the event conditions get tough in Hong Kong. Simply by investing $50,000 in a teak plantation, they obtain residency, and don't really care whether they make money on their investment or not. They look on the $50,000 as an insurance policy. At least one American resident of Costa Rica is taking advantage of this situation. He purchased a large cattle ranch, planted teak, and now has salesmen in Hong Kong, soliciting investments in his project.

Having said all of this, I need to add that reforestation projects aren't just a matter of deciding to do it. You need to present a plan of the area and how you intend to go about it, and this must be prepared by an approved forestry technical expert (a member of the Forestry Professionals of the General Forestry Office). The property, once planted can be resold, as long as the purchaser agrees to continue with the reforestation project.

Going into Business

Most North Americans who go into business in Costa Rica don't bother using the $50,000 investment laws, since most of the tax advantages accrue to any qualifying business, and since a Costa Rican passport isn't much of an enticement to those already holding U.S. or Canadian passports. Residency papers can be obtained under the *residente rentista* provisions of the laws (explained in Chapter Twelve).

Anyone who owns a business is permitted to import items necessary to operate the business, without the usual import duties. This can be important. For example, while the owner of a motel or other tourist facility is restricted in the importation of an automobile, he is given tax breaks when importing a passenger van because he needs it to transport clients. The owner of a farm can buy a pickup or four-wheel-drive vehicle at reduced duties, because it's necessary for operation of the farm. For this reason you see many four-wheel-drives wheeling about the country, even in places where such a vehicle really isn't necessary; they are cheaper than regular automobiles.

For that matter, it isn't even necessary to become a resident to own and manage a business. Since most businesses are registered in the name of a corporation, a foreigner holding tourist papers can effectively control and work in the enterprise. While it is against the law for a non-citizen to work at an ordinary job without permission, it's perfectly okay to manage your own corporation. Some discretion is required here, however, since part of the scheme is to create jobs. I know of at least one case in which a foreign couple built a small business and managed it entirely by themselves (working very long hours, incidentally). Some local government officials hinted that perhaps they should hire some help, and were slow in granting permits as a way of reinforcing the hint until the couple finally hired a much-needed assistant.

Many North Americans have done quite well in Costa Rican business ventures. They bring enthusiasm, expertise and imagination, often recreating successful enterprises they operated in their home country. Foreigners are particularly successful in tourist-oriented businesses because they understand the wants and needs of other foreigners when visiting Costa Rica. Restaurants and bars seem to be popular ventures. However, the exceptionally high failure rate of this kind of business should worry investors. Motels, hotels or bed and breakfasts fare better, and real estate sales and development have produced some fabulous success stories.

One example of innovative thinking in business opportunities is an iguana farm. Looking like miniature dinosaurs, iguanas are considered gourmet food in some quarters, and apparently make good pets. The Costa Rica iguana farm was started by Dagmar Werner of the Green Iguana Association, and has earned her the nickname of "Iguana Mama," for her efforts to convince Ticos to try iguana farming as an alternative to cattle. Costa Rica is a growing economy; as it grows, so will opportunities for new businesses and acceptance of new ideas.

Buyer Beware

However, it is just as easy to lose money in Costa Rica as it is back home. For a stranger in a foreign land, it's even easier. You must know what you are doing. Ray Nelson, manager of Alajuela's Welcome Center, a firm specializing in travel, real estate and business investments, says, "My best advice is to come here for six months, and look around. Study the existing businesses and find out why some are successful and why others go belly-up. Above all, don't jump into a business just for the sake of being in business—particularly a business that you don't know much about."

One feels a dynamic sense of progress in the air in Costa Rica. This is the country of the entrepreneur. This is a country of wide-open opportunity, cheap land, dependable labor and honest government. Modern-day Costa Rica is reminiscent of the old frontier days of the U.S.A. and Canada, full of success stories about North Americans who've opted to "start all over again." But there are also horror stories. Because of Costa Rica's liberal attitude toward foreign business ventures and sometimes lax regulation, a surprising number of foreigners feel as though they have complete freedom to operate as they wish. Costa Rica draws more than its share of swindlers, crooks and con artists. A prime example of audacity: the *Tico Times* recently exposed a Canadian who tried to cash a fake check for $9.6 million dollars. It was drawn on the U.S. Treasury Department as an *income tax refund*! When the bank turned them down, the ambitious swindler and his accomplice fled the country.

The Costa Rican government does what it can to keep on top of swindlers, but its impossible to do much more than prosecute crooks *after* the damage has been done. For this reason, look very carefully at any business deal presented to you. All too often, ostensibly honest businessmen surprise everyone by turning out to be swindlers. Make sure you have a good, English-speaking lawyer check with all the proper government agencies and verify the integrity of your deal before risking your hard-earned money.

Agriculture as an Investment

Because of incredibly rich soil and year-round growing seasons, Costa Rica is an agricultural paradise. The country is checkerboarded with crops of all descriptions. Just about anything grows here, with bumper crops the rule rather than the exception. Rich volcanic soil and a rainy season that coincides with the peak growing season makes farming a dream in Costa Rica. Therefore, agriculture would seem to be one of Costa Rica's best bets for investment. It is, actually, but it can also be Costa Rica's biggest investment disaster for novice farmers and for those who do not understand the ground rules. Just because crops grow well doesn't guarantee you are going to make money.

Ray Nelson warned against going overboard on farm and agricultural investments, particularly for those new to this field.

"Farming is a great way to go broke even if you are an experienced agriculturist. There are too many unknowns, and too many marketing problems. If I had invested the same amount in real estate as I spent trying to get an orange grove started, I would be a rich man by now," he said wryly.

Newcomers are bombarded with brochures, advertisements and lecturers, all promising huge profits from oranges, macadamia nuts, black pepper and other such crops. Seminars on teak, mahagony and other exotic woods tempt investors with promises of 30 percent return on the dollar. Most of these promotions feature absentee management; you put up the dough, the company handles the rest. Other investors plan on living on the property and actually doing the growing, harvesting and marketing all by themselves.

Of course, growing and harvesting are the nitty-gritty of agribusiness, but a third factor, marketing, is truly the key. Without a marketing strategy, all your efforts in growing oranges or bananas are in vain and your crops a waste, except for whatever you and your family can eat. One farmer said, "If you don't have a contract, you are banging your head against the wall. What are you going to do with a field full of pineapples without buyers? Local marketing is the only way to move them, but there is only so much local demand. Bananas are the country's top crop, but a little guy can't compete with the huge multinational corporations. Coffee growing is a small-scale operation, that's true, but today's world price is so low that you can't make any money."

One ex-farmer narrated some problems he encountered trying to farm profitably in Costa Rica. "We had some great orchards, with good production, but we couldn't get marketing contracts. Local markets can absorb only so much citrus fruit, and high export costs kept our products out of range for foreign markets. The only money appeared to be in marketing juice. So a few of us citrus farmers decided to invest in a juice extraction plant. But, before it could be completed, a government plant went into operation, causing our project to go bankrupt."

Next he tried growing starfruit. "We did great at first, because we were the first to put it on the market. But the problem was, a starfruit vine bears a thousand fruit, and each fruit has enough seeds to grow a thousand plants. Before long, starfruit flooded the market and we couldn't give it away. Then we looked toward Europe as a market for starfruit juice. That worked out great for a time, but competition reared its head again. European buyers began demanding concentrate rather than juice, and we couldn't afford to build a concentrate plant."

A long-time Costa Rica resident who dabbles in agriculture for fun, advised, "It's a mistake to blindly take the word of promoters and developers who claim huge returns from agricultural projects. If you don't know Spanish and don't understand Costa Rican labor laws or the legal system, you are going to have a tough time under the best of circumstances. If you don't understand the problems of production and marketing, then you have no business trying to be a tropical agriculturist." He added that even if an investor is an expert in these fields, he shouldn't buy a farm unless he is prepared for continuous, personal, hands-on management. "Absentee ownership seldom works," he emphasized.

But what about all of these advertisements for plantations of high-profit crops? Listed here are some problems and questions related to me by farmers.

Black pepper at one time was indeed a profitable crop, but East Indian overproduction has dropped the price. Buyers are insisting on low prices because they use black pepper as a loss leader in their marketing strategies. **Jojoba bean** production was once popular, but like many other crops, jojoba wasn't native to this area and a glitch in the climate killed off most of the trees in one season. **Macadamia trees** take a long time to produce, and then are susceptible to pests; the wrong spray can kill them. **Hawaiian papaya** is becoming popular for shipment to Japan. But this market is very selective, with buyers hand-picking and accepting only about 30 percent of the crop. Another problem with papaya and other crops is that Japan and other countries usually insist on certification of medfly-free crops. "This is the roughest part, getting medfly-free certification. It's difficult enough in places like California or Florida, and extremely difficult in Costa Rica," said Ray Nelson.

What about teak plantations? This is the biggest push in Costa Rica at the moment. According to promoters, this is a sure-fire venture that will pay huge dividends. One company advertises that a $6,500 investment "will earn almost $300,000 over a ten year cutting period." I asked an American agriculturist about this. This was his opinion: "First of all, teak isn't native here, and nobody knows what the production will do or what kind of wood it will produce. It takes about 15 to 25 years for the trees to be big enough for harvesting, and we won't know for sure until then. That is a long time to wait for profits. Then, another unknown is what the government's view toward harvesting crops will be 15 years from now. They are giving big tax breaks and incentives for teak as a reforestation project. Suppose they decide to put restrictions on how much wood can be harvested and when?" Another problem with teak, according to some experts, is that it doesn't grow well in wet climates like that of the Caribbean coast.

Tax Havens, Offshore Corporations

For a variety of reasons, banking secrecy laws such as those in Switzerland attract a great deal of interest among certain folks who have motives for hiding assets. As far as I know, there is no law against this as long as these accounts aren't used to defraud creditors or to avoid paying taxes. Like Switzerland, Costa Rica has very strict rules on non-disclosure of bank accounts.

An interesting angle of financial secrecy is the use of Costa Rican "offshore" corporations. Like bank accounts, these corporations can be started by anyone—citizen, resident or tourist—and are supposed to be totally secret. My understanding is that it is extremely difficult to discover who actually controls one of these corporations. In fact, the legal term is *sociedad anónima* or "anonymous society." Corporation names are appended with "S.A." instead of "Inc." as is the custom in the United States. One example of a legitimate use of a corporation is when buying or selling real estate. If the property belongs to a corporation, transfer of ownership is simple. You simply transfer the corporation's stock; the property belongs to whoever holds this stock.

Before we go any further, we need to understand a few crucial points. First of all, I am not an attorney, and even if I were, you would be foolish to accept legal advice from a book—particularly when it comes to activities as complicated as offshore corporations or foreign banking practices. Secondly, while most corporations and bank accounts in Costa Rica are legal, used for perfectly legitimate purposes, the ones used for illegal schemes are occasionally toppled, sending an overly-creative schemer to jail. I suspect that what happens is the corporation originally starts off with legal goals in mind, and then branches out into a small tax fraud which grows until it gets out of hand. Some schemes are so obvious that the IRS has little trouble spotting the smoke and flames. My final point is a reiteration of the first: I am not a lawyer, or in any way urging readers to get involved in offshore corporations or secret bank accounts. I am merely reporting what Costa Rican residents and attorneys have passed along to me. I have no way of knowing if what they tell me is true, whether it is legal, or if it is as easy as they say. Remember the old adage: "If it sounds too good to be true..."

Traditional tax havens like the Cayman Islands, Switzerland, Luxembourg, the Channel Islands, and the Netherlands Antilles, have always tempted those looking for ways to hide assets. I've been told that medical doctors routinely hide as much of their holdings as possible in these places to avoid disaster should a multimillion-dollar malpractice suit top their insurance limits. Like the aforementioned countries, Costa Rica maintains a strict policy of banking and commercial secrecy. The amount of money you have in a bank account is supposedly sacrosanct and unavailable to anyone, including the U.S. Internal Revenue Service. One banker told me, "If I disclosed information about someone's account—even to a policeman or a government official—I could go to prison." The *Tico Times* illustrated this point with a story about a suspect who was accused of stealing and forging checks. The crime could easily be solved if authorities had access to bank records, to see whether the suspect deposited the stolen checks to his bank account. But bank officials refused to help the police solve the crime, because in the process they would become criminals themselves!

Do not think that this secrecy has deterred the IRS from looking about, and I suspect not without some success. Sometimes the fraud is so transparent that all the secret bank accounts or anonymous corporations in the world wouldn't help. But the Costa Rican government firmly holds the line on secrecy and has resisted vigorous pressure from the U.S. government. Those using corporations claim that "this country provides an almost perfect setup for hiding money from the prying eyes of the IRS." The thing that bothers me about this statement is the phrase "almost perfect." Before taking a chance on going to taxpayers' prison, I need to hear the phrase *"absolutely* perfect."

Again, not all offshore corporations are for the purpose of avoiding taxes. As far as I know, there is nothing illegal about a U.S. or Canadian citizen owning majority stock in an offshore corporation as long as profits are reported and taxes are properly paid.

Costa Rica's corporate structure allows any person (Costa Rican or not) to control a company without his name appearing in the public records. A Costa Rican lawyer (who must be a specialist in this) sets up a corporation without the real owner's name ever appearing in the record. It is set up as a *socidad anónima con acciones al portador* (anonymous society with all stock owned by the bearer). This means that although there is a legal president, secretary and treasurer (often simply employees of the attorney), the actual ownership of the corporation is invested in whoever physically has the stock certificates in his or her pocket or safe-deposit box. Even the attorney has no way of knowing whether the original client still owns the stock. This system is not permitted in the United States but apparently is perfectly legal in Costa Rica.

A corporation is free to engage in many types of business activities, both in Costa Rica and in other countries. Theoretically, because it is considered a "foreign corporation" as far as the IRS is concerned, it pays no taxes in the United States. Because it is a Costa Rican corporation, it pays little or nothing on what it earns outside of Costa Rica. This doesn't relieve the individual of the responsibility of reporting his income and paying income taxes in his home country.

An example of an illegal activity: A person bought some artwork some 30 years ago for $25,000. The value has increased greatly—to the point that a buyer offered $500,000 for the painting. But capital gains taxes could eat as much as $180,000 of the selling price. So, the painting is sold to a Costa Rican corporation for $30,000 and the seller pays taxes on his $5,000 capital gain. When the corporation sells the painting for the full price, the money goes into a Costa Rican bank account (which belongs to the original seller). Will this work? I don't know. I wouldn't have the nerve to try anything like this; just my luck I'd be caught, and besides, it is highly unlikely that I will ever own a painting worth $500,000!

A network of corporation lawyers in Costa Rica, mostly in San José, specialize in this area of law, charging from $500 to $2,000 to form a corporation. While they claim they never counsel their clients to break the law, they also admit that their job is to do whatever the client requests. "I'm only concerned with Costa Rican law," one of these lawyers told me. "Whether my client pays all of his income taxes is between the client and his government."

Chapter Ten

Ecotourism

Tourism has become Costa Rica's second industry, bringing in even more cash dollars than coffee exports, and soon will eclipse the number one crop: bananas. Its importance as an economic resource cannot be overstated. As pointed out earlier in the book, visitors come here to enjoy a unique combination of climate, tourist facilities, gorgeous beaches *and* Costa Rica's ecological wonderland. Therefore, with a new awakening of environmental awareness on the planet, it's no surprise that Costa Rica attracts large numbers of affluent visitors who insist on seeing these wonders first hand, sights not available anywhere else on the tourist circuit except in a zoo or a greenhouse arboretum. They go out of their way to come here, to enjoy the sensation of walking through a rain forest, to catch sight of a quetzal bird, to listen to the bizarre calls of howler monkeys. Accommodations are a secondary consideration for many of these visitors. If they seek discos, shopping and spiffy beach front hotels, they don't need to travel all the way to Costa Rica. They travel here for something special. They are willing to pay well for the privilege of viewing tapirs, ocelots, wonderfully colored butterflies and marvelous flowering trees, all in their natural settings. The phenomenon of nature pilgrimages is called *ecotourism*.

Investment Possibilities

An intriguing feature of ecotourism is that it doesn't necessarily require an enormous investment in land and accommodations. Traditional tourist resorts, in order to attract visitors, must invest heavily in great views, beach access, tennis courts and golf courses, luxury rooms and first-class restaurants. Then, after they've sunk a fortune into a project, there's always a danger of someone building an even more expensive resort next door to lure away clientele. The facility must be top quality and well-maintained to stay even with today's competitive market. Without something special, tourists have little reason to patronize a particular resort.

Ecotourism, however, is a game played in a different league. Those quetzal birds, boa constrictors and red macaws that visitors seek are rarely found living next to a resort hotel. The only Jaguars they'll see are parked in front of the Hilton. Instead, ecotourists search out those facilities located *away* from fancy hotels, night life and golf courses. The best nature preserves are located on land high in the mountains or on isolated beach coves far from paved roads, miniature golf and other necessities of civilization.

Land for ecotourism developments can be incredibly inexpensive because it has little commercial or agricultural value and is of interest only to ecologists and special types of tourists. It isn't necessary to provide nightlife, high-tone restaurants and deluxe accommodations for these visitors. In fact, most would be disappointed if they found them. They didn't travel half-way around the world to boogie all night in a disco or hit golf balls on a manicured fairway. If they have to travel over rocky, muddy roads to arrive at their nature accommodations, so much the better. This adds to the feeling of isolation from civilization. If getting there requires an hour's boat trip, having to wade the last 50 yards to get to shore, ecotourists don't complain. It's part of the adventure.

Rustic Accommodations

If regular tourists were told that their room will be small and sparsely furnished, that they must use a community bathroom and showers, that dinners will be mostly rice, beans and fish— they would laugh in derision at the thought of paying $120 for a room. After all, in Escazú, they can find delightful little hotels at $35 a night, with genuine hot water in a private bathroom. But at an ecotourism development, they're happy to share the bathroom, thankful there is a room available. Some places put guests in tents, where they sleep on cots, share outdoor showers and are served simple food—for $38 per person. And they love every minute of it. In ecotourism you have two choices: either you put up with what is available or you don't enjoy the ecological experiences Costa Rica has to offer.

Ecotourism dining rooms operate on the same premise. Instead of a fancy menu with a long list of gourmet selections, the kitchen serves one meal for everyone. The food is tasty and well-prepared, that's true, but from management's position, very efficient and cost-effective. Ecotourists don't complain if *gallo pinto* is served three times a day, if fried yucca and plantains replace baked potatoes or if they're served smoked pork chops instead of steak. After working up an appetite slogging through dripping forests or climbing mountain trails in search of elusive butterflies, everything tastes great!

In addition to getting into business with the lowest possible investment, entrepreneurs derive satisfaction from working toward the preservation of earth's environment. If they didn't feel that way, they probably would have gone into some other endeavor. Visitors feel they, too, are contributing to a better world by supporting environmental understanding and education. The Costa Rican government welcomes and encourages this type of development. Some ecotourism projects have gotten off the ground through grants from U.S. government agencies or from conservationist groups.

Following are three example of ecotourism developments. One features a high forest setting, another is on a beach and a third is an experimental farm project.

Ecoadventure Lodge

The first example is Ecoadventure Lodge. Located in the mountains above Lake Coter, a few kilometers from Lake Arenal, Ecoadventure Lodge has 300 hectares of primary forest plus another 300 hectares in citrus and pasture. According to our guide, this forest is unique: transitional between a cloud forest and a lowland rain forest. It combines features of both environments. World-famous Monteverde forest is about 40 miles to the south, but at a higher altitude and with more clouds than rain; Ecoadventure's mountain top location catches a *lot* of rain! The rainfall during our visit was phenomenal, but mostly happened in the evening with sunshine at least part of the day. Included in the cost of a room is a set of rubber boots and yellow rain parkas for each guest.

This particular project is operated by three Costa Rican businessmen who were originally assisted by a grant from the U.S. Agency for International Development (AID). Previously it had been a marginal cattle ranch with the uncleared forest as a bothersome adjunct. The price of the land was exceedingly favorable since the forest was worthless for cattle production and because the government wouldn't permit the remaining trees to be harvested. A token herd of cattle is maintained as an example of how cattle production radically changes the environment. A few horses are also kept for guests to ride on the many trails through the area.

As you walk across a grassy field from the lodge, the forest appears as a towering green wall in the distance. Suddenly, as you step into the forest, you can't help but feel a clash of emotions and an awesome wonder at the dramatic change in your surroundings. The shock almost blurs the mind. From a tranquil meadow, you've just stepped into a primeval wilderness. You almost expect to see a broad-chested jaguar pacing past, or an iridescent quetzal bird fluttering through the air (entirely possible, by the way). A boardwalk trail prevents damage by foot traffic as it leads you through a dense growth of vine-tangled trees, where moss-draped shrubs and broad-leafed philodendrons struggle upward, seeking the sunlight that weakly penetrates the thick forest roof. Once the initial surprise wears off—when the forest becomes familiar and friendly—another shock takes over: the horrible realization that before cattle became king in Costa Rica, *most* of the country looked *exactly* like this! This awareness is what ecotourism is all about—making the world mindful of the difference between how our world once was, and where it is headed, if we don't take steps to prevent disaster.

The developers did a good job in constructing a 25-room lodge, rustic and perfectly suited to its surroundings. The rooms are small and bathless; guests use communal showers and bathroom facilities. Money saved on plumbing was spent to provide a large dining area and meeting room, complete with bar and fireplace—a wonderfully suitable place for sitting around and discussing the day's events. Besides a lone pool table, the only other recreational facilities provided are a guitar and a selection of paperbacks.

The point is, instead of investing in high-rise hotel construction to attract visitors, this ecotourism venture only needed a minimum outlay to get into business. The staff, except for kitchen and housekeeping help, are trained ecologists who earn their pay by conducting nature tours through the rain forest or river trips in the lower elevations. Ecoadventure Lodge is a perfect example of how tourists are more than willing to pay first class rates for rustic accommodations and put up with inconveniences in exchange for adventure. They slog through mud, suffer insect bites and get rained on; they not only enjoy it, but recommend it to their friends! For information: Ecoadventure Lodge, P.O. Box 6398-1000, San José, Costa Rica. Tel.: (506) 21-4209, FAX: (506) 21-4209.

Rainbow Adventures

Another example of ecotourism is located on the beach in an isolated cove on the waters of Golfo Dulce, near the town of Golfito in southwest Costa Rica. Getting to the lodge, called Rainbow Adventures, requires either a seven-hour drive from San José or a one-hour flight on SANSA, and then a 35-minute ride in a motor launch from Golfito. This boat ride is itself a nature experience, with glimpses of leaping dolphins and schools of tuna skimming the surface, and a unique view of pelicans roosting in trees by the water's edge. (Somehow, I never thought of pelicans roosting in trees, I always assumed they slept on the shore or floated on the water. Who would have imagained that pelicans have condominiums?)

Local folks refer to Rainbow Adventures as *Arco Iris* (which means rainbow). The setting is 1,000 acres of virgin rain forest fronting a mile-long, private beach on the sheltered waters of the gulf. The unique feature about its setting is that, like nearby Corcovado Park, it combines the environment of a rain forest and a dry forest. Many plants and animals common to both environments thrive here, as well as some species which have evolved in special ways to adapt to the special conditions here.

The lodge sits half-hidden from the water's view by lush tropical growth. A small circle of landscaping and gardens surrounds the main lodge as the forest closes in on three sides, the calm waters of the gulf spreading out in front. The forest climbs a low mountain that begins a few meters behind the lodge, and the sounds of toucans, whiteface and howler monkeys remind you that you are indeed in the jungle. Rooms in the main lodge have private baths and the two-bedroom cabins (hidden from view of the lodge) have one bathroom each. The buildings are constructed of native hardwoods by staff carpenters who also make furniture to complement the lodge's antique furnishings. On display is an assortment of Precolumbian art, the largest private collection in the country.

The surroundings are deliberately kept natural, with as little interference as possible from human intrusion. Behind the lodge, a jungle trail winds up the mountain through virgin forest. "This environment is identical to the Corcavado Forest Park," our guide explains, "but the only people who ever enjoy it are the relatively few clients who visit the lodge. The environmental impact of just a few visitors is thus minimal."

Rainbow Adventures was started by Michael Medill of Portland, Oregon. When asked how he decided to turn his private home into an ecotourism lodge, he replied, "It wasn't a hard decision to make. Everything was so natural and untouched that I began inviting friends to come and enjoy it. Originally, my goal in Costa Rica was fruit exportation to the States. But as more and more business guests and friends began dropping in for visits and longer stays, I decided to begin charging money. Then, even more people came. Before I knew it, I was in the hotel business, and I love it! The nice thing about ecotourists is, they come here to enjoy themselves by involving themselves in nature and the environment."

For more information: Rainbow Adventures, 5875 N.W. Kaiser Rd., Portland, OR 97229. Phone: 503-690-7750, FAX: 503-690-7735.

Botanical Gardens

Around the bend from Rainbow Adventures, on another sandy cove, is yet another ecotourism idea that may someday provide an interesting living for a North American couple. Ron and Trudy McAllister found this little niche of paradise some years ago. It had been a farm, and already had many trees and food plants in place. Among other plants were coconut trees, yucca and chayote, several kinds of bananas, vanilla, pineapple and pomegranates. They moved onto the property and began collecting other tropical plants to add to their gardens. Enormous breadfruit and breadnut trees provide shade for exotic flowering ginger plants, and beds of green onions, sweet peppers and yams supply fresh veggies for the table. Some of the plants are quite unusual. For example, they grow what they call cilantro and basil plants, which look to be totally unrelated to the plants we know, yet the flavor is exactly the same. Over the past 15 years, their gardens have become so extensive that they have to hire people to keep up with the work.

The botanical gardens became well known and drew visitors to Golfito who wanted to see this marvel. So many started coming, that the McAllisters decided to start charging a fee and to try and turn their hobby into an ecotourism business. Visitors receive an extensive tour of the property, conducted by Trudy, and are treated to some tropical foods that are rarely tasted by those who live in temperate climes. Contact with the botanical gardens is through neighboring Rainbow Adventures.

Centro Ecologico La Pacifica

An ecotourism facility doesn't have to be on the ocean or in a cloud forest to be informative and enjoyable for ecotourists. A third example of an ecotourism development is at La Pacifica, about four miles north of Cañas, in the dry forest area. Almost all of the forest in this area long ago was destroyed to make grazing land for cattle, yet at La Pacifica Ecological Center some 387 acres of the forest remains. Another hundred hectares have been planted with natural trees, with more planned. Nature trails along the Corobici River provide first-hand forest experiences, with frequent sightings of rare birds and dry-forest animals.

The interesting thing about this type of development is that it integrates a working cattle ranch and an experimental farm with tourism. Guests stay in luxury cabins in a lovely setting, grouped about a swimming pool and an international-cuisine restaurant. The project's orchards supply mangoes, plantains and bananas, and its gardens produce asparagus, chayotes, maracuya and all varieties of tropical foods for the table—with a minimum of chemicals used to control pests and weeds.

One of the aims of La Pacifica (besides making money) is to demonstrate how a Costa Rican family can do quite well on a small plot of land—cultivating fruits, vegetables, herbs and flowers—not only for their own use but for sale in the domestic or foreign markets. Local people are becoming quite interested in this project, learning that this kind of farming can support more people than cattle ranching, with much less detriment to the environment. For more information: Phone 69-00-50.

Environmental Wear and Tear

It's only fair to point out that many environmentalists are concerned that Costa Rica's ecotourism boom is endangering the very ecosystems that bring tourists in the first place. Monteverde cloud forest is a good example. A few years ago, only a handful of dedicated biologists and students walked the trails of Monteverde to savor its unique treasures. In 1973, just 300 visitors arrived during that entire year. By 1991, the numbers increased to well over 30,000! There's no question that large numbers of people tramping through the forest every day frighten away some of the fauna and cause unintended damage because of the heavy foot traffic. Recent visitors have said they were shocked to discover that birds and animals that used to be common are becoming difficult to spot.

However, I believe that with the growing number of ecotourism facilities, the total number of tourists will be spread over more sites, in more regions of the country. The Cordillera de Talamanca area, for example, which is virtually unvisited, holds wonderful potential for ecotourism projects. Diversity should lessen the impact on any one location, since most ecotourist developments can accommodate a comparatively small number of visitors. Whether we like it or not, folks will come to Costa Rica to commune with nature.

Chapter Eleven

Hiring Help

During World War II, the Costa Rican government, under Rafael Angel Calderón Guardia, (the father of today's president) passed a series of progressive labor laws which are still on the books, and are strictly enforced. These laws seek to avoid conflicts between workers and employers by setting out concrete employment rules and a system of wages and benefits. In effect, these laws take the place of union contracts between worker and employer, thus guaranteeing individual workers benefits they probably couldn't negotiate on their own. If you look at the rules from the viewpoint of the worker, they are only fair, and certainly not unreasonable from the viewpoint of a fair employer.

Therefore, hiring a maid, a gardener, or an employee in your business involves more than a simple understanding about wages and conditions as is the custom back home. Because we North Americans aren't used to such formal relations with employees, and because we will likely be hiring workers, even if just domestic help around the house and garden, the rules need to be spelled out in some detail. Following the laws to the letter prevents serious and unexpected problems.

Briefly, here are some of the ground rules. The employer is responsible for making social security payments for an employee as well as deducting contributions from the employee's wages. All workers are entitled to paid vacations. After a 30-day trial period of employment, an employee is entitled to severance pay as well as notice before being laid off. A Christmas bonus is not a gift or a nice gesture, but is required by law. The employer is required to give three months of maternity leave at half-pay. All of these rules are detailed below, and should be studied carefully before hiring any help.

Good Labor Relations

Recently I spoke with a lady who was visiting Costa Rica with the intention of starting some kind of business. "When hiring workers," she said, "I understand that the secret is to just hire them for 89 days, and then lay them off. That way you aren't responsible for benefits such as severance pay, vacations and such. Once they work 90 days you are obligated; so you simply hire new workers every 89 days!"

This upset me, and I told her so. Although her information was incorrect, that wasn't the point. The Costa Rican people work very hard for a fraction of the wages employees receive in the United States or Canada, and the law guarantees them certain benefits. It seems repugnant to me to try and chisel them out of their rightful wages. Attitudes like this can do nothing but tarnish the reputations of other North Americans. Those who have lived here for a long time generally try to pay their help a little *more* than the law requires. "I try to make it so my maid can't *afford* to quit," said one lady. "She is wonderful, and I couldn't stand to lose her."

The word quickly gets around the neighborhood if you are a good person to work for (or a chintzy one). If you have a bad reputation, your job applicants will be those who can't hold a job elsewhere. Then you wonder why your employees are lazy, don't show up half the time or have a tendency to steal!

After I gave the newcomer a piece of my mind about her attitude, she explained that she had heard that if you lay a worker off after they've worked more than 90 days, you must pay eight years salary as severance pay. She heard wrong; the facts are: for each year worked, an employee is entitled to severance pay of one month's salary—up to a maximum of eight months pay. That is eight *months* salary, not eight years! From a worker's point of view this is only fair. Let's suppose that after eight years of faithful service, it becomes necessary to let your housekeeper go. For eight years, the severance pay amounts to about $1,000. Does that amount sound outrageous for eight years of loyalty and hard work? If it does, then maybe you deserve workers who are lazy, don't show up half the time or have a tendency to steal!

Conditions of Employment.

1. Length of employment. The first 30 days of employment is a trial, and either employer or worker can terminate without notice. However, vacation pay and *aguinaldo* (Christmas bonus, described later) must be paid in addition to wages if employee has worked over 20 days in that month's time period. Thereafter, for each month worked, one day's vacation pay is due, amounting to two weeks of vacation for a full year's work. Many employees, either by custom or through union contracts, receive three weeks vacation. My understanding is that an employee may work through his vacation, providing he receives an additional day's pay for each day worked. (I'm not a labor lawyer, however, so don't hold me responsible if my understanding is incorrect.)

2. Wages. Minimum wages depend on the job and the skills required. A chauffeur, for example gets $121.60 a month, and a farm worker $88.38 a month. An interesting facet to the wage structure is that a maid, gardener or chauffeur who lives in your home is considered to be receiving an additional 50% of their salary as "payment-in-kind." In other words, if you pay a live-in maid $100 a month in wages, the actual salary is considered to be $150, or 50% more when figuring benefits. This is important, because the gross salary (salary plus payment-in-kind) is used to figure the aguinaldo, social security payments and severance pay. A catch here is that an hourly employee who regularly receives a lunch at your home, is also considered to be receiving a 50% in kind, so your Christmas bonus, severance pay and vacation pay has to be based on this. If you feel like you are already paying the hourly employee enough, you can save money by *not* offering him or her a sandwich at lunchtime!

3. Working Hours. The maximum for domestics is 12 hours a day, although almost nobody expects this. The standard is usually an eight-hour day, five-day week. For regular employees, work on Saturday and Sunday are at double-time rates.

4. Social Security. An important obligation for employers, one which is taken quite seriously by the government, is social security payments. This very important institution pays for health care, sick leave and disability pensions. You, as an employer *must* pay 14 percent of the gross salary and you *must* deduct 9 percent of the worker's wages and pay both portions of the tax to the *Caja Costarricanse del Seguro Social*. Make sure your employee understands that you are withholding the money from his check, or his share could come out of your pocket. Within eight days of hiring an employee you must register his name with this bureau.

This is extremely important, because should an employee become ill or injured, you could be liable for the medical bills, and 50% of his or her pay for the duration of sickness (for life, should the disability be permanent). Once registered, you are only liable for 50% pay for the first three days; Social Security takes over for the rest of the time. To prevent abuse of this law, you, as the employer, are entitled to demand a health certificate from the worker *(carnet de salud)* when he or she is hired, and every six months thereafter. This is provided at no cost to the employee by the Seguro Social Hospitals.

Pregnancy is another problem, not only for the maid but for you. Employees are entitled to a month's rest before the baby is born and three months afterward—half of the salary to be paid by the employer and the other half by the government. By the way, firing a maid for being pregnant is frowned upon, and you will need to validate your reasons for firing her for reasons other than pregnancy.

5. Christmas Bonus *(Aguinaldo)*. Sometime between the first and 20th of December, employees are due an aguinaldo. For those who have worked a full year previous to December 1st, the bonus is a month's pay (including payment-in-kind). For those who work more than the 30-day trial period but less than a full year, the payment is prorated over the time they worked. Thus, a person who works three months is 3/12 of one month's. Remember that employees who live in, or who regularly receive at least one meal a day, also get a Christmas bonus on the payment-in-kind, or an additional 50 percent.

6. Notice and Severance Pay. Employees employed more than 90 days and less than a year are entitled to a two-week notice before being laid off. Over a year, a one-month notice is required. If you don't or can't give notice, you must pay the employee full wages for the notification period.

Unless an employee quits the job, you are obligated to pay severance pay at the following rate of pay: up to three months, none; from four to six months, two weeks pay; between seven months and one year, one month's pay. Then, you must pay an additional month's pay for each year worked or fraction over six months. In no case can this payment be more than the equivalent of eight months salary.

Again, remember this is based on gross pay, including 50 percent payment-in-kind. It doesn't matter if the worker immediately finds a new job, you still have to pay.

A worker can be fired at any time during the first 30 days for any reason, with no obligation other than the aguinaldo and wages due. Furthermore, a worker who fails to give notice (*preaviso*) before quitting forfeits the aguinaldo.

Employee Obligations

The worker can be held responsible for damages they have caused, whether intentionally or due to imprudence, negligence or inexcusable neglect. A domestic worker can be discharged when "notorious lack of respect or civil treatment is shown," which should be backed up by witnesses. In this case, the severance pay is not paid. You had better have good proof, because the Ministry of Labor tends to side with the worker in doubtful cases.

When an employee is laid off, it is usually a good practice to make things crystal clear by having him or her sign a statement (in Spanish) to the effect that all benefits have been paid. Include the severance pay, vacation pay, Christmas bonus and any salary due up to the time of separation. Have the employee sign the document in front of a witness. Should the employee be quitting voluntarily, be sure to note that in the document.

Wages

If you are in a business and hire help, you need to keep up with the current wage structure. Each section of the country issues a list of minimum salaries every January and July. Wages are adjusted twice yearly, according to the increase in cost of living. The following chart lists a few representative wages in effect in the Nicoya area as of January 23, 1992. It was issued by *La Jefatura y el Departamento de Inspección de la Sucursal de Nicoya*. The wages have been converted to dollars.

Typical Daily and Monthly Wages in Costa Rica*

	Daily	Monthly
Farm quality inspectors	$ 6.52	$130.40
Farm workers	5.12	102.40
Fishermen and heavy farm work	6.83	136.60
Graphic arts, optical lens technicians	11.12	222.00
Workers in chemical industries	7.10	142.00
Semiskilled workers	5.66	113.20
Unskilled workers	5.18	103.60
Truck or bus drivers	6.23	124.64
Domestic chauffeur (with meals)	6.17	123.34
Domestic servants (with meals)	4.27	85.47

* In dollars

A doctor who works for the national hospital system earns between $500 and $1,000 a month, and most college professors earn less than $500 a month. Some occupations are paid by piecework; coffee pickers, for example, receive 92 colónes per box. Those North Americans who have successfully operated their own businesses unanimously say that paying well over the minimum wage means happy employees who are loyal and hardworking.

Chapter Twelve

Becoming a Resident

When I first visited Costa Rica, immigration rules were rather strict. A Canadian citizen was permitted a 90-day visa, an American citizen only 30 days. Before you could get a visa or tourist card, you needed to show a return ticket and enough money to last the stay. A 30-day extension could be applied for, but it was easier to take a bus to Nicaragua or Panama, stay overnight and apply for another 30-day visa. I heard stories of visitors who overstayed their limit being placed on the next plane or bus out of the country with a "no return" stamped on the passport. Why Canadians were permitted longer visas always puzzled me. It was tough for United States citizens who wanted to spend a winter in Costa Rica's balmy spring and summer weather.

Today, anybody with a passport gets a full 90 days, just for the asking, just for stepping off the airplane! A two-month extension is also easily obtained, bringing you a five month stay. A trick is to wait until *after* your 90 days have expired—this is okay—and apply around the end of the fourth month. By the time you get the 60-day extension, you end up with a hassle-free, six-month stay in Costa Rica. That takes care of the winter, plus part of fall and spring! I have to admit embarrassment when I contrast the openness of the Costa Rica government with the closed-door policy the U.S. embassy shows to Costa Ricans who want to visit Disneyland or Las Vegas. In order to receive a visa, a Costa Rican must visit the embassy, hat in hand, and try to prove beyond a shadow of doubt that he or she has every intention of returning to Costa Rica, and has no possible motive for staying in the United

States. It must be a humiliating experience to be denied a visa because your job doesn't pay a high enough salary to convince an embassy employee that you are not a potential "wetback."

Actually, for North Americans, Costa Rican immigration rules are even more liberal than I've just outlined. If you stay longer than permitted, the penalty is a weak fine of less than $5 a month for the overstay plus purchasing an exit permit for about $7.50, or in an extreme case, possibly $40. You don't even have to go to the ICT to apply for the permits; a travel agent can take care of it for a few dollars. I've met folks in Costa Rica who came several years ago on a tourist card and are still here. One couple bought land, built a motel and restaurant and are operating a business, never so much as asking government permission. My attorney says he has at least one client who hasn't bothered to renew his tourist card in five years.

Understand, I'm not recommending that anyone overstay their visa or try to ignore Costa Rican laws. I'm simply reporting how the laws are being enforced at this point in time, and how they are being applied toward foreigners with the wherewithal to support themselves, who may invest much-needed capital in the country, and who won't be taking jobs from citizens. Stricter enforcement could happen in the future, just as is the case for Nicaraguans and Panamanians who have slipped across the border as economic refugees. Even if the government cracks down, you still have the option of driving to the border, staying out of the country 72 hours and then returning for another five- or six-month sojourn. Very liberal.

Legal Technicalities

When the 30-day rules were in effect, just about the only way Americans could enjoy more than a short visit was to become either a *pensionado* or a *residente rentista*. Today, with six-month stays completely legal, the necessity of obtaining legal status is not as pressing as it once was. For someone like myself, who can be satisfied with living half the year in Costa Rica and the other half in his home country, there is no clear advantage to becoming a legal resident. One can own property or a business and can travel about the country with nothing more than a tourist visa. On the other hand, there are restrictions and obligations on foreign pensionados and rentistas—not ponderous ones, but which involve a certain amount of red tape. For example, you must prove a certain amount of monthly income has been deposited in a Costa Rican bank. You must provide police certification of good conduct on a periodic basis, and you must live in Costa Rica for at least four months of the year in order to hold on to your residente status.

For those who will be staying pretty much full time in Costa Rica, or for those who plan on entering business and working as a manager in the business, the residente option is probably the best way to go. Once you have the papers and as long as you fulfill the obligations of residency, you are completely legal and are enjoy all of the rights of a Costa Rican, except for the right to vote.

For years, those valuable duty-free imports of automobiles and household goods were major reasons for wanting legal residency. Although it appears these exemptions are gone, government officials assure pensionados that they are looking for ways to compensate for the loss of these benefits, and that foreign residents will still be welcome as in the past. These tax-free imports have been a point of contention between Costa Ricans and foreign residents, with the local people complaining that it is unfair to pay more taxes than foreigners. If the government follows through with plans to reduce import duties by four-fifths, imports will be more affordable for all. All hope of reversing the legislative decision to revoke the exemptions isn't lost, however; local retirees are planning an appeal to the Supreme Court.

Becoming Residents

Immigration, pensionado and rentista applications are handled by the Costa Rican Tourist Board (ICT). Basically, they recognize two classes of residentes. One consists of retired people with a pensions of $600 per month or more. The second category is for those who are not retired, or who don't receive a government pension; they have to prove $1,000 a month guaranteed income. This money must be deposited in a Costa Rican bank and proof shown to the government every year. No law says you can't take the money out right away or that you have to spend all of it; you only have to prove you've brought that amount into the country. For a married couple, the person without the income is considered a dependent, so no extra income is required.

To make application, you can either do it yourself or hire someone to go through the red tape for you. It requires a $100 deposit and about $30 in fees, stamps and forms. It takes about a year before the approval comes through, but in the meanwhile, your residency status is legal. The process is best started in your home town, in your home country, since you need a statement from the police department there that you are not a criminal. You also need a health certificate from a U.S. or Canadian doctor. It's much easier to get these at home than by mail from Costa Rica. These documents, along with your birth certificate, marriage certificate and a proof of income, are then passed along to the proper officials.

Pensionado and Rentista Association

Most people find it convenient to let an attorney or someone familiar with the process handle things for them. Yes, some individuals have done it on their own, but you'll hear sad tales of woe from those who have tried it without knowing what they were doing. Few people enjoy standing in line, facing the indifferent attitudes of some clerks or the hard-to-understand questions and information in Spanish. One way to avoid this is through the Costa Rican Pensionado and Rentista Association. This organization specializes in obtaining residencies and charges very reasonable fees, considering the amount of time you save. Membership is $50 for a provisional membership, entitling you to apply for residency through the group, to attend social events and meetings. My recommendation is to give them a call at 011-506-33-8068 (FAX 011-506-22-7862) and ask what kind of documents you are going to need to start the process and then contact them when you arrive. Their offices are conveniently located on the mezzanine of the same building complex as the government Department of Pensioned and Annuitant Residents—the ICT Building on the corner of Calle 5 and Avenida 4.

Further benefits are: the organization will make sure your annual papers are up-to-date; translate and notarize your documents, renew the required Costa Rican I.D. card; help you get a driver's license and other special permits, and assist you in buying an automobile. They will do English-to-Spanish translations, notarize documents and authenticate a photocopy of your resident's carnét so that you can leave your original at home.

Members are eligible to receive doctor and hospital care in the National Health Services System, under terms of a special contract. This relieves you of the obligation of standing in line each month to make your payments. They pay it on a three month basis and send you proof of payment for the current month, which entitles you to medical service. The Association also publishes a newsletter, the *PenRen News*, six times a year. It claims to represent more than 50 percent of all current pensionados and rentistas, and as such, engages in lobbying actions in the legislature and mounts legal challenges to laws which may be harmful to their members.

Resident Investor

An additional category of interest to those who are not retired, but want to invest in the country, is the *Resident Investor* status. Here again, an attorney should be hired to take care of the details and paperwork, but the general idea is as follows.

The minimum investment is $50,000. The venture must be of a type endorsed by the ICT as being of national interest: projects related to agriculture, industry, tourism, housing and businesses of that nature. If the money is invested in an existing company you need to submit the latest balance sheet of the company and a statement indicating its profit and loss situation. This needs to be certified by an authorized public accountant. If this is a new corporation, a certified copy of the incorporation papers must be presented.

As is the case with pensionado or rentista applicants you'll have to have birth certificates, marriage certificate, police good-conduct report, a pile of stamps, photos and all the other stuff required of applicants. I've been told that the yearly four-month stay in Costa Rica is not mandatory as it is with other classes of immigrants, but please don't hold me to this.

The entire question of whether to become a legal resident or to visit using a tourist card is something that varies with the individual. Some feel that five or six months is all they want to stay there, so why bother with the red tape of papers? Others plan on making Costa Rica their primary home and therefore see benefits in becoming *residentes*. It all depends upon your circumstances.

Chapter Thirteen

Spanish and Bilingual Schools

Because of Costa Rica's high literacy rate and excellent educational system, more people speak English here than in any other Latin American country. When you try practicing your Spanish with folks you meet, you'll often be surprised when they insist on speaking English; they love the opportunity to practice with a native English-speaker. This is good news for most North Americans; they can get by without having to learn another language. Indeed, many live in Costa Rica for years, never learning any more words than needed to deal with the gardener or the gas station attendant.

Yet, knowing the language opens many doors that would otherwise be closed to you. Being able to communicate with *anybody* instead of looking for someone who speaks English permits interaction with a whole new set of people—potential friends and acquaintances. Fortunately, Costa Rica is a great place to learn the language.

An excellent way to study Spanish and to learn about Costa Rica at the same time is to enroll in one of San José's many Spanish language schools. Language acquisition is big business here, with at least 20 schools in and around San José offering intensive Spanish classes. Throughout the country, individuals give private, one-on-one Spanish lessons. Some schools keep class size to three or four students, thus insuring each person maximum attention from the teacher.

People come from all over the world to combine a tourist vacation with learning Spanish. Corporations send executives and sales trainees to San José to study. Some countries send embassy and consular personnel here to learn Spanish before reporting to their posts in Spanish-speaking countries. Your fellow students usually turn out to be a very interesting group.

Most schools offer a program which includes living with a Costa Rican family. This is a valuable experience for anyone thinking about moving to Costa Rica or spending long periods of time here. By interacting with a local household, you learn how to cook Costa Rican food, where and how to shop, how to deal with servants—those ordinary, everyday routines of life that are so different from back home.

By combining school with the recommended home-stays with Costa Rican families, the learning process speeds up; you are in a round-the-clock Spanish environment. Weekend excursions with teachers and fellow students to various tourist locations combine learning and vacation into a very pleasant package. Many schools include tours of farms, factories, archaeological sites, museums, conservation projects, national parks and other places of ecological and cultural importance as part of the curriculum.

Schools, Facilities and Tuition

Listed below are some of the language schools and tuition charges. These costs were current as of spring of 1992, and will undoubtedly rise with world inflation. In addition to the tuitions quoted here, most schools have flexible courses by the week, day or hour. Unless stated otherwise, home-stays are not included, however any of the schools will gladly place you in a Spanish-speaking home with two meals a day and laundry. Home-stay meals are often not served on Saturday and Sunday; arrangements may have to be made individually on this. Many schools include free airport transfers. At least one will pick you up at your door every morning, take you to school and return you in the afternoon.

Academia Costarricense de Lenguaje. Intensive course, four hours daily plus home-stay with two meals a day for $975 per month. Includes cultural activities, such as music, drama, dancing, Costa Rican cooking and excursions. Apdo. 336-2070 San José. (506) 21-16-24. FAX: (506) 33-86-70.

Academia Smith Corona. Specializing in crash courses for tourists. Two weeks of three hours per day, $90. Located in downtown San José. Apdo. 4592-1000, San José. (506) 22-46-37.

Academia Tica. Minimum course of 20 hours, three hours a day, for $120. Home-stays available at $10 per day with three meals. Excursions optional. Located in Guadalupe, a short bus ride from San José. Apdo. 1294-2100, Guadalupe, San José. (506) 34-06-22. FAX: (506) 33-93-93.

American Institute for Language and Culture. One-on-one instruction, 15 hours weekly at $700 a month; small group instruction $500. Home-stays $90 a week extra. Apdo. 200-1001, San José. (506) 25-43-13. FAX: (506) 24-42-44.

Central American Institute for International Affairs. Complete package including home-stay, cultural and sightseeing activities, airport transfers, for $840 a month. Apdo. 10302-1000 San José. (506) 55-08-59.

Centro Cultural Costarricense-Norteamericana. Five-week course, three hours daily, $280. Special rates arranged. Individual tutorials, $15 an hour. Located in San Pedro and also in Paseo Colon. Apdo. 1489-1000, San José. (506) 25-94-33. FAX: (506) 24-24-80.

Centro Lingüístico Conversa. Four weeks at three hours a day at San José campus for $307. At Santa Ana campus the instruction is eight hours a day, with home-stay, transportation and excursions for $1,455. Apdo. 17-1007, Centro Colon. (506) 21-76-49. FAX: (506) 33-24-28.

Centro Lingüístico Latinoamericano. Located near Alajuela, $900 tuition includes daily transportation, home-stay with three meals a day for four weeks of five hours a day. Optional excursions. Apdo 151, Alajuela. (506) 41-02-61.

Centro Panamericano. Monthly cost of $1,000 covers 120 hours of instruction, textbooks, home-stay, an excursion transportation and airport transfers. Located near Heredia. Apdo. 947-1000 San José (506) 38-05-61. FAX: (506) 33-86-70.

DALFA Spanish School. One month of four hours a day, weekend excursions and cultural activities for $1,100 including home-stays. Located in suburb southeast of San José. Apdo. 323-1011, San Francisco de Dos Rios. (506) 26-85-84.

Forester Instituto Internacional. Four weeks, four hours a day, plus field trips, textbooks and home-stays for $1,120. Located in San José. Apdo. 6945-1000 San José (506) 25-31-55. FAX: (506) 25-92-36.

Institute for Central American Development Studies. One month, four-and-a-half hours daily, for $892, including home-stay with three meals, field trips and lectures. Apdo. 3-2070 Sabinilla, San José. (506) 25-0508.

Instituto Britanico. Three-week course, three hours daily, including field trips for $1,000 including home-stay. Intensive course without excursions $875 including home-stay. Apdo. 8184-1000 San José (506) 34-90-54. FAX: (506) 53-18-94.

Instituto Universal de Idiomas. Tue., Wed., Thurs., six hours a day, $95 a week; Mon. thru Friday, three hours a day, $155 for two weeks. Four weeks with home-stay $630. Apdo. 219-2120, Francisco de Guadalupe. (506) 57-04-41.

INTENSA. Intensive programs of two weeks, four hours daily for $542 including home-stay. Located on northern part of San José. Apdo. 8110-1000, San José. (506) 25-60-09. FAX: (506) 39-22-25.

Latin American Instuitute of Languages. Four hours daily for four weeks, $575. Home-stays available at $105 a week. Apdo. 1001-2050, San Pedro. (506) 25-24-95. FAX: (506) 25-46-65.

Mesoamerica Language Institute. Four hours daily instruction, $80 per week. Home-stays and excursions optional. Apdo. 300-1002, San José. (506) 33-77-10.

Kindergartens, Elementary and High Schools

Recently, a friend came to me, obviously distraught. "Tell me about schools in Costa Rica," he demanded, "I'm seriously looking for an alternative to the school system here in the United States. I need to find some place where my kids have a chance to grow up safe and sane." It turned out that a young boy in his children's school had been robbing other children at knife-point, and hadn't been discovered until after he had attacked a dozen or so victims. Another boy had been caught passing out samples of drugs to his classmates. "I'm ready to go anywhere to give my kids a chance," my friend insisted.

While I wouldn't want to send anybody off to a foreign country just for the sake of the children, it's my understanding that Costa Rica does have a lot to offer in the way of private education. It's also my observation that drug use and juvenile delinquency is much less of a problem than in the United States. Juvenile gangs and graffiti are either non-existent in Costa Rica or else I've missed seeing them.

In the San José area, there are 19 English or bilingual private schools. Some schools present classes half in Spanish, half in English, others are basically English-language schools. Some offer classes from pre-kindergarten through high school, others just the first three to seven grades. The all-English schools are very popular with upper-class Costa Rican families because they are seen as prep schools for U.S. universities. Just to give an idea of costs, herewith are a few examples of schools in the San José area.

The **Country Day School** is a prestigious institution in Escazú, with classes pre-kindergarten through the 12th grade. It is Costa Rican accredited and has 650 students, with classes all in English. The enrollment fee is $300 a year plus $3,510 tuition for grades one through 12. Kindergarten and preparatory school is $1,810 for a half day.

The **Costa Rica Academy** is another popular school which charges similar tuition. It is accredited by Costa Rica and in the United States by the Southern Association of College and Schools. It's located in Ciudad Carari, west of San José, on the way to the airport.

The largest academy is **Lincoln School**, in Moravia, on the northeast side of San José, with 1,600 students. Tuition for high school is $128 a month; for grades seven through nine, $93 a month; and lower grades slightly less. **Escuela Britanica** teaches half in English and half in Spanish, kindergarten through 11th grade. It's located in Santa Catalina on San José's west side and has 800 students. Grades nine through 11 require $147 a month tuition, lower grades less. Most schools charge an enrollment fee or a one-time family membership fee in addition to the tuition.

Universities and Foreign Students

Students from abroad are welcome at Costa Rica's many universities. There are four public universities and nine listings for private institutions. The largest of the schools is the **University of Costa Rica** (UCR), with about 35,000 students. Most of the Costa Ricans have scholarships and pay little or nothing. Located in San Pedro, on San Jose's northeastern edge, tuition for resident students is about $70 a semester; foreign students are more, with rates available on request.

The **Universidad Nacional** has about 13,000 students and has several campuses scattered about the country as does UCR. Private universities offer programs ranging from MBAs to degrees in theology, tropical agriculture and conservation. Most welcome foreign students, charging tuitions of $100 per class and $5,600 for an MBA degree.

Chapter Fourteen

Guatemala

Guatemala is separated from Costa Rica by three countries, 400 miles and five centuries of social change. Guatemala is so different from Costa Rica it's difficult to believe they share the same planet. While Costa Rica thinks European, with modern-day world views, Guatemala persists in its mysterious, Precolombian past. Indigenous tribes, clinging to customs and language of the ancient Mayas, have yet to catch up with the 16th century much less prepare to enter the 21st century. Although a layer of modernity blankets parts of the country, the covering is quite thin, with the old civilization surfacing wherever the fabric is frayed.

Those who cannot visualize life without cable television, well-stocked supermarkets and civilized conveniences in every direction will, of course, look upon Guatemala as a quaint place to visit, but clearly not a place for long-term living. On the other hand, there are some people who can envision life without television or miniature golf. Those who enjoy shopping in native markets, who prefer a laid-back and tranquil existence to modern-day routine, wouldn't exchange Guatemala living for anyplace else in the world.

Guatemala has that same picturesque charm and colonial atmosphere that made Mexico a retirement haven for so many North Americans starting in the 1940s. The economics of retiring in Guatemala also lags several decades behind today's prices, with a cost of living reminiscent of the 1940s. Here a couple can live well on a Social Security check *and* put a third of it in the bank every month! Single people find nice accommodations for $120 a month, including three meals a day. This is truly a country suspended in time, a place unique in all the world.

Guatemala versus Costa Rica

Guatemala is more than twice the size of Costa Rica. Its scenic wonders are no less striking. A major difference is that Guatemala lacks the alluring beaches, bays and protected waters that draw throngs of tourists to Costa Rica. This suits most North American residents just fine; reduced tourism means quieter and less crowded village streets.

This doesn't mean tourists are scarce. On the contrary. As peace and tranquility return to the countryside, tourism is on the rise. Guatemala attracts a different type of visitor than does Costa Rica. People don't come here in search of discos, night clubs and beach entertainment. They want to savor Guatemala's unique atmosphere of other-worldness, to connect with the mysteries of a vanished civilization, to enjoy a slow pace of living. Since Guatemala lacks beach front developments, most foreign residents choose to live in the higher, mountainous regions. The weather here is even better than Costa Rica's highlands because it is less humid.

Another difference is that North Americans aren't spread out all over the country; instead they congregate in three main locations: on the outskirts of Guatemala City, in the town of Antigua or at Panajachel on the shore of Lake Atitlán. The average annual temperature is around 75 degrees in these places, with thermometer readings in the 80s uncommon. Every day is shirtsleeve-comfortable. Winter or summer, a sweater or sports jacket is appropriate for evening wear and if you sleep with the windows open, a blanket feels good. In the high mountains, early morning frost isn't unusual.

Tropical Lowlands

A strip of low country runs along the Pacific coast, some 200 miles long by about 30 miles wide. This is a very sparsely populated region of cattle ranches and fields of bananas, sugar cane

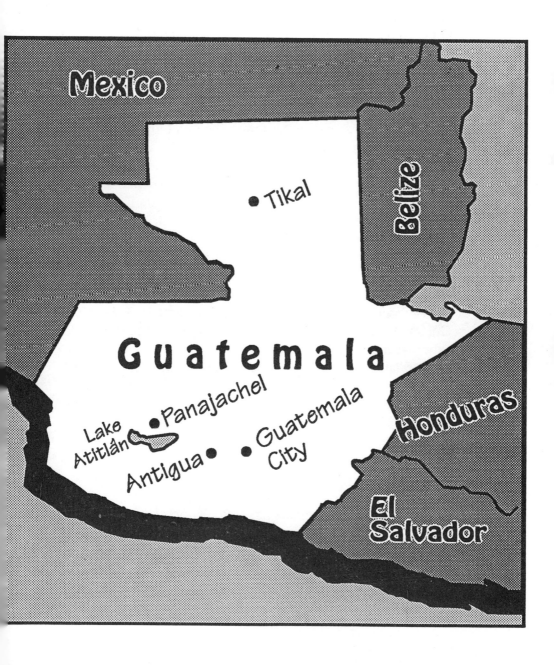

and tropical fruits. Highland residents occasionally visit the beaches near the Guatemalan towns of San José and Iztapa for a dip in the ocean, then quickly return to the comfort of their highland homes. This area is unlikely to attract many foreign residents in the near future. Perhaps a few agriculturists might be interested in the Pacific coastal lowlands but it's too hot and humid for most folk's taste.

If you look at a map of Guatemala—one printed in Guatemala anyway—it would appear that the country also has a long stretch of Caribbean coast. The map shows offshore reefs, islands and cays stretching north for many miles, all the way up to Mexico and the Yucatán Peninsula. Although the Guatemalan government refuses to admit it, this land actually belongs to the nation of Belize, the former British colony which was recently granted independence. That's why they insist on including Belize as a part of Guatemala. The people living in Belize, mostly English-speaking Blacks whose ancestors came from Jamaica, emphatically refuse to recognize any connection with Spanish-speaking Guatemala. Even though there is no chance that Belize will ever give in, the Guatemalan government stubbornly refuses to recognize Belize's independence. At times there have been problems for tourists crossing the border into the Petén area from Belize.

Guatemala's undisputed portion of the Caribbean coast is very short and unsuitable for long-term living or retirement. The major population center, Puerto Barrios, is a shipping port, and not actually on the Caribbean; instead, it's in a protected bay on the Gulf of Honduras. For Caribbean beaches, foreign residents usually travel to Honduras or to one of the small islands off the coast of Honduras or Nicaragua.

Magnificent Weather

Like Costa Rica, Guatemala has two distinct seasons: a rainy winter and a dry summer. The residents also transpose the meanings of summer and winter with "winter" meaning June, July and August, and "summer" being December, January and February. The peak tourist season falls in the dry season, December, January and February, when vacationers come to enjoy the spring-like weather. But year-round residents claim that the rainy season is the best. "That's when flowers are at their peak, when everything is fresh and when days are delightful," is the way one retiree put it. "Although it is beautiful here in January, I can hardly wait for the rains to begin in May. Days are always sunny and the rain falls at night when I'm sleeping." She pointed out that many evenings can pass without any rain at all. Even in the rainy season, the precipitation isn't unbearable. The average yearly rainfall around Guatemala City is 47 inches per year—about the same as Philadelphia. The heaviest rains fall in June and September, with ten inches average for each month; I've seen it rain that much in *one night* in Houston! In Antigua, one of the most popular places for North Americans residents, the total is a mere 37 inches a year. That's less rain than falls on Oklahoma City (but no snow).

Mountain Country

Other similarities between Costa Rica and Guatemala are volcanic mountains and forest-covered lowlands. More than 30 volcanoes rise to high, pointed summits, providing dramatic backdrops against the azure-blue skies. Several are continually active, some issuing steam, or tossing into the air red-glowing boulders which can be seen in the evening with the aid of binoculars. A popular pastime for audacious tourists is climbing these volcanoes. The easiest is Pacaya Volcano (8,370 feet above sea level), located south of Lake Amatitlán. The climb to the summit takes less than two hours, starting from San Francisco de Sales. A small crater has been active there since 1975, a favorite place to photograph the boiling lava in its center. (This is what I hear; my passion for volcano-climbing is quite minimal.)

Deep canyons slice through this high country, forcing roads to wind up and down the steep mountains and through narrow passes. Luxuriant vegetation covers all, with swift streams and tumbling brooks carrying water to the villages below. Indians farm the steep hillsides, terracing the land and living much as their ancestors have for the past two millennia. Since these mountain slopes are not easily cultivated as part of a large farm, they are worked as family plots with the same technology the Mayas used before Europeans arrived. Sometimes fields are so steep, farmers are in danger of falling out of their fields and crashing into a neighbor's ranch. Tropical crops grow lushly in the rich volcanic soil, with coffee, pineapple and cashew nuts favorite harvests.

The natives who work these small fields present a very interesting sight. Their everyday wear is eye-catching and colorful as they dress in bright, hand-woven textiles. No matter how hard they work, the clothes seem to remain clean and vividly colored. Each village and each region has its traditional and distinct woven patterns that remain virtually unchanged after five centuries of European occupation. Those who know what to look for can tell not only which tribe and village an Indian is from, but also the martial status of the person. For example, from the design woven into a man's costume you know whether he is married, how many children he has and how many of them are married. This probably keeps them from hanging around singles' bars.

The Petén Region

While much of Guatemala is mountainous, a major geographical feature in the northern part is a flat, forest-covered, limestone plain similar to that which underlies Mexico and Belize. This is the Petén, the heartland of the ancient Mayas. The Petén's rain forests and jungle, and an occasional humid savanna, are reminiscent of Brazil's Amazon basin. This region accounts for one-third of the country's land, yet it supports a tiny fraction of the total population. A few people harvest rubber, hardwoods and chicle, or work subsistence farms slashed and burned from the forest.

Long before the Spanish came, cities like Tikal, Uaxatún, Piedras Negras and hundreds of others flourished throughout the Petén. The population density was at least 20 times what it is today. Archaeologists estimate that over 3,000 Mayan ruins in the Petén area alone have never been investigated.

The city of Tikal covered 50 square miles, with a population estimated at 55,000, equal to any world capital at that time, a thousand years ago. Temples rising to the height of modern

20-story buildings, cement causeways and ornately carved palaces now sit abandoned, covered with forest. Mayan architects designed water systems, aqueducts and irrigation systems that can still be used today. Their mathematicians developed a calendar even more accurate than the one we use today, one which predicts eclipses of the moon and sun for a million years into the future. Because of their extensive trade routes, the Mayas are often called the "Phoenicians of the New World." According to one expert, as many as 4,000 Mayan canoes were at sea at any one time, trading honey, wax, parrots, feathers, rubber, cotton and jade. They ranged as far south as present-day Colombia and north, up the Mississippi River to trade with the Mound Builders of Missouri, Tennessee and Oklahoma. Rubber balls and parrots were traded with tribes as far away as Arizona. All of this occurred while Europe was languishing in the stagnation of the Dark Ages.

The most important vestiges of the Maya era are their present-day descendants. After 500 years of European occupation, the Mayas manage to retain their identity, language and customs intact, and display a dignity that is truly admirable. They break into smiles readily, and their children are so cute that it's hard to resist the urge to give them hugs. This comes from a guy who normally doesn't like to be bothered by kids!

Naturalists' Paradise

Guatemala shares another characteristic with Costa Rica: an abundance of wildlife and marvelous rain forests. A visit to famous Mayan ruins, such as Tikal, offers a unique opportunity to combine archaeological explorations with natural history tours. Tikal is set in a 576 square kilometer protected park, home to over 200 resident bird species. Colorful and weird-looking toucans with enormous bills of bright yellow, orange, green, and red are rather common. As you trudge along the jungle trails you'll see flocks of native turkeys, similar to North America's wild turkey but vivid in color, sporting a blue head, orange skin flaps and a gold and bronze body. Scarlet macaws, blue-crowned parrots and numerous other varieties of parrots call raucously from the tree tops. Coatimundis calmly amble along in front of you and monkeys will sometimes throw small fruit in your direction as an indication of their annoyance with your presence. Jaguars and ocelots patrol the area, but are rarely seen by humans; were it not for their tracks left in the soft parts of the trails we'd never know they were there. Guatemala is the only country in Central America where you still can see a tapir in the wild, and occasionally you might catch a glimpse of the rare, endangered Quetzal bird which is being protected in the high, misty forests of Baja Verapaz.

An inventory of Guatemala's forests includes 8,000 species of plants, including 600 varieties of orchids. Orchids of one kind or another exist in nearly every life zone from sea level to 11,000 foot mountain tops. Flowers, brilliantly colored butterflies and the constant twittering of birds complete the scene.

Guatemalan Ecotourism

With regional peace making remote parts of the country accessible to tourists once more, a fledgling ecotourism industry is beginning to take off. Where Costa Rica's ecotourism combines beaches and tourism, Guatemala combines ecological wonders with intriguing archaeological sites, rich in both natural and historical treasures. Tikal's palaces and pyramids have drawn tourists for years, but only recently have a handful of entrepreneurs started to package these historical attractions with Tikal's marvelous rain forest surroundings. For years tourists have gazed at the temples in rapture, almost unaware that the rich tropical environment is as unique as the ruins themselves.

At this point, I am not aware of many North Americans launching ecotourism projects in Guatemala, although there may well be a few. The role of tourism, outside of the three areas discussed in the next chapters, is too new to comment on. Before investing in any kind of ecotourism project, an investor needs to study the situation very carefully and check with all pertinent government agencies.

Economics

One Guatemala attraction is an incredibly low cost of living. Prices of many goods and services here are as they were in the United States decades ago. The currency is the *quetzal*, which in the spring of 1992 was valued at about 20 cents U.S. or five quetzales to the dollar. For those who live in a non-tourist manner, a quetzal goes very far indeed, with a purchasing power often equivalent to a dollar in the United States. For example, about two blocks from the Guatemalan tourist ministry in Guatemala City, I had a lunch consisting of a wonderful chicken soup flavored with cilantro, a *milanesa* (breaded veal cutlet) and sauteed Swiss chard with rice. The meal came with a glass of *horchata*—a lightly sweetened drink made of whipped rice and cinnamon. Since I was thirsty, I also ordered a beer. The whole thing came to 6.75 quetzales—just $1.35!

Several foreign residents reported their grocery bills were between $100 to $150 a month. They said they could cut this considerably if they chose to eat as the local people do. After all, $100 is far more than most Indian families earn in a month. Checking food prices at a supermarket, I came up with the following list:

Supermarket Prices

	Quetzales	Dollars
Round Steak, lb.	8.94	$ 1.79
Filet Mignon, lb.	10.89	2.17
Chicken, lb.	4.33	.87
Spinach, lb.	1.87	.37
Smoked chicken, whole	17.78	3.45
Green onions, lb.	.97	.19
Celery, lb.	1.33	.27
Cauliflower, lb	1.63	.33
Tomatoes, lb.	.47	.09
Broccoli	1.47	.29
Potatoes, lb.	.60	.12
Milk, 1/2-gallon	6.29	1.25
Coca Cola, 2 liters	3.00	.60
Eggs, dozen	5.20	1.04
Vodka, Smirnoff, 1 liter	25.00	5.00
Rum, Bacardi, 1 liter	14.00	2.80
Cigarettes, Marlboro, carton	35.90	7.18

Of course, anything imported is quite expensive. Cigarettes appear to be cheap by our standards, but at 71 cents a pack they are far too expensive for ordinary Guatemalans. You rarely see one of them smoking.

Labor is so low-paid it is embarrassing. Local retirees tell me that they pay 75 quetzales, or $15 a week for a girl to do the cleaning. A gardener is expected to put in an eight-hour day for $18 a week. Building materials are quite inexpensive, with cement blocks priced at 20 cents each compared to $1.10 each in the United States. A qualified bricklayer charges 20 cents a block to lay them, or $2.80 a square yard. These are reasons why a nice home can be built for well under $20,000. As an indication of how low-cost Guatemala is, the government only requires $300 a month income for a foreigner to become a permanent resident. Compare this with $1,500 a month in Mexico or $600 a month in Costa Rica.

While it's true that some foreigners are attracted to Guatemala because of low prices and inexpensive living, most say they would live there regardless of cost. They point out the perfect weather, the picturesque surroundings and the peaceful atmosphere. "Guatemala is as different from my home town of Cleveland as summer is from winter," is the way one expatriate put it. "I wouldn't consider returning to Cleveland for anything more than brief visits to see the grandkids. I absolutely love it here!"

Health and Medical Care

As you might expect in an underdeveloped nation, water is safest boiled, and routine precautions must be taken in the kitchen. However, the problem isn't nearly as serious as it is in some third world countries. Where North Americans tend to live, the water is generally safe to drink from the tap, but many prefer to treat it anyway. After a while, food-handling precautions become second nature. I've visited Guatemala many times, and I've never contracted any sickness.

Medical care is as inexpensive as other goods and services in Guatemala. According to a man who lives in Panajachel: "I'm perfectly satisfied with local doctors. There are three of them here, and in Sololá, about a 10-minute ride by bus, there are two hospitals. One is run by the government and is free. The other is a Catholic hospital where you have to pay a little money. The problem with the free hospital," he explained, "is that you take a number, no matter how serious your case, and you wait until your number comes up or until you die—whichever happens first. Also, the conditions aren't exactly the best; no blankets on the bed and things like that. But it *is* free." Another resident said, "For something really serious you go to Guatemala City to the hospitals there. A private room costs $12 a day with color television." He told of a friend who had a stomach operation which cost a total of $6,000. It would have been $30,000 to $40,000 in the States.

Dental work is likewise inexpensive and of good quality. One woman told of having root canal and cap done—140 quetzales for the root canal and 90 quetzals for the cap, or $46 for the whole thing. "Compare that to your dentist's bills back home," she said. A periodontist who graduated from Harvard operates a dental clinic in Guatemala City.

One man, a WWII veteran, said a representative of the U.S. Embassy comes periodically to Panajachel to speak to the American residents to describe their rights and discuss problems. During the last visit, the veteran was told that in the event of a serious heart attack, the Veterans Administration was prepared to send a helicopter to Panajachel to fly him back to Guatemala City, and they would make sure he got back to the States if necessary.

Historical Accidents

Guatemala's present-day cultural atmosphere is best understood by looking at history. Unlike Costa Rica—which was isolated and neglected for hundreds of years—Guatemala was settled early; within months of the conquest of Mexico, Cortez's soldiers found their way to Guatemala. They immediately divided the land into large parcels which they generously awarded to themselves. They became lords over the peaceful, easily-defeated Maya Indians. While pioneer Costa Rican settlers struggled to wrest a living from small, family-operated farms, the conquerors of Guatemala enjoyed servants, mansions and rich fields tilled by squadrons of peons. Traditions of feudal aristocracy imposed by the Spanish, influence economic and social conditions even to this day. Seventy percent of Guatemala's farmland is in the hands of only two percent of the population. Over 60 percent of the people are pure Indians—the largest percentage in any country of this hemisphere—yet these Indians receive only 10 percent of the country's income. Guatemala's chasm between rich and not-rich is so broad that neither can see the other side. In the center of this void is a tiny middle class, too small to form a bridge between super-rich and poor. This has been a problem over the years, the basis of much civil strife.

The majority of the remaining population are mixed Indian and European. When they speak Spanish, adopt European dress and customs, they're called *ladinos*. They live side-by-side with the *indios* (Indians), but in totally different universes, as if invisible to the other. Many Indians speak no Spanish, or if they do, in a kind of patois. Among themselves they speak one of the 23 different Quechua dialects. Few can read, and few have ever watched television. Essentially, they are living five centuries in the past.

Social Groups

Few North Americans fit into any of Guatemala's three social categories. Few of us are wealthy, at least by our standards, even though we are considered extremely wealthy by the vast majority of the ladinos. Few North Americans speak Spanish well enough to merge into their society anyway. As for the indigenous caste, almost no non-Indian can communicate in any of the Maya dialects. While ladinos and indios have little in common with each other, they have even less in common with us; they feel uneasy in our presence. There is a growing Guatemalan middle class, but it is so small that we seldom come in contact with its members. The wealthy are unapproachable, protected by their closed social circles.

Therefore, making friends among Guatemalans is all but impossible on anything more than a superficial level, except under special circumstances. This is a major difference between Guatemala and middle-class Costa Rica. In Guatemala, we North Americans become dependent upon fellow countrymen or Europeans for social contact. Foreigners tend to cling together in Guatemala. It is true that a few North Americans enjoy living in the smaller villages and work at making contacts with the natives. Some show great dedication to helping the Indians better themselves; others live in villages simply to absorb the exotic atmosphere. Most, however, prefer to live where other English-speaking North Americans live. Places such as Chichicastenango, Quetzaltenango and other equally unpronounceable locations, make wonderful places to visit on fiesta days, but few foreigners will consider living there until a critical mass of English speakers grows to make a viable society.

I've met several North Americans who have married Guatemalan women and have built a very successful life within the Guatemalan community, but the women are all of middle-class background and they speak perfect English. That's another story.

Personal Safety

What about crime in Guatemala? "Everything was fine until about six months ago," said one of the Gringos as we sat on a park bench in front of a fountain in the central square of Antigua. "But since then, we've had lots of robberies, with teenagers brandishing knives and demanding money. At least one person was hurt when he was thrown to the ground after refusing to give money to the punks."

This was indeed upsetting news, since I had been wandering about Antigua, day and night, with a feeling of complete tranquility. I asked if the crime situation were such that they were thinking about moving away.

"No, it's not *that* bad," said one man, a Canadian, "You just have to watch your wallet and be careful about which part of town you go walking about after 10 p.m. Actually, most of the victims had been drinking a bit, and should have known better. But it is definitely getting to be a problem."

He then told me about a notice at a local restaurant that caters to tourists, a notice that warned of a band of teenagers who had been hassling tourists, and threatening them with knives. I went to the restaurant and copied down the message. It had been dated January 1, 1992, just a week earlier. Next, I decided to confront the local tourism office and the police department to see what they had to say.

At the tourist office, I expected the chief of the tourist police to gloss over the problem, or even deny that it existed. The chief of police turned out to be a very attractive lady of about 35 years, Vivian Pinot, a lawyer as well as a police officer. I read the warning notice to her and waited for a reaction.

"I was not aware of that notice," she said, "but what it says is true. That is exactly why I am here. But I have only been here for two weeks. If you ask about town, you will learn that things are much better now, and if you ask two weeks from now, you will hear that things are even safer. In six months, things will be absolutely tranquil." She said that she knew exactly who had been robbing tourists. "Some were from Guatemala City, and we've run them out of the area. The others know we're watching them closely. That's why the robberies have stopped."

She went on to explain that this is a pilot experiment by the government of placing specially trained "turismo" police in areas of high tourist activity. "I brought 20 specially selected officers, highly paid, all of whom speak English, to straighten out the situation. In addition, all of them had expressed an eagerness to live in Antigua and to make their homes there. That's important."

She pointed to three maps on the wall of her office. One marked the areas where robberies had occurred; another showed where the special police patrol during the daylight hours and the third where they patrol at night. She said that in addition to automobile patrols, she is instituting foot patrols to help insure the safety of the people.

Her enthusiasm was obvious. "It is my dream," she said, "that tourist police will soon be stationed in all areas of the country where foreigners live and travel."*

Crime in Guatemala City is another story. Like all large cities, the more people the higher the crime rate. Here, the most common offense is pickpocketing, a crime that is fairly easy to prevent, if you simply keep aware and continually be on the alert when wandering about crowded, downtown streets. After while, it becomes second nature to walk with one hand on your wallet. Pickpockets don't bother the wary and careful traveler; there are too many careless, unthinking ones to prey upon. It's also a given that most pickpockets work the downtown streets. In suburbs or on the fringes of the city, pickpockets are rare to non-existent.

Dining in Guatemala

The worst thing about many Guatemalan restaurants is the coffee. Although coffee is the country's most important crop, and even though the quality of Guatemalan coffee is superb, for some unexplained reason, many restaurants serve *instant coffee, Guatemala* rather than the real thing! When asked about this, several restaurant owners told me, "Our customers prefer Nescafé!" He seemed to consider instant coffee a status symbol. Once in a while you'll find a restaurant serving real coffee, and what a treat! I have a suspicion that higher quality coffee is exported, so local people can only buy the cheaper grades—and perhaps that's why they prefer instant coffee.

Guatemala has several very interesting regional dishes which are influenced by pre-European cuisine. In some ways, Guatemala's cooking is similar that of neighboring Mexico. But there are significant differences in preparation. For example, both

---

*   She was successful; tourist crime in Antigua almost disappeared under her direction, but male chauvinism was too strong and Vivian was replaced by a man.

countries love tamales. But Guatemalan tamales are usually steamed in banana leaves instead of corn husks. The *masa,* or dough, is made with corn flour instead of the Mexican *nixtamal,* or hominy meal. Mexican tamales are traditionally loaded with chili; Guatemala tamales contain little or no chili. The difference is remarkable. Guatemalan cooks seldom use mouth-burning chili to cancel out the flavor combinations in their food, preferring milder herbs and natural flavors.

Another dish common to both Mexico and Guatemala is Chicken Mole (pronounced mó-lay), yet the recipes are totally different. In Mexico, the sauce is made with chocolate, chili and ground seeds of one kind or another—a ghastly combination which I've never understood. *Chocolate?* Mole sauce totally over-powers the flavor of the chicken as well as paralyzing your digestive system. Yet I was served a delicious chicken mole in Guatemala, so good that I coaxed the recipe from the cook. It is made by blending tomatillos (those small green tomatoes that come with a husk on them), a sweet bell pepper, lots of garlic and fresh cilantro in blender. After the chicken is boiled, just before serving, make sauce of chicken broth, chicken bullion, the blended mixture and a little corn flour. The same cook showed me a Guatemalan way of fixing hamburger: simply sauté it with finely chopped watercress and garlic, giving it a most unusual flavor combination.

Transportation

For some strange reason, taxis are an expensive way to get around Guatemala. This is very puzzling. It can't be due to costly high equipment costs; the cabs are mostly very old and decrepit 1960s and 1970s U.S. models—Chryslers, Pontiacs, Chevys and the like. It can't be because of high maintenance costs; they do precious little of that.

One time I took taxi to the airport, the first one I could flag down, and told the driver I was in a hurry because I figured with luck we could arrive with about eight minutes to spare. The cab was in horrible condition—an antique 1954 DeSoto—with the transmission slipping out of gear every few seconds, rattling, bumping and stalling at every stoplight. A very weak battery added to the anxious tension, never sure if the engine would start. All I could do was sit on the edge of my seat, sweating anxiously, ready to jump out and help push-start my cab. Fortunately the plane was half an hour late in departure; so I made it with 20 seconds to spare!

On the other hand, buses are incredibly cheap. For example, from downtown Guatemala city to the suburb of Vista Hermosa, it costs $8 by taxi, but only eight cents by bus. Although I enjoy a cab driver's jokes and hysterical laughter, I'll take the eight-cent bus ride any time. Rental cars in Guatemala are prohibitive. You can rent a car and driver for what you have to pay.

Chapter Fifteen

Guatemala City

Guatemala City would seem to be an unlikely place to spend a winter or to retire. Although some parts of the city are attractive, elegant looking and pleasantly landscaped, most neighborhoods are rather tawdry, with unkempt industrial areas mixed with humble housing. Most long-term visitors spend as little time here as possible, making immediate tracks away from the city in search of a place to live.

Yet there are those who absolutely love the excitement and stimulation of a big city. Not just any city, mind you, it has to be a special city. I have to admit that places like Paris, Manhattan, Mexico City or Buenos Aires stir something inside my breast. The cosmopolitan, sophisticated way of life does something for my spirit that I can scarcely describe, much less explain. I've met folks who feel so strongly about city living that they would no more consider leaving Manhattan or Mexico City than they would give up their citizenship. Despite New York's reputation for crime and traffic, some people adore the place and feel sorry for those who can't afford to live there.

Parts of Guatemala City also have this special ambiance of elegance, sophistication and convenience, albeit on a much smaller scale. You'll find gourmet restaurants, boutiques and fashionably dressed people—not nearly as many as in Paris or Buenos Aires of course, but the ambiance is there, and costs are scaled down. A number of North Americans live in these elegant zones. Many work for the embassies or for international corporations, and others who once worked there are now retired.

The nicer residential areas are on the edge of the city and beyond, places suitable for foreigners. Besides marvelous views of the city and its environs, with volcanoes looming in the background, living in these areas bring peace and quiet, no traffic jams, and excellent shopping. The only time residents actually have to visit the downtown sections is to conduct business at the Embassy or take care of the continual paperwork and tangles of red tape at the immigration offices.

These neighborhoods are unique in Guatemala in that middle- to upper-class Guatemalans live here, neighbors with North Americans. This is one of the few places where one might make Guatemalan friends, where neighbors deal with foreigners as equals. Let's take a look at three lifestyles on the fringes of Guatemala City.

Vista Hermosa

This exceptionally beautiful neighborhood is on the western edge of the city, where the streets begin climbing toward the mountains. I visited one couple who live here in Zona 15, a deluxe district known as Vista Hermosa (beautiful view). Broad boulevards with large trees and tasteful landscaping give the neighborhood a pleasant ambiance. Commercial buildings are modern, constructed of steel and cement as required for earthquake safety. Private residences are elegantly designed, often with high walls surrounding the property, as is the fashion in Latin America. The unmistakable aura of wealth and quality is clearly evident.

Jim and Rita live on the ninth floor of the Vista Hermosa complex, a private condo conveniently built above a deluxe shopping mall. The supermarket here is huge, stocked with almost anything you might need. If you can't find it in the supermarket, you can browse through dozens of other shops, on several different levels which sell luxury goods and necessities, from clothing to perfumes. If you can't find what you need in this building, you probably didn't need it in the first place. The residents' guarded parking lot is on the third floor for additional security. In order to visit one of the condos, you must pass a guard who announces your presence over an intercom and closed-circuit TV to obtain permission to enter the residential part of Vista Hermosa.

Their apartment has one of the best views I've ever seen. From a broad balcony you can see the cathedral domes and downtown office buildings off in the distance. You can also see the yards of private homes, many with swimming pools, some truly mansions, half-hidden by tall palms and flowering trees. Verdant mountains circle the city to complete the dramatic scene.

The couple lives in their Guatemala apartment for half the year, returning home to Alabama every summer to take care of business. Rita is originally from Guatemala. Their three-bedroom apartment has a bath for each bedroom, a large living room, a dining room, a good-sized kitchen and a maid's room. I was impressed, to say the least. How much is the rent?

"When we first leased this place nine years ago," Jim said, "the rent was only $225, but now we're paying $300." He admitted that this was probably a low rent, because he has heard that others in the building are paying $600 and sometimes $900 a month. No matter what the rent, this is living in luxury and dignity, in a style impossible to duplicate except in such an affluent neighborhood.

How did Jim happen to move to Guatemala for retirement? After his first wife passed away, he met a lovely Guatemalan lady who was visiting friends in New Orleans. When they decided to get married, she urged him to take a look at Guatemala as a place to retire. When he saw the Vista Hermosa neighborhood, he was convinced. The only problem with the arrangement is that Rita doesn't like the heat and humidity of Alabama's summers. "I'm used to perfect weather," she explains, "So, I feel very happy when we return to our home here in Guatemala."

When I inquired about their budget, they were unable to say how much they spend every month. "We've never kept records, but we know it costs much less here than in the United States. *Much* less." They did say that their electricity was about $14 and that their cable TV hookup is $15 a month.

Renting a House

Frank, who used to work for a United States-based petroleum company, came to Guatemala about four years ago for a visit, and decided to stay.

When asked how he decided to retire in Guatemala, he replied, "I had a wonderful job, but the bottom fell out of the oil market a few years back. I wasn't old enough for Social Security, yet I discovered that I was too old to find another good job. I had a moderate Air Force pension, but that wouldn't be enough to retire on. After trying some low-paying jobs, someone mentioned that Guatemala was the place to go. After talking it over with my wife, we decided to pack up everything we could get into our car and head for Guatemala. I've never regretted it."

They prefer living quietly, economically, away from the hustle and bustle of the city. So he and his wife found a place far up in the mountains, with a lovely view of the city. Their three-bedroom home rents for only 700 quetzales ($140) a month. There is also a maid's quarters, but his wife Grace chooses not to hire maids; she doesn't care to have someone underfoot. "I've always done my own housework, and even though we could afford it, I would feel foolish hiring someone to do my work."

When asked how far his Air Force pension was taking him, Frank said, "My pension is only about a thousand a month, but out of that, I'm able to save four hundred! And, I'm living well! I put all of my stock dividend income away, and when my Social Security begins rolling in, I plan on banking that as well. "When asked how his wife adapted to Guatemala living, he said, "At first, she wasn't sure. She wanted to go back. But I kept saying, 'just wait a little longer before we decide.' Now, she feels as I do, she doesn't want to move back. This is our home. We love our fabulous climate, where we are comfortable throughout the year. We were used to hot summers and cold winters where we came from. People are lovely and they make you feel at home. Every day is fascinating and a new adventure." When asked for advice to others, he said, "Come and visit, and you'll stay!"

Suburban Mountain Living

San Cristóbol, on the west side of city, sits high on a mountain slope that overlooks the entire valley. This is representative of several subdivisions that take advantage of a view, peace and quiet and clear air. Presently there are two sections of San Cristóbol, one which is pretty much completed, and an undeveloped part, farther up in the hills. If the newer section turns out as nice as the original development, it will be gorgeous. The streets, sidewalks and utilities are in place, and a scattering of expensive-looking homes provides a clue as to the how the final development will look.

Given the low costs of labor and materials, the size and quality of these homes will be impressive indeed. Here, $20,000 will build a lovely house; $35,000 almost a mansion. I looked at one place, higher up the mountain—almost on the crest of the ridge—priced at $120,000 dollars. For Guatemala, that sounds expensive, but this was an enormous house, situated on about 20 acres of landscaped grounds surrounded by a cement-and-wrought iron fence. There were several outbuildings, fountains and housing for a staff of servants. (If you buy a place like this, you will need plenty of servants.) I counted eight to ten bedrooms—who knows how many baths—plus a dining room large enough to host Fidel Castro's army. Nothing seemed real; it was like a Hollywood movie set. My mouth sagged open as I looked about the property, recalling that my neighbor's home in California—a one-bedroom cottage on a tiny lot—recently sold for $150,000 *more* than the asking price of this mansion!

Hillside subdivisions are popular with those middle-class Guatemalans who can afford to move away from the city's traffic snarls and noise. My personal inclination would be to look at one of those neighborhoods where homes are under construction, where families have already moved into their homes. This way you can determine what kind of people your neighbors will be. If you buy into a neighborhood where most people are super-rich, or where none speak English, you could be lonely. In the areas I visited, I found several middle-class, English-speaking families, and others who speak Spanish and who are delighted to have neighbors with whom they can practice their little-used English.

Lots in subdivisions of this nature are inexpensive, ranging from $5,000 to $10,000 and will probably go up in value as the subdivisions begin filling up. A nice feature about living on a mountain slope is that every home has a view—guaranteed.

It was here in San Cristóbal where I visited a retired Oklahoman and his Guatemalan wife. They live in a white stucco home overlooking the city. From their broad deck they have a marvelous view of the city—a view which matched Jim and Rita's view, but with a different perspective. The downtown area is so far away you can barely distinguish major landmarks. But volcanoes and verdant mountains more than compensate for this. By night the city lights below sparkle like a blanket of stars, and in the distance red fire from a volcano is visible without the aid of binoculars.

"I wouldn't trade Guatemalan retirement for anywhere else in the world," said Jerry, as he gazed out over the gorgeous panorama of green-clad mountains, tall volcanoes and the city of Guatemala in the distance. We've lived in this house for two years and we are very happy."

His wife Sonia is originally from Guatemala City, of a middle-class family, and has a college education. Jerry comes from Oklahoma City where he worked in the restaurant and food business for years, until automation and new ways of dealing with the public began to make his job uninteresting. He decided to take an early retirement and cash in on his company profit-sharing plan. "It wasn't a fortune," he pointed out, "but I figured I could get by."

When asked why he chose Guatemala for retirement, he replied, "Actually, I had no intention of coming here. I had read a lot about Mexico as a retirement location, but I knew next to nothing about Guatemala. So I went to Mexico to begin my search for a place to retire. Luckily, I ran into this lovely little lady." He smiled affectionately at his wife. "Sonia was working in Mexico City as a secretary when we met. After we dated a couple of times, I asked her to marry me. When we came to Guatemala City to ask her family's approval, I fell in love with the country. We forgot all about Mexico."

The house, of earthquake-proof cement and steel-reinforced concrete block, is in an area under development. Most of the lots in the subdivision are still for sale. A profusion of flowers, shrubs and trees, broken by an occasional house, give the area a combination rural-suburban air. It's far removed from the hustle and bustle of the city, away from the noise of diesel buses and exhaust fumes, yet only a 20-minute drive to the American Embassy or the Guatemala Retirement offices. A continual breeze wafts through the windows (screenless, for houseflies and mosquitoes are rare).

"When we bought this place, it wasn't finished. We had no electricity or telephone, not even glass in the window frames. That was no problem, since it never gets cold enough to really need windows. So we moved in anyway. We made do with kerosene lamps and candles—no problem. The first thing we did was order glass for the windows. Then came plasterers and bricklayers to complete the walls and outside, and gradually things came under control. As soon as we finished up the maid's quarters, we hired a girl to help out. Then we planted our garden and lawns."

Jerry proudly showed off the various plants in the garden, from bromiliads to orchids, from chayote to some strange plant that is used for scrubbing one's back in a shower. He explained that Sonia's cousins, who live in various parts of Guatemala, are continually bringing some new, exotic plant to add to his collection. A pair of ducks waddled about the yard, loudly quacking "in English." As Jerry explains, "I brought the ducks from Oklahoma and they've never quite learned to quack in Spanish."

While they have a view of Guatemala City, it is seldom necessary to go downtown. Within a short distance of their home they can shop at any number of small, family-run markets, or they can go to either of two large shopping centers, complete with modern supermarkets. The latter have anything one might need, from food to hardware. Clothing shops sell both imported and locally made garments.

My next question was, how much would I have to pay for a home like this, with a view like this? "The total investment was about $18,000 dollars," Jerry said proudly. "It still isn't done, because I want to add another floor with a wider living room to take advantage of the view." To buy one like this, already completed in the development, would probably cost less than $30,000.

What does it cost to live in this style, in a nice house with two servants? They graciously figured out their budget for me. They pointed out that it included some unusual items. For one thing, Jerry presents his mother-in-law with 300 quetzales a month to help out with her expenses ($60). Another unusual item is school expenses for three Guatemalan kids who otherwise might not be able to go to school. His totals are listed below:

A Guatemalan Monthly Budget

Housekeepers (two of them)	* 275
Food	1200
Mother-in-law	300
Electricity	85
Water	35
Propane	32
Telephone	25
Bus to school for kids	20
School tuition, 2 kids at 160Q each	320
School tuition for 1 kid (kindergarten)	75
School tuition Jerry (Spanish lessons)	332
Gasoline expense	500
Gardener (part time)	50
Cable TV	35
Total	3,284 quetzales
In dollars	$656.80

*Amounts in quetzales, at five to the dollar

"This is just for basic items." said Sonia. "It isn't that we can't afford to spend more than this." she emphasized. "There is just nothing else we need." They do have automobile maintenance and those other unexpected items which are always cropping up. But with good bus transportation, they only use their Jeep for pleasure rides into the country or an occasional trip to San José (on the Pacific coast) for a swim in the ocean.

School Project

One item on their budget attracted my curiosity. Why tuition for three children? It turns out that public education is not exactly free in Guatemala. The government provides teachers and buildings, but parents must pay expenses like lunches, books and supplies. In addition, all children must buy uniforms. Even though these items don't amount to very much money, for some poor families it is impossible. Students feel pressured to drop out of school, go to work and help support the family. Public school classroom sizes are around 75 students, so the learning environment isn't very good. To make matters worse, even when poor children manage to go to school, many are too malnourished to concentrate or study.

For quality education of any kind, a private school and tuition is a must. Jerry and Sonia picked a school with a combination academic-trade curriculum; one that teaches boys to be cabinetmakers and girls to be tailors so they will be able to earn an income while going to college. Then they asked the school to recommend some children who were intelligent, but who would have to drop out of school if they couldn't get some support "For only twenty dollars a month, we can keep a kid in school! We can actually make a difference, and change someone's life," Jerry said thoughtfully. "For only twenty bucks!"

San Lucas Sacatepequez

Farther up the mountainside are a couple of small villages that have attracted some North Americans retirees. My favorite has the tongue-twisting name of San Lucas Sacatepequez, a pre-Conquest town about 15 miles from the city at an altitude of 6,940 feet. The reason these villages around San Lucas are exceptions to the rule that small villages aren't appropriate for foreign residents is that many middle-class Guatemalans live here—as well as a few rich ones—so North Americans feel comfortable and report that making friends with neighbors is rather easy. Since San Lucas Sacatepequez is an easy half-hour commute to the heart of the city and since buses run frequently, this village is becoming increasingly popular with foreign residents. The altitude keeps temperatures in the low 70s or high 60s during the day, perfect for those who love cool weather.

Every Sunday, San Lucas Sacatepequez hosts a famous outdoor market, which is well worth a visit. In addition to a bounteous selection of fresh tropical fruits and garden vegetables, there are two excellent but rustic restaurants that serve intriguing native dishes. Marimba and folkloric music by local musicians provide wonderful entertainment as you dine. Families from Guatemala City come here regularly to enjoy a luncheon of *carne asada* cooked over aromatic wood coals or the special pork tamales wrapped in banana leaves. A trip to Guatemala is not complete without a good sampling of tamales!

North American Society

English-speaking residents aren't nearly as numerous as in Costa Rica or Mexico, yet they have their own network and social groups. A weekly newspaper called *Aquí Guatemala* is published by the American Society. The newspaper is full of information about upcoming events, what other organizations are doing in Guatemala as well as a classified section listing rentals and services to residents. A newsletter called *This Week* presents news and in-depth analyses about Guatemala as well as the rest of Central America. Write to Apdo. Postal 1156, Guatemala City, Guatemala, C.A.

Chapter Sixteen

Antigua and Panajachel

The other viable places for long-term residency or retirement are the towns of Antigua and Panajachel. Both locations have North American colonies and both have strong boosters, with enthusiasm for their choice of residence.

My first reaction to Antigua was one of nostalgia. It took me back to my youth, when as a teenager I first visited the traditional Mexican village where my family maintained a weekend home—an ancient adobe with two-foot thick walls and a tile roof—a place called Tequisquiapan. Those were the days before cars, buses and trucks clogged the highways; when small-town streets were paved with cobblestones or plain dirt. Those were days of tranquility, low costs and simple living, before major industrialization, unmuffled motorcycles and overcrowding.

When the antiquated bus from Guatemala City rolled into Antigua, rumbling past centuries-old buildings, stone walls and pastel-colored homes, I felt as if I had found something I had lost somewhere in the distant past. Old colonial buildings with arches covering sidewalks, tree-shaded parks, quiet byways and the sounds of birds singing in the square, all reinforced this impression. Antigua is an old, old town, suspended in time.

Indians in colorful costumes spread their wares on the sidewalks, selling hand woven fabrics, carved or painted wall decorations and pottery made in traditions of centuries past. The array of native arts and crafts is moderately priced, but do bargain and do not pay the first amount asked; the sellers enjoy the process of settling upon a fair price. Brilliantly colored and uniquely patterned fabrics are especially popular. Indians in nearby villages weave these fabrics on hand-looms just as they have for centuries, the technology unchanged from Precolombian times. Check out the jackets, blouses, skirt tapestries and blankets.

Thick-walled homes and buildings, painted light pastel colors, topped with red tile roofs, dignify the town and symbolize stability. The occasional clatter of hoofbeats against stone paving echoes through the streets as burros trudge along, bearing loads of firewood, produce or grain, unmindful of competing rubber-tired vehicles zipping past. Automobile traffic here has a long way to go before reaching a critical mass. Drivers don't have to circle the block in search of a parking spot, they simply pull up to the curb, shut off the engine, and go about their business. Life in Antigua proceeds at a slow, relaxed pace.

A Touch of History

In 1524, just a couple of years after the conquest of Mexico, Captain Pedro de Alvarado, deputy of Hernán Cortéz, conquered this area and established his headquarters. After a volcanic eruption destroyed the first settlement in 1543, the capital was moved to the Panchoy valley, and Antigua was born.

One of Cortez's non-commissioned officers, Bernal Díaz de Castillo, was given land in Antigua. He spent his last years here writing his famous chronicle of the conquest, *La Historia de la Conquista de Nueva España.*

Antigua soon became one of the most important cities of the New World. By 1543 it governed a vast area from the Yucatán and Chiapas in today's Mexico, south to what is now Panama. Antigua very early established itself as a center of culture and learning. Its university was the third in the entire western hemisphere. Its printing plants gained world recognition for fine book publishing and expert lithography. Outstanding architects came from Spain to design buildings of remarkable beauty—ornate and baroque, of massive construction, designed to withstand the continual earthquakes of this region. Modern-day architects and historians marvel over Antigua's unique 16th century homes that feature a curious corner window faced with wrought-iron grills—something found elsewhere only around Cáceres, Spain. Apparently these homes were built to order to please powerful conquistadores who insisted that things look exactly as they remembered back in the Estremadura region of Spain.

Because the Panchoy Valley was subject to earthquakes, the city was laid out with wider streets than usual, with ample parks and squares strategically placed about the town to accommodate sleeping out during time of tremors. Then, as today, folks accepted earthquakes as a common fact of life. (By coincidence, as I was typing these thoughts into my manuscript, a slight tremor jiggled my desk and chair. It came from a 6.9 quake centered near Eureka, California, about a three-hour drive from my Oregon home base.)

By the year 1773, Antigua was one of the largest and most beautiful cities in all of the Spanish colonies. But, suddenly, in that fateful year of 1773, an incredibly strong earthquake tossed the Panchoy Valley about like a maid flipping a bedspread. The exact magnitude is unknown (long before anyone thought of measuring), but judging from the ruins of those buildings—many virtually untouched since that fateful day in 1773—the force must have been colossal. Massive buildings with masonry walls eight feet thick cracked and crumbled as if they were of adobe clay. The quake was so bad, the people so frightened by the disaster, that the Spanish Viceroy ordered the town to be abandoned. The capital moved 25 miles to the east, to the site of what is now Guatemala City.

This abandonment is largely responsible for the impression that Antigua is suspended in time. People were very slow in returning. Gradually, they moved into some of the relatively undamaged homes and began turning a ghost town back into a place of human habitation. Sprawling ruins of churches, convents and government buildings remained undisturbed over the centuries, with huge chunks of ceiling arches and broken columns strewn about auditories, patios and courtyards. They remain silent testimonies to the power of Mother Nature.

Repopulating Antigua

Before and during World War II, tourism started to come into its own in Antigua. Retirees from the United States and Canada heard about its charms and came to visit and to stay. Hotels and businesses opened, attempting to draw tourists with conventional neon signs, billboards and other curses of development. But in 1944 the government realized what a prize they had in Antigua and prohibited modern construction and banned flashy signs. By law, old buildings must be restored to their original condition, or when that isn't possible, left exactly as they fell during the big quake. Today, Antigua is more like an original Spanish colonial town than any other place in the world, relatively untouched since colonial times when inhabitants walked away in despair.

Wealthy families from Guatemala City were among the first to recognize Antigua's charm and established weekend homes here. They remodeled old 16th century homes which had survived the quake, turning them into mansions. Wealthy North American retirees joined the restoration movement, along with not-so-wealthy compatriots who began refurbishing the less elegant homes. By the end of the 1950s, Antigua had acquired a reputation as a Gringo retirement haven.

This trend slowed during the days of civil strife, although those who lived there through the troubled times report that they experienced nothing but peace and tranquility. Today, as calm promises to settle over the country, Antigua is regaining its reputation as a place to retire or a retreat to spend pleasant months basking in its tranquil and picturesque setting. More and more North Americans are staking out claims to old homes and transforming broken ruins into lovely homes. With Guatemala's low cost of labor and materials, this is possible even for those who are not wealthy.

From Guatemala City

Antigua is easily reached by catching one of the rattle-trap buses that leave every few minutes from the terminal at 18th Calle in Guatemala City. Just tell the taxi driver, *"Terminal de bus para*

Antigua, por favor." (Bus is pronounced *boose* in Spanish.) A "terminal" by the way, is seldom a building in Guatemala, but usually just a place where buses park at the end of their run. There are no posted schedules, but you know which bus to take because the driver and his helper start shouting out their destinations a few minutes before they are ready to leave. If a bus is going to Guatemala City, for example, they will shout, "Guate! Guate! Guate!" (Pronounced *what-tay*, which is how Guatemalans refer to Guatemala City.)

There are other places in the city where you can catch the bus as it makes its way toward Antigua, but it's best to board at the terminal; that way you are assured a window seat and won't end up being the third passenger on a two-passenger seat. If you have luggage, the driver's helper will put it on top of the bus, in a secure area; you won't have room inside except for what you can tuck under the seat or carry on your lap. The trip takes between 45 minutes and an hour and is very interesting, particularly if you have a window seat. Most of the trip is over a divided, four-lane highway. By the time you reach Antigua, you will understand how sardines must feel.

Since several buses travel for the same destination at the same time, it's fun to watch the interaction between competing drivers and helpers. Each bus driver does his best to pull ahead of the bus in front so he can pick up waiting passengers before the other bus can get there. The helper's job is to lean out the door shouting the bus's destination so there can be no mistake. (The bus stops wherever a person waves to indicate that he wants a ride.) When one bus manages to pass another, there is a wild honking of air horns, shouts of derision and gesturing by the helpers, who defy gravity as they hang out the permanently open doorway. They must enjoy their jobs immensely. The price of this trip is a mere 2.50 quetzales, or 50 cents American.

Alternative modes of transportation will take you between Antigua and Guatemala City, but they are more expensive, and not significantly quicker. Passenger vans make the run, leaving from the better hotels on a daily basis. Your desk clerk can make arrangements. There is also the option of taking a taxi, for about $70, not too bad if the ride is shared by four or five passengers.

However, most taxis running around Guatemala aren't any better or newer than the buses.

The bus ride ends either at Antigua's terminal or on one of the main streets, occasionally at the *Parque Central* or Central Park (it would be called a *zócalo* in Mexico). This park, just one of several lovely ones in Antigua, is a wonderful introduction to the town. This is the focal point for foreign residents and local people alike. Its lofty trees, plush flowering shrubs and convenient benches make a great place to sun, meet friends and exchange travel stories. A baroque fountain, designed by a European architect in the early 1700s, is the centerpiece of the park, everything radiating out from there. Surrounding Parque Central is a square of 16th and 17th century buildings, most of which have been reconstructed using original facades, some of which were undamaged by the 1773 earthquake. Heavy stone archways front many of the buildings forming a shady arcade over the sidewalks. A half-block away from the square are other buildings, still in ruins after more than two centuries.

Oddly enough, the earthquake's destructive evidence is part of the town's charm. A number of churches have been left pretty much as they were the day of the earthquake, with only a wooden grating keeping people out of the ruins. Some churches, convents and monasteries display their destruction as public monuments.

Accommodations

Antigua has a good selection of hotels, ranging from $5 to $125 a night. But I much prefer to stay in a *pensión*: a private home converted into a tiny hotel, typically with no more than four rooms for rent, often serving a simple breakfast. This makes a pleasant and quiet place to stay while looking for an apartment or a room with a private family. A good place to look for either a pensión or a private-family room is at the tourist office on the northwest corner of the square. The director, *don* Benjamín, speaks excellent English and knows the best places to direct you. A nice room will cost between $10 and $20 a day.

Those who spend a few months or more will naturally prefer an apartment or a house. I spoke with several seasonal visitors about their housing and they reported monthly rents ranging from $90 to $500. The $500 rent was for a large old home, complete with patio and bougainvillea-filled garden. The $90 was for a small efficiency apartment, perfect for a single person (although a couple was renting it at the time).

All complained of the high costs of rents compared to the previous year. "Last year we paid $80 for our place," said one couple from Nevada. "This year the landlord charged $135, and after we've only been in there one month, he's raising it to $180! We're looking for another apartment, but so far we can't find one as close to the square as we'd like." They described their place as a large, two-bedroom apartment with wrought-iron balconies in front of each bedroom. It was just two blocks from Parque Central, and the price included a cleaning lady one day a week.

The farther you go from the center of town, the less expensive the accommodations. However, you are also farther from other English-speaking residents, from the supermarket and non-native shopping. Most try to stay within a ten-block radius of the Parque Central.

Social Groups in Antigua

The English-speaking community is divided into several distinct groups that do not often mix socially. One group is known as the "regulars," those who either live in Antigua permanently or who return annually to spend part of year. Many regulars own their own places. Theirs is a closely-knit circle which meets socially in private homes, entertaining behind high stone walls. Because tourists and occasional visitors are continually coming and going, the regulars have a reluctance to make friends with those who will be gone in a few weeks. In that respect, it's rather like a high-class Florida resort community, where residents and tourists live in totally different worlds and rarely mix on a social basis. Many people in this social circle are affluent, and the group includes wealthy Guatemalans who also regularly live in Antigua.

I visited the homes of two year-round residents, both families living in marvelously restored mansions. Both places were built in the 1600s and had survived the big quake of 1773 in more or less good shape. One couple, during the course of restoration, decided to break the large house into three sections, with two small rental units besides ample living quarters for themselves. "That way, when we have family and friends to visit, they have their own space," they explained. "During the summer, we usually rent the apartments to school teachers. In the winter, we do quite well renting them by the week to tourists." In accord with 1700s style, the home was built around a large interior garden. The small apartments are across the patio from the owners' four-bedroom living area, providing privacy for all. When I inquired as to how much they figured it costs to live there for the winter, I was told, "We've seldom spent more than $1,000 a month, and our rentals bring in more than that."

Both homes I visited were furnished with period antiques, lending an air of elegance that borders on opulence. Even though antique furniture is far less expensive here than in, say New York City, this obviously represented a tremendous investment, and price probably didn't enter into the picture. Both households employed domestic workers who were continually busy scrubbing, waxing and cleaning.

In the second home, two Indian girls (in colorful costume) worked full time keeping the marble floors scrubbed, the woodwork polished and the brass work gleaming. Another woman, a *ladina*, worked as a cook and housekeeper. A full-time gardener kept up with the flower beds and lawns that filled the large patio. He trimmed the grass with expert swipes of a long machete, just as neatly and precisely as if he had used a lawn mower. When I remarked about how picturesque the Indian girls were in their tribal costumes, my hostess said, "Once I tried to get them to wear ordinary clothing—those long, wrap-around blankets they wear for skirts look awfully stiff and uncomfortable. I bought them uniforms—nice flowing skirts and lacy blouses. But the next day, they were wearing their wrap-around skirts and woolen overshirts. They claimed that the loose-fitting skirts made them feel as if they were naked and immoral."

This family has lived in Antigua for several years, buying their house after the husband took an early retirement from a large corporation. I wanted to discretely inquire about their monthly budget, but I couldn't bring myself to do it. The Mercedes-Benz in the garage and their general luxurious lifestyle made me think that they probably didn't keep track of such things. I did find out that the total cost of the four full-time servants was less than $200 a month. "We pay them more than our neighbors do," she said, "and instead of working 12 hours a day, six-and-a-half days a week, we let them go home when they are finished with their work, usually after six or seven hours, and they get Saturday and Sunday off."

Snowbirds and Tourists

A second social set consists of those temporary residents who arrive every fall and return in the spring—the "snowbird" set. They usually rent apartments, small houses or rooms in private homes. Social activities center around the Parque Central, in surrounding restaurants or in ad-hoc travel groups. Often their apartments are too small for large-scale entertaining, so restaurants or Parque Central benches become their meeting places or reception salons. Making friends among this group requires little effort; everyone seems eager to socialize and make new friends. A simple "good morning" and a smile is all it takes. Tourists here for even a two-week stay have no problem finding friends among this group of temporary residents.

Overlooking the park, under an arcade near the southeast corner of the square, the San Carlos restaurant is well known to tourists, snowbirds and seasonal residents as a place to meet newcomers, plan sightseeing trips to neighboring villages or simply to quaff a few inexpensive beers and exchange gossip about absent members of the impromptu social group. A long table in San Carlos' front-and-center is traditionally reserved for snowbirds, and it's generally filled by noon. Yet, there's always room to pull up another chair or two. Individual members change from month to month, but the group lives on from season to season.

Doña Luisa's restaurant is the "in place" for a hearty breakfast or lunch at reasonable prices, making it popular with language school students and tourists alike. The setting is in the patio of an old mansion which has a balcony jutting out all around the dining area. Artists, writers and musicians can often be found here, discussing their latest projects. A hearty breakfast costs about $2.50 and $4.00 buys a delicious and filling lunch.

An important feature of Doña Luisa's is the large bulletin board near the entrance. Since the local tourist publication comes out monthly and has few classified ads, Doña Luisa's bulletin board fills the need for an up-to-date information center. Notes tacked to the board tell you what apartments are available, who is giving guitar lessons, who wants companions for a trip to Tikal, who is selling a bicycle, where to buy a second-hand car or just about any other piece of information you might need to settle into Antigua.

Across the street is Mistral's, a restaurant-bar that features a large-screen television and satellite dish. This is an extremely popular (and noisy) place during Super Bowl, World Series or play-off time. When no sports activity is being featured, American movies are shown in a theater-style lounge.

The Flor restaurant is another meeting place for North Americans and has an excellent menu. This is the unofficial center for Peace Corps volunteers when they come down from their nearby training camp. You are likely to find a table of them almost any night of the week. You'd never guess that Ricardo, the Flor's owner, is Guatemalan from his accent. (He went to school in New York and Denver.) At the time I interviewed him, he was in the process of building a new home on the outskirts. "Of course, it has to be colonial style," he said, "so building costs are more expensive than they normally would be. But the whole thing will cost only about $15,000, so I'm able to pay cash as I go along. The beauty of it is, when it's finished, it will be paid for!"

Language Schools

Still another social group consists of language students who attend one of the many Spanish schools. A large percentage of Antigua's English-speaking residents at any given time are students. More than 30 Spanish language schools in Antigua make teaching Spanish the town's largest business enterprise, a virtual industry. Students from all over the world come here to take advantage of inexpensive, quality instruction. Some schools feature individual instruction—one teacher for each student—at a tiny fraction of what an ordinary, multi-student classroom tuition would cost in another country. For example, the most expensive school in Antigua charges $35 a week for individual instruction of four hours a day, five days a week. That's only $1.75 an hour—which has to cover the school's overhead as well as paying the teacher's salary!

The schools encourage, almost insist, that students stay with Spanish-only families to speed up language acquisition. Students are forced to become totally immersed in the language. The going rate for board and room in Antigua (in spring, 1992) is just $120 a month! When you add the average classroom tuition of $120 a month—for seven hours a day, five days a week of intensive training—that brings one month's basic living costs to just $240. That's less than they'd spend for groceries back home! It's small wonder that Antigua's language schools are so popular.

But not all students live this way. I heard from one retired couple who decided to drive their motorhome to Guatemala and study Spanish for a few months. Instead of an apartment, a hotel or a room in a private home, they made their headquarters behind a Texaco gasoline station. "It was a new, modern station with space for three campers," they said. "We had water and electric, and use of the cold shower in their restroom (cleaned daily). On one side of the motorhome was a lawn; in front of us was the Ramada Inn; the rear of the motorhome faced a horse farm."

They decided to attend the *Projecto Linguistico Francisco Marroquín*, one of the more expensive schools, where the U.S. government sends its employees to study Spanish. They describe their experiences as follows: "Our school consisted of four buildings scattered throughout the town, most of which were formerly homes of wealthy families. All rooms open onto the interior courtyard. Students work one-on-one with a teacher. One student-teacher pair occupies each room. The room contains one small table, two wooden chairs and a 40-watt light bulb. The windows, in general do not have glass, but rather shutters and the requisite iron bars to prevent intruders.

"On top of each table is a pile of blank newsprint sheets which serve as "blackboards." If there are more students than rooms, tables are also scattered along the covered walkway surrounding the courtyard. Those students who return week after week can request specific teachers and/or rooms, which means the new students generally spend the first week in the courtyard.

"School occupied the majority of our waking hours. We attended seven hours a day, five days a week, with a two-hour break for lunch. We were so saturated with Spanish that studying at the break was impossible. At night we did a few chores, rushed home to dinner, and then studied .

"At first, the teachers spoke slowly and distinctly to us. But by the time we left, they were speaking at nearly normal speed and we were really grasping their thoughts. It was truly amazing how much clearer all of the native people were speaking compared to how they used to speak when we arrived just two months before!"

Rooms in Private Homes

Private home room-rentals create a significant source of income for Antigua, with many families hosting students and visitors. The extra money helps the economy, raising the general level of prosperity throughout the town. In addition to language students, many seasonal visitors prefer to rent rooms in private homes rather than bother with an apartment or house. A large number of single men, often divorced or widowed, as well as a few couples and single women, take advantage of this inexpensive lifestyle. The higher the rent, of course, the better the accommodations and the more edible the food. At the low end of the scale, accommodations are quite rustic and likely to be occupied by backpackers who consider wall-to-wall floors a luxury.

While I was interviewing a newly-divorced man from Illinois about his lifestyle, he suggested that I rent a room with the family he was living with and see for myself. There happened to be a vacant room in the house and the landlady is always willing to rent by the day until a permanent tenant appears on the scene. The cost of one night's lodging and a hearty breakfast: 25 quetzales, or five dollars. For $120 a month, a boarder receives three meals a day. "The food is good, " my friend insisted. "Beans and rice at every meal, of course, including breakfast, but the landlady is a great cook and serves typical Guatemalan dishes you can't find elsewhere. She makes a chicken cooked in a sauce of ground pumpkin seeds and fresh cilantro that is absolutely wonderful." How much was it costing him to escape Illinois winter by staying in Antigua? "Last month I spent about $100 over my $120 for the room. But I wasn't particularly trying to scrimp, there was just nothing else I happened to need."

The house was about five blocks from the Parque Central. A pleasant elderly lady greeted me with a bright smile, but her dog, which looked suspiciously like a pit bull, greeted me with a low growl that rumbled deep in his chest. The house dated from the early 1700s. It had two patios, one for the kitchen and the owner's living quarters. The second patio had a dining room and four rental rooms facing it. My room was huge, at least 20 feet square with a ceiling that was close to 20 feet high. The furnishings were massive, and marked with wear of many years. The featured pieces were a large armoire and an old-fashioned cabinet with a door that opened to display a chamber pot. (That's right; for $120 a month, you get no private bathroom.)

"The bathroom's right around the corner," explained my friend, "but I wouldn't use it late at night, because the dog is always roaming around the patios. The lady claims he's harmless, but I don't like the way he growls at me." I took his advice and didn't take any chances with the dog.

Backpackers

The last group of foreigners, present everywhere in Guatemala, is the backpacking set. In Antigua, they make their headquarters by day in the Parque Central; in the evening they frequent one of the disco bars closer to the bus terminal. Loud music, shouting and sounds of full-bore laughter give away the locations at any time after nightfall. Most of these visitors come from Europe—Germany, Switzerland, Italy or England. Of course, Canada and the U.S.A. are well represented, too. English seems to be the common language, with heavily accented conversations punctuated by loud rock-and-roll music coming through the open doorways of the bars, along with an occasional odor of some burning substance that doesn't quite smell like Lucky Strikes.

Backpackers patronize the $3-a-day hotels or the less-expensive rooming houses, and prefer to eat in the open market, or *mercado*, where they dine for pennies, or perhaps picnic in the park rather than pay restaurant prices of two or three dollars for a meal. It's a totally different world, one of adventure and fellowship that I wish I could have experienced at that age (long before anybody thought of backpacking). It's a pleasant crowd that treats members of my generation with polite but distant deference when we enter one of the bars for a short dose of earsplitting music and a glass of beer. We exist in different universes.

Panajachel

One other practical place for long-term living or retirement is Lake Atitlán, principally in or around the town of Panajachel. (The accent falls on the last syllable: *Pan-a-ha-chél.*) "The most beautiful lake in the world," is the way novelist Aldous Huxley described Lake Atitlán, and that's the description found in most of today's travel guides. If this isn't the most beautiful lake, it certainly ranks near the top of the list. Encircled by mountains with three sharp volcanic peaks presiding over all, reflecting on the lake's crystal-clear waters, Lake Atitlán is truly a sight to remember.

Sitting at an altitude 4,700 feet, the villages around the lake enjoy a superb, year-round climate. As one American retiree says, "There are certain inconveniences here, but the weather is perfect and I sleep under a blanket every night of the year. That helps make it all worthwhile." The waters are famous for tasty black bass which is served in local cafes and restaurants. The lake also provides opportunities for water sports such as boating, swimming and water skiing.

In addition to Panajachel, there are a dozen smaller towns around the lake, exceptionally picturesque and populated with

Indians, most of whom are involved in weaving or farming. A few foreigners live in the villages, and perhaps more will someday, after peace and quiet totally take over the land.

Considering the lake's natural beauty and its pleasant spring-like climate, the total population is surprisingly sparse. Panajachel, the largest town, has but 5,000 people and that probably counts in much of the surrounding area's population. This community is as different from Antigua as you can imagine. Instead of Antigua's old-world charm, with dignified Spanish-colonial homes, Panajachel and surrounding villages are basically Maya Indian, with just a smattering of European residents. Panajachel's building style is utilitarian, without much thought given to style or aesthetics. Many buildings are of raw cement block or hand-hewn wooden planks. The main street is totally lined with rickety booths and stands displaying colorful weavings.

When Antigua was founded in the 1500s, Panajachel had been a thriving Indian commercial center for several centuries. Ignored by the Spanish over the years, it remained Indian up until the present time. Most foreigners here are temporary—visiting for a few weeks or months, with a minority in permanent residency. That's not because of the climate or hospitality, but because Panajachel is a long way from the civilized amenities of Guatemala City (a four-hour bus ride), and rather isolated. After a period of time enjoying the sights, studying the Indian culture and interacting with other foreigners, visitors tend to drift back to Antigua or Guatemala City.

The vast majority of the people on the streets, at least 90 percent, are pure Maya Indian, most of whom speak very little Spanish. Women wear traditional, colorful costumes of hand-woven fabrics. Men wear a curious type of woven pants, pink and intricately designed, under a dark brown skirt. (Yes, I said skirt!) Indians from surrounding villages carry large bundles of merchandise either on their heads or in homemade wheelbarrows to market in Panajachel. They sell retail to tourists and wholesale to buyers from the capital. Everything from archaeological treasures to woven "panama" hats are on display. The biggest volume of goods are the weavings of the Lake Atitlán region, sometimes shining with silver or golden thread. The colors and the embroidery work are dazzling.

On Panajachel's side streets you find numerous rooming houses, bungalows and houses scattered about town, catering to tourists and long-term vacationers. Hotels are plentiful, ranging from very expensive to moderate in price. Longer-term residents rent apartments, condos or cottages, which are sometimes grouped about to form a closed compound. Some long-term residents opt for houses or small farms on the outskirts of town. Those who own permanent homes in town usually hide them behind lush gardens and landscaping. Some homes are of modern construction, sometimes colonial-style with tile roofs.

Because the lake provides an inexhaustible supply of water, many people have pumps at the water's edge sending a steady stream of water for irrigating plants and gardens. Flowers grow in profusion here. Purple, red and yellow bougainvilleas, brilliant red poinsettias and purple hybiscus-like flowers bloom everywhere, all year long. Instead of bushes or vines, these plants grow into full-fledged trees. Particularly dramatic is a huge tree with brilliant orange flowers mixed into the deep green foliage.

Panajachel's climate is even more spring-like than Antigua's or Guatemala's, if that's possible. The nights are certainly cooler, with a sweater needed after 6 o'clock, but shirtsleeves and swimming suits comfortable all day. The lake is unpolluted and excellent for swimming, with a fresh-feeling temperature to the water—not cold, but not warm, either.

A major difference between here and Antigua is the lack of a town square where foreign residents can congregate. Instead, restaurants and private homes serve as social centers. Antigua's San Carlos restaurant is replicated in Panajachel by the El Patio, El Chisme and the Mayan Yacht Club restaurants. These places have wrought iron tables and large umbrellas for shade. Every day, around noon and then later about 5 o'clock, you'll find a gathering of *Norteamericanos* chatting, gossiping and discussing world events. Curiously, as isolated as Panajachel is, there is an excellent cable system, complete with Cable News Network, so current world events are eagerly discussed over coffee or beer.

The meeting places for the younger set is a series of bars along the lower part of Panajachel's main street (toward the lake).

Retirement in Panajachel

When I brought up the subject of retirement in Central America, one man who has lived in both Guatemala and Costa Rica said, "No question in my mind, I love it here best." He told of moving to Panajachel about four years ago from Costa Rica's Turrialba. "I came for a visit, but when I returned to Costa Rica I began packing things for a permanent return here." When asked why, he replied, "Costa Rica is beautiful, that's true, but it's just as beautiful here. And here everything costs one-half to one-third as much. I rent a large house for $175 a month, which I couldn't find in Costa Rica for twice that amount."

What about safety? Again, safety is relative; we all know that crime in the United States is growing out of sight, so it would be unrealistic to expect a place like Panajachel to be totally crime-free. Still, even though crime rates are lower here, it won't do to gloss over the problem. When a group of American retirees were asked to comment on crime in Panajachel, they were in general agreement that violent crime was relatively rare, but that one had to keep a sharp eye out for break-ins.

One man said, "My house was broken into three times in the past three years. As a matter of fact, one occurred just two weeks ago."

Another man at our table said, "Yes, but that's because you have no security system. If you are going to live outside of town, you need to have a wall around your property or else some live-in help. Me, I've never been burglarized."

A couple volunteered: "We don't expect trouble, mostly because we live in a compound of six bungalows and the owner of the property keeps a sharp eye on things." They all agreed that pickpocketing is a serious problem here for tourists, yet noted that none of them had been victimized. You learn rather quickly to take precautions against this kind of crime.

Renting a Home

Local property owners much prefer renting to mature North American retirees. As a rule, we have a reputation for being quiet, responsible and usually improve property rather than allowing it to go downhill as some other classes of tenants tend to do. There is a general feeling that some of the Europeans—the younger set—come here to take advantage of cheap living and often get involved in drugs and destructive parties.

One of the long-term residents graciously invited me to his home on the outskirts of Panajachel. Wallace (Wally) was renting a place on the edge of what once was a coffee plantation, now a multi-purpose farm. When he parked the car in its usual place in front of the house, the place could not be seen; it was hidden by a screen of trees, shrubs and flowering plants. A small stream, which the gardener used to irrigate the garden, ran through the property. He did this by scooping water with something that looked like a shallow pan and then throwing it over the plants. Incidentally, this is probably the identical way crops were irrigated back in Precolumbian days. Lines of water channels, each about a foot wide and a foot deep, cut across fields in rows spaced apart half the distance of an easy throw, so water can be scooped onto the crops. On this particular farm the Indians were harvesting string beans and potatoes, with one plot ready for planting some other crop.

Wally's house is a simple, concrete block affair with a lightweight corrugated roof, the kind popular in earthquake country. Its arrangement is unusual because the bedroom and kitchen are combined. A bathroom and a large studio-living room completed the layout. A retired art professor, Wally's hobby is restoring Mayan pottery and sculptures. "I buy partially destroyed pieces in the marketplace," he explained, "something with a clue as to what they originally looked like. Then I go to work. Once they are dug out of the ground, they have no archaeological significance, so I don't feel I am doing anything wrong, and I never represent my work as anything but a restoration."

The gardener is paid by the woman who owns the property; he takes care of her place as well as Wally's. His salary is 60 quetzales a week ($12) for an 8-hour day. A maid comes in one day a week to clean and do laundry for 10 quetzales a day ($2).

Owning a Business

Harold, a German who worked as a photographer in his home country, related his experiences as a businessman and told how he made the decision to leave Germany and move permanently to Guatemala. "My wife and I made a vacation trip to Guatemala and we discovered Panajachel. We fell in love with the place and tried to think of some way to earn a living here and not have to return to Europe. We noticed there were no Chinese restaurants here. So, we decided to try opening a Chinese restaurant."

He admitted that they had absolutely no experience in either the restaurant business or Chinese cooking. "But we've done just fine. The secret to our success is our employees. We treat them better than any other business in town. Instead of paying just minimum wage, like most restaurants, we also give them 10 percent of our receipts. Every night, just before we close, everybody gathers around as we count the money. You can see the pleasure on their faces. Their enthusiasm is unbelievable." He said that working seven days a week became a bit tiring, so he wanted to close the restaurant one day a week. But the employees objected strenuously. They didn't want to lose the extra money. "You stay home," they insisted, "and *we'll* run the place!"

Peace Corps

Guatemala is the location of an important branch of the Peace Corps. This is one country that can greatly benefit from the enthusiasm, energy and expertise of young American volunteers. Although most of them are young, there also happens to be an older caucus of volunteers who bring just as much enthusiasm, energy and expertise to the field.

The Peace Corps training headquarters is located on a mountainside not far from Antigua, in a small village called Santa Lucía

Milpa Alta. I went there to interview John Dwyer, a retired publishers' representative, who decided that a two-year adventure helping others was just what his life needed now that his kids were through college and he had no more heavy responsibilities. The Peace Corps compound consists of several buildings—classrooms, offices and dormitories. Excitement was running high because the 15-week training classes were drawing to a close and field assignments were being handed out. Soon everyone would know where they would be spending the next two years of their lives. I could hear feverish shouts of, "Oh boy! I'm going to San Fulano! Where are you going?" The excitement was contagious. Those in the same age bracket as John were just as exhilarated as the youngsters.

When I asked John how he "fit in" with the younger crowd, he replied, "My fellow Peace Corps Volunteers are a very nice group. It's interesting to me, the friendships I am building with people just out of college. They invite me on their trips, to their parties and share their fears and joys. I find the experience just delightful."

John's assignment was in a place called Jutiapa, in the southeastern section of the country. Later on he wrote to tell me of his experiences. "I am finding it very interesting and have met some very nice people. This is real 'cowboy country' complete with horses, pistols and cattle drives. Just the other day, the newspaper *Prensa Libre* said that Jutiapans are known for taking the law into their own hands—'shades of Tombstone.'" His assignment is to work with agricultural cooperatives located in the mountains about an hour away from town. His project is teaching workers to operate the new equipment and training people for administration, accounting and marketing. He pointed out, "As many of the co-op members are illiterate, it can be challenging. And as my agricultural background is virtually nil, I have a lot to learn, but it's a great experience."

While his work is interesting and his new friends are delightful, John makes an interesting point about adjusting to a non-English-speaking environment. He said, "During our training, we were surrounded by bilingual personnel, which made communications simple when one tires of speaking Spanish—we simply toss in a few English words. But in Jutiapa it is always Spanish, and this leads to some stress. Time will, of course, take care of the problem, but in the meantime one needs patience."

The Peace Corps is a very interesting alternative for foreign living and doing something constructive and worthwhile at the same time. The Peace Corps actively solicits older volunteers, by the way. According to the program director in Santa Cruz Milpa Alta, about 10 percent of the volunteers are over age 50. These are folks who not only have valuable experience to share with others, but when retired, can afford to work for the small payments available to the volunteers. Most college graduates are too interested in launching a career and a family to afford two years working for a Peace Corps pay. Volunteers receive $200 a month (plus a vacation allowance) and a bonus at the end of the tour of duty of $5,400.

Interestingly, the Japanese also maintain their own version of the Peace Corps in Guatemala. There are quite a few of them stationed about the country—young, eager, with the same look of serious dedication as our own Peace Corps volunteers. However, one suspicious Gringo said, "I wonder if they are here to help, or merely taking inventory!" Since we North Americans are used to Japanese visitors to our country speaking perfect English, it is somewhat surprising to discover that few Japanese Peace Corps members in Guatemala speak English, but all have been trained in Spanish. I spoke with one young lady on a bus ride back in the hills, and found out that in college, her expertise was in textiles. When I ask her if she was teaching the Indians Japanese textiles technology, she replied, "Oh, no. They are teaching *me* how they do *their* weavings." I suspect that someday soon we'll be seeing Guatemalan Maya patterns with "Made in Japan" labels.

Chapter Seventeen

Guatemalan Residency

When you enter the country, you will be given a visa good for a 90-day visit. A Guatemalan consulate can grant a five-year, multiple-entry visa, but it is still only good for 90 days at a time. The crazy thing is, even though *you* receive permission for a 90-day stay, your car permit is issued by another bureau of the government and is good for only *30* days!

It turns out that visas are given out by *migración* (immigration) but car permits are given out by *aduana* (customs). As in most Latin American government entities, common sense doesn't enter into the situation. But don't despair. At the end of 30 days (apply earlier, of course) you can request an extension at INGUAT office in Guatemala City and you will receive a car permit that equals the time on your visa. Then, at the end of 90 days, you can apply for another visa of 90 days at which time you will receive a car permit for the same amount of time. You may be wise to hire a *tramitador* to help you. Some travel agents can take care of your car papers; inquire about town until you find one who is willing to help.

After the second car permit expires (and if you want to stay in Guatemala longer) you must take your car out of the country for a few days before bringing it back. This is best done by going back to Mexico, or by crossing into Honduras and enjoying a few days at those beach areas on the Honduran coast of the Caribbean which are popular with North Americans who go there to give their autos an "out of the country" experience.

One day, in Panajachel, I noticed a friend driving with Canadian plates on his car. I knew he wasn't from Canada, and he told an amusing story to explain the foreign plates. "I had to take the car out of the country for two days before bringing it back. So I left it in a government storage lot across the border in Mexico. But when I returned, my New Mexico plates had disappeared. I complained to the government employee who ran the lot. He said that he couldn't find any New Mexico plates to give me, but that I could pick out any other plates in the lot that I liked. The Canadian plates looked nice, so he removed the them from the unfortunate Canadian's automobile, put them on my car, and I was on my way back to Guatemala!"

Legal Residency

The government of Guatemala is delighted to have you apply for resident or retirement papers. After all, you will be contributing to the economy with your pension money, and you will be a desirable, law-abiding citizen. Despite the government's desire to have you as a resident, an ossified bureaucracy makes it difficult at every turn. You will be referred to one office after another to have your papers perused, stamped and then sent on to another office. There is a better way: hire a *tramitador* who will stand in line for you, who knows all the crazy ways of bureaucrats, how to cut corners, and which lines to stand in. As one retiree applicant said, "The $20 that it cost me to have a tramitador take care of my papers must have saved me two days of standing in lines." They are easy to find; when you approach a police station or a government agency, or anywhere the red tape is long with lines to match, you will be besieged by a crowd of tramitadores, waving credentials as they solicit business.

It isn't unusual for the final papers to take as long as 18 months to be completed. However, there is no problem with having to leave the country during this wait; you will be given papers to cover you until the bureaucracy finally comes through. A friend told of an amusing incident which occurred at INGUAT offices in Guatemala City. A lady from Chicago decided she wanted retire in Guatemala. So she sold her house, put her furniture and belongings in storage and caught the next plane for Guatemala City. She breezed into the INGUAT office with a handful of documents, birth certificate and other papers which she supposed she would probably need. Apparently, she expected to be given her retirement papers immediately, because she had instructed her taxicab driver to wait for her!

An American retiree, a veteran of Guatemala's bureaucracy, smiled at her naivete, and said, "Lady, my advice to you is this: Go back up to the States with all your papers. Find a Guatemalan consulate and start all over again. While they're working on it, you can come on back to Guatemala, find yourself an apartment or a house, and just forget about it until it happens."

One problem is that all documents must be translated into Spanish by a certified translator, preferably at a Guatemalan consulate in the United States. The consul knows exactly what to do and in what order, so you are relieved of a lot of worry, trouble and wear and tear on your feet.

Retirement in Guatemala

Because retirees make a such a positive contribution to the economy and development of a country, the Guatemalan government, back in 1973, decided to codify the rules and regulations so that those considering retirement would understand the procedure. These rules are contained in a booklet titled, "Law For Resident Retired Citizens and Rentiers," which be obtained by writing the following addresses, or appearing there in person:

Guatemala Tourist Commission, 299 Alhambra Circle, Suite 510, Coral Gables, FL 33134. TEL: (305) 442-0651, 442-0412, FAX: (305) 442-1013. Or: Instituto Guatemalamalteco de Turismo, Centro Civico, Cuidad de Guatemala, Guatemala, Central America. TEL: (502-2) 31-13-33, FAX: (502-2) 31-88-93. This booklet explains in detail what needs to be done to become a resident or a retiree.

There are two categories of residents under the law: *Resident Retired Citizens*, those who have been pensioned or retired by governments or private companies, and *Resident Renters*, those 50 years of age or older, who are not retired, yet receive steady, permanent income from outside the country. To fit into one of these categories, you must provide documentary proof showing you have at least $300 U.S. dollars a month which can be used for living expenses inside Guatemala.

Once granted, residency provides substantial tax benefits. The law reads as follows: "Persons covered by this law shall enjoy exemption from custom duties, charges and surcharges, sales taxes and any other kind of selective consumer taxes which may be created in future up to the amount equivalent in national currency of $8,000 (U.S. dollars) for importation of their household effects. This amount could be divided into several parts, according to how the importation is carried out, within the first year of residence." These goods must be for personal use, and if they are sold within three years of entering the country, any taxes which were exempted would be due.

You may either import, or purchase in Guatemala, a vehicle for personal or family use, free of all taxes. This can be done every four years. Of course, if you sell it before the four year-year period, you will owe import duties. If the vehicle is stolen or destroyed in an accident, you can buy another tax-free.

Your retirement income is also free of income taxes. But you must deposit a minimum of $300 every month to your Guatemalan bank account as proof that you have enough for living expenses. If you return home for an extended period, you have to show proof of at least six months of deposits in advance to cover your absence. In order to keep residency papers current, you are not allowed to stay abroad for more than one consecutive year.

Foreign residents are not entitled to work at a job without government permission. Excluded from this prohibition are those who, in the opinion of the Ministry of Economy, invest in activities that are beneficial to the country. That means if you invest in a business that helps tourism and provides jobs, you can work in that business. I know several foreigners who say they've had no problems going into business.

Chapter Eighteen

Traveling to Central America

Three practical modes of travel will take you to Central America, to either Costa Rica or Guatemala: by airplane, by automobile or—for the exceptionally hardy—by inter-city bus. It's theoretically possible to travel as far as Guatemala City by train, but the logistics of doing this are best left to wild adventurers who are willing to put up with incredibly uncomfortable and unreliable facilities.

Another mode of transportation, the passenger-carrying freighter, is all but out of the question nowadays. Waiting lists are said to be six months to a year. However, freighters are commonly used by North Americans living in Costa Rica to deliver household goods, automobiles and other items too large to carry on the airplane or to pack into the car. By the way, you can have your automobile delivered by airplane! One man reported that it cost $1,200 to have a VW flown from Miami. By ship, it would have been about $400.

Central America by Air

The quickest and easiest way to get to Central America is by air, but of course this restricts the amount of belongings you can take—things you may need for a long-term stay. A number of airlines run regular service to Costa Rica: American Airlines, United, and Continental, among others, and inexpensive Canadian charter flights fly from Vancouver and Montreal. Mexico's Mexicana Airlines flies both to Guatemala and Costa Rica. In addition, several Central American airlines, such as

TACA, Aviateca, COPA and SAM, fly from Miami, New Orleans, Houston and Los Angeles. These local lines sometimes offer bargain rates, but your travel agent may not be willing to spend the time asking about them. Check directory assistance for their 800 telephone listings. Costa Rica's own airline, LACSA (now mostly owned by the Japanese), generally beats the prices of the U.S. airlines, but its lower-priced fares involve stopping several places along the way. On my last trip from Los Angeles, we stopped in Acapulco, San Salvador, Managua and finally, San José!

My experience with travel agents is that they can't always find the cheapest way to travel. You can often save money by calling the airlines yourself and asking their best rates—preferably well in advance—and either make your own reservations or inform your travel agent so he or she can make them for you (costs the same either way). I saved $160 on my last Costa Rica tickets this way. You may spend some time on the phone, listening to boring music while waiting for a clerk, but in the end you could save dollars.

For a combination Guatemala-Costa Rica trip, LACSA offers a stopover in Guatemala for only $50 over a regular round-trip fare to Costa Rica. This is an excellent way to see which of these countries is the best for your long-term living, retirement or investment options.

Costa Rica's Airport

Costa Rica's international air terminal is the Juán Santimaria Airport, near San José. It's a clean, modern place where customs inspection is relatively easy. Any time I've passed through customs, the agents weren't the least bit curious about what was in my luggage. A second international airport is scheduled to open in 1993 near the northern city of Liberia. This will relieve congestion at the San José facility, and make it easier for tourists to visit Pacific beaches such as Flamingo, Nosara and Sámara. This will definitely boost the economies and make a stronger case for paving the roads along the Nicoya Peninsula coast.

Taxis to downtown San José or any other place on the Meseta Central are plentiful and prices competitive. It usually costs $8 to $12 to a destination in downtown San José. (Taxis aren't permitted to go to more than one hotel or address per trip.) If you don't have much luggage, you could take a bus to downtown San José or nearby Alajuela for less than half a dollar.

Money changers hang around the taxi stand, so this might be a convenient time to change a few dollars into colónes if you don't want to wait until you get to your hotel. Be cautious though; some of these guys are quick-change artists. Know exactly how much money you give them, and count your change carefully. Having a calculator in your hand makes them think you know what you are doing. They usually don't want travelers checks, by the way

Guatemala's Airport

The international airport in Guatemala City is a small facility and it's not very complicated to get through customs. Immediately upon disembarking, you'll see a branch of the Guatemalan Bank where you can change money or travelers checks. As always, when you change money in public place, tuck it into a secure place on your person and be specially cautious when in a crowd. Above all, don't put it in your wallet and then into your hip pocket. I haven't heard of people having problems at the airport, but I would be astonished if someone's pocket *doesn't* get picked from time to time.

Taxis are always lined up at the exit, so you'll have no problem getting to your hotel or to the bus depot if you are continuing on to Antigua or Panajachel. From the airport you shouldn't pay more than 40 quetzales, about $8, to go downtown. But make sure that the driver agrees with you on the amount before you enter the cab. Incidentally, taxi drivers in Guatemala are unusually gregarious and jovial, especially if you understand even a little Spanish. They seem to enjoy telling jokes and then laughing uncontrollably at the punch lines, pounding the steering wheel in hilarity—no matter whether the passengers get it or not. I've found them to be very helpful and have seldom felt cheated.

Driving to Costa Rica

One of the first questions folks ask when thinking about spending time in Guatemala or Costa Rica is: "Can I take my car there?" The answer is, "Yes, but it isn't easy."

A few years back—before the turmoil in Central America—I made an automobile trip to Costa Rica and thoroughly enjoyed it. The roads were fairly good—as long as you didn't travel at night—and the scenery very exciting. Every day was a new adventure, a new challenge, full of photographic opportunities and pleasant encounters with local people. The most annoying part of the journey was the long wait and inconvenience while crossing from one country into another. (This hasn't changed.) Sour-faced officials examine your papers with suspicious eyes, then hand out a sheaf of forms to be filled in triplicate and then rubber-stamp everything in sight. (Oh, how they *love* rubber stamps!) You go from one official to another for what seems an eternity. Finally, you are allowed to leave the country, only to drive 50 feet into the next country and start the process all over again at the next customs office.

However, all the problems in Guatemala, El Salvador and Nicaragua brought tourist automobile travel to a virtual standstill. Even then, some folks continued to drive, merely changing the route somewhat. They traveled the Pacific coastal route through Guatemala, avoided El Salvador by detouring through Honduras, and then carefully skirted trouble spots in Nicaragua. Ironically, when the Sandinistas took over in Nicaragua, travelers reported that the only easy border crossings were into and out of Nicaragua. Apparently, the Sandinista customs inspectors were somewhat laid back, casually waving Costa Rica-bound tourists on through, saying, "Have a good trip! Maybe General Somoza took the rubber stamps when he went into exile.

Driving Once Again Feasible

Today, the outlook is considerably brighter in Central America. Again, tourists routinely drive the Pan American Highway, as far as Costa Rica, and even into Panama. With a peace accord in El Salvador, cessation of hostilities some time earlier in Nicaragua and with Guatemalan officials negotiating with its rebels, most of the region is peaceful.

Driving the Pan American Highway isn't easy, mind you, but then it never was easy. This isn't a journey to be taken lightly. We're talking mile after mile of marginal highways, poor hotel accommodations, frustration and red tape at every border crossing. Yet I interviewed a half-dozen people who made the trip in early 1992 and all shrugged off these inconveniences. They felt that the important thing was that they were able to get their vehicles and belongings through intact. All described their trip as an adventure they wouldn't have missed for anything in the world. The secret is to "hang loose" at the customs stops, don't get upset and try to laugh at the process. A few five-dollar bills handed out from time to time helps smooth problems.

A family of three related their experiences in April of 1992, as they drove a pickup on their fifth trip through Central America. They reported to the *Tico Times* that 95 percent of the highway was in good condition, and that the six border crossings consumed an average of two hours each. They spent about $150 in fees, stamps and bribes. The husband summed up by saying, "At no time did we sense danger from criminal attack... The trip is feasible, and even though a bit tiring, it is almost never boring! We can recommend it to anyone who has a bit of Spanish, a measure of patience, a dependable vehicle, at least seven days and upwards of $1,000 to invest in such an experience."

On the Road

From the U.S. border at Brownsville to Costa Rica, the drive is 2,300. From Mexicali, the distance is 3,700 miles. Your car should be in good condition, with new tires and spare, an emergency tool kit, road flares and flashlights with extra batteries. Unleaded fuel is available in Mexico, but seldom in other countries. If your car is set up for unleaded gasoline, check with your dealer for a conversion package which allows the engine to burn leaded fuel efficiently. Be aware that when you return, the catalytic converter will probably have to be replaced.

You must have a valid U.S. passport, and although visas aren't required, it's a good idea to get them from the consulates before you leave if possible; you'll save time and bribery money at the borders. Mexican, Guatemalan, Costa Rican and Honduran tourist offices and consulates have free road maps for the asking. Before making any plans, check with these consulates for any new rules, or any recent problems for travelers.

Don't forget car insurance. Your U.S. or Canadian policy isn't recognized south of the border, but do carry proof that you *have* a valid policy. You will need to buy a special insurance policy for Central America. *Before* you cross into Mexico, contact Charles Nelson of Sanborn's Insurance, at (512) 686-0711, or write to P.O. Box 310, McAllen, TX 78502. This company can write Central American policies by telephone and will take credit cards. For a 15-day policy (which should be more than ample time to drive all the way to Costa Rica) the cost of full coverage on a vehicle valued at $12,000 would be $201. For 15 days of liability-only, the cost is $49. If your vehicle is financed, you'll need a notarized statement from the bank or finance company stating you have the permission to take the vehicle out of the country. Best have it notarized at a Mexican consulate if at all possible. Mexico has been cracking down on cars coming into the country to combat a rash of stolen automobiles.

Through Mexico and Guatemala

The first country to cross is Mexico. You will be issued a tourist card at the border, or you can obtain one in advance at your nearest consulate by showing your passport. Driving through Mexico is, in itself, no small chore, and you should figure three days at a minimum to make the trip. You will probably take at least a week, enjoying a mini-vacation, visiting Mexico's recreational and historical sites.

Never drive at night—in Mexico or anywhere in Central America. As explained in my book *RV Travel in Mexico*, Mexican (and Central American) highways are generally in fair condition, but they are built as cheaply as possible. The road definitely ends at the edge of the pavement; when there are shoulders it's purely by accident. In the dark, you have no idea what lays beyond the pavement—a stretch of dirt, gravel, or a two-foot dropoff. There are no high-speed highways on this route, and four-lane roads are almost unknown.

Guatemala

The recommended place to cross into Guatemala is near Tapachula, Mexico—at the Guatemalan town of Tecún Umanán. Good overnight accommodations can be found in Tapachula, to be ready for the Guatemala run in the morning. Do your crossing early, since the border is closed for siesta from one to 3 p.m.

A typical border crossing is described by Karen Bonis as she and her husband Scott drove their large motorhome into Guatemala: "From the center of town we followed a steady stream of taxis filled with customers, heavy trucks and cars down a pot-holed highway to the border a few miles south. We crossed a little river and immediately were deluged with young men wanting to change money and lead us through the maze of admittance procedures for Guatemala. We exchanged a few dollars and hired a young man who led Scott into a small building to pay the bridge tax. They were gone an interminable amount of time, during which I tried unsuccessfully to stop several young men from washing our windows with oily rags, while telling young beggars they weren't going to get any dollars from me. Finally Scott and the young man returned, clutching papers and we went another hundred yards forward to a modern building where a large sign said "fumigación." They were in this building an even longer amount of time. Occasionally they would reappear at the rig, clutching even more papers. Eventually someone sprayed the tires and underside of the motorhome and then we were confronted by customs inspectors. They weren't happy about the two TVs, didn't like the cellular phone and were adamant about not allowing the CB radio into the country. It turns out that CBs are illegal in Guatemala because they don't want rebels in the hills to get them. It was now well into siesta, but fortunately, no one seemed to take a break. The inspectors grabbed lunch from various food stands lining the road and continued working. Scott disappeared into the building and was gone for well over an hour negotiating with customs. He returned smiling; we would be allowed to move in just a few minutes. But the inspector returned to look at the car we were towing. Another problem. Only one vehicle per driver allowed. After showing the inspector my license, and offering to drive the car across myself, and solving a few more problems, we finally received permission to enter Guatemala. It was a short haggle over the price with our young man who helped us, settling on $5.00 U.S. which Scott felt was worth the price." The total time spent crossing: four-and-a-half hours; about par for the course.

The drive down Highway 2 into Guatemala City takes about five hours, and is not nearly as picturesque as the traditional route through Huehuetenango. But this is the safest and best way to go. The pavement, according to one traveler, "gives new meaning to the words chuckholes, rough and narrow." Even so, this is better than trying the Huehuetenango route.

To Costa Rica

From Guatemala City to Costa Rica, you have two choices: through Honduras or through El Salvador (which will include a few miles through Honduras). The shortest, quickest route is through El Salvador, yet until the cessation of the civil war here, most drivers preferred the slow, safe route through Honduras. Nowadays, recent travelers describe driving El Salvador as uneventful.

The drive from Guatemala City to the city of San Salvador takes about six hours, depending upon the delay at customs at the border. My inclination would be to get an early start and drive across El Salvador in one day, crossing into Honduras before dark. Another early start in the morning should get you through Nicaragua and into the comfortable safety of Costa Rica. Try to have a full gas tank before entering Nicaragua since gasoline shortages aren't unknown. It's only a 190-mile trip from the Honduran border to the Costa Rican border.

Before attempting the short route through El Salvador, make inquiries in Guatemala City, preferably talking to tourists who have made the trip. Even though drivers report feeling safe driving through El Salvador, I'm not sure I'd have the nerve to try it until things have been peaceful for a while longer. The route through Honduras is far safer even though it's a longer trip and the country is full of greedy and corrupt cops.

To get from Guatemala City to Costa Rica via Honduras, you have two choices. One way is through Copán where you might want to pause to visit those famous Mayan ruins on the way. Make sure that the border officials know you are going to *cross* Honduras and not just visit the ruins for a day; otherwise they will give you temporary papers. Stretches of this road are much slower going than on the other route, and you end up going through San Pedro Sula, and then on to the Honduras capital city of Tegucigalpa. From there you cross into Nicaragua on Highway 3 and head for Chinandega and León. The other route through Honduras is through Agua Caliente, and on to Nueva Ocotepeque, where you'll find satisfactory accommodations if you need them.

Crossing Honduras

When entering Honduras, be prepared to hand out money to various officials and perhaps some who are not officials, but who simply dress in a quasi-uniform and take full advantage of your not understanding the process. There are always kids hanging around who, for a fee, will run your passport and car papers around to the places where they will be rubber stamped, have stamps affixed and signatures scrawled upon them. Unlike the *tramitadores* at the Guatemalan border, these guys are as crooked as the officials you are dealing with, and probably split the bribes after you've gone. It's difficult to tell which are legitimate charges and which are *mordidas* or bribes. The total cost is several times what it would be if you were to stand in lines and bumble about for yourself. It's a tough decision to make, hire one or not; if you speak Spanish you're probably better off without a tramitador.

However, one recent traveler reported that the border officials wouldn't deal with him until he hired a tramitador!

One piece of paper is extremely important in Honduras: the *transito*, or traffic permit, a document that gives you permission to drive your car through Honduras. I believe the cost is $10, but if you don't have one, expect a $10 payoff every time a cop stops you. The cop cars have *transito* written on their sides, so they are easy to spot. The problem begins at the border, where the man who hands out transitos has a tendency to take your money, pocket it and forget to give you the transito. Make sure you actually have it before leaving customs!

When in Honduras, keep one eye on the speedometer, because radar traps are everywhere. Watch for traffic control roadblocks with *alto* signs (stop signs), which are deliberately placed inconspicuously in hopes that motorists will go through them for another $10 or $20 fine. Even if nobody seems to be around, stop anyway. One man said he stopped, but because a bus was in the way he pulled around it and parked a few feet past the line of the roadblock. Another $10 fine. Asking for a receipt is an exercise in futility, but do bargain for the fine. If the cop suggests $20, you know you can probably get away for half that.

Central America by Bus

Although tiring and tedious, it's entirely possible to travel to Guatemala by bus, and many adventurous travelers do so. For the exceptionally adventurous, it's possible to travel all the way from the Mexican border to Costa Rica by bus. In Mexico, buses run regularly and are inexpensive. But the long trip to the Guatemalan border requires numerous changes and long hours of sitting on a cramped bus. Mexican first-class buses are okay, often having a bathroom, stereo music and sometimes even an attendant serving coffee and soft drinks. Guatemalan buses are another story. Most are old and rickety machines, long ago discarded by U.S. school districts. The only modification is the addition of wider seats, permitting the squeezing of three passengers into each seat. Passengers on the aisle end up with half of their bottoms hanging over empty space. If at all possible, when making trips longer than an hour, try to get one of the newer buses with regular seats, or else try to be first on the bus so you can get window seats. And, be very careful of your wallets and purses as in any crowded place.

From Guatemala City, the bus becomes another adventure. The bus line going between Guatemala and Costa Rica is the *Ticabus* company. Service was suspended through El Salvador for a time, but now that things are peaceful, Ticabus once again operates fairly modern, air-conditioned equipment. The trip to Costa Rica takes three days of driving six to eight hours a day, with overnight stops in the cities of San Salvador and Managua.

This is not a trip for the timid, fussy or overly fastidious; hotel accommodations are exceptionally rustic, and you will feel constrained to stay near your hotel and/or the bus station. I don't advise exploring San Salvador or Managua except in the company of other bus passengers—Central Americans who know what they are doing.

Each terminal supports a definitely second-class hotel, which passengers call the *Ticabus Hilton*. To say the Ticabus Hilton's facilities are spartan would be charitable. Furnishings consist of twin beds with rock-hard mattresses, two worn sheets and a couple of disreputable-looking pillows. Oh yes, a few hooks to hang clothes on. You must hurry to get in line to rent one of these rooms or else you'll have to go to a nearby hotel. You may want to do that anyway. The advantage of staying in the terminal is that you don't have to tote luggage back and forth to a distant hotel, and you can be first in line for seat assignments the next morning. The fun part of this bus trip is making friends with the other passengers. While having lunch at the rest stops, the passengers make plans for having dinner together at the next overnight stop. By the time you reach San José you will have made many friends and will probably have an invitation or two to visit a Costa Rican family. None of the daily bus rides are much over six hours, so it really isn't tiring. This trip isn't for just anyone; you need a real appetite for adventure!

Appendix

Business Contacts

American Chamber of Commerce of CR: P.O. Box 4946, San Jose, (Tel: 3321033).
Asociación Nacional de Fomento Economico: Apdo. 3577, San Jose.
Camara de Azucareros: Camara de (Comerciantes) Detallistas; Centro Nacional de Productividad Industrial, Apdo. 1858, San Jose.
Camara de Industrias de Costa Rica: Camara de Comercio, Calle 1-3, Avenida FG. San Jose.
Costa Rica Export Investment Promotion Center: International Trade Mart, New Orleans, LA 70130. (504) 529-2282.
Dirección General de Aduanas: (General Customs Bureau), Ministerio de Hacienda, Avenida 1-3, Calle 14, San Jose.
Economic Development Offices: Washington D.C. c/o Embassy of Costa Rica, 2112 "S" Street, N.W., 20008. (202) 328-6628.
Ministerio de Industrias: Apdo 5001, San Jose.
U.S. Foreign Service: Embassy with a Foreign Commercial Service Post in San Jose, Avenida 3 and Calle 1. 33-1155.

Costa Rican Consulates

Albuquerque: Consulate General, 7033 Luella Anne Drive N.E., Albuquerque, NM 87109. (505) 822-1420.
Atlanta: Honorary Consulate, 3815 Presidential Parkway, Suite 102, Atlanta, GA 30340. (404) 457-5656.
Boise: Honorary Consulate, 3705 Lemhi St., Boise, ID 83705. (204) 345-4128.
Buffalo: Consulate, 5370 Siegle Rd., Lockport NY 14094 (716) 625-9692.
Chicago: Honorary Consulate General, 8 South Michigan Ave., Chicago IL 60603. (312) 263-2772.
Cleveland: Honorary Consulate, 23811 Chagrin Blvd., Cleveland OH 44122. (513) 521-2160.
Denver: Honorary Consulate General, 2045 Franklin St., #1105, Denver, CO 80205. (303) 839-5522.

Houston: Consulate General, 3000 Wilcrest, Suite 145, Houston, TX 77042. (713) 266-0484.

Las Vegas: Honorary Consulate, 4154 Seville, Las Vegas, NV 89121. (702) 458-4139.

Los Angeles: Consulate General, 3540 Wilshire Blvd. Ste. 404, Los Angeles, CA 90010. (213) 380-7915, FAX (213) 380-5639.

Miami: Consulate General, 28 West Flagler St., Suite 806, Miami, FL 33130. (305) 377-4242.

Milwaukee: Honorary Consulate, 130 West Lexington Blvd., White Fish Bay, WI 53217. (414) 332-0376.

New Orleans: Consulate General, World Trade Center Bldg. 2 Canal St., New Orleans, LA 70130. (504) 525-5445.

New York: Consulate General, 80 Wall St., Suite 1117, New York, NY 10005. (212) 425-2620

Philadelphia: Consulate, 335 E. Main St., Moorestown, N.J., 08057. (609) 235-6277.

Pittsburgh: Consulate General, 1164 Harvard Rd., Monroeville, PA 15146. (412) 856-7967.

Portland, Oregon: Honorary Consulate, 2050 N.W. Lovejoy, Portland, OR 97209. (503) 224-0103.

St. Louis: Honorary Consulate, 929 Fee-Fee Rd., Suite 200, St. Louis, MO 63043. (314) 434-6300.

Salt Lake City: Honorary Consulate, 686 N. 1300 West, Salt Lake City, UT 84116. (801) 539-1284.

San Diego: Consulate General, 4201 Caledonia Dr., San Diego, CA 92111. (619) 277-9447.

San Francisco: Consulate General, 870 Market St., Suite 546, San Francisco, CA 94102. (415) 392-8488.

San Juan, Puerto Rico: Consulate, Calle 32 No. 327, Jardines Metropolitanos, Rio Piedras, PR 00927. (809) 758-6301.

Seattle: Honorary Consulate, 344 37th Avenue West, Seattle, WA 98199. (206) 284-7219.

Springfield, Mass.: Honorary Consulate, 52 Mulberry St., Springfield MA 01105. (413) 781-5400.

Vancouver, Wash.: Honorary Consulate, 11011 N.E. 64th Ave., Vancouver, WA 98665. (206) 694-4027.

Washington, D.C.: Consulate General, 1825 Connecticut Ave., NW, Washington DC 20009. (202) 234-2945.

Canada: Embassy of Costa Rica, One Nicholas St., Suite 1515, Ottawa, Ontario K1N 7B7. (613) 234-5762.

Real Estate, Investment and Retirement Contacts

Beaches of Nosara, Paulina Anderson, Apdo. 38-5233, Nosara, Nicoya, Guanacaste, Costa Rica.

Ray Nelson, Apdo 1268-4050, Alajuela, Costa Rica, C.A. Telephone and fax number is 41-11-41. One block down from park, about 50 meters to right, next to Alajuela Travel Agency, Agencia de Viajes, Alajuela, S.A.

Forever Yours, 1491 West 5th Ave., Eugene, OR 97402, (800) 578-6535. Conducts tours emphasizing adventure, learning and discovery, to explore possibilities of retirement and investment.

ICIA Retirement Seminars, offering 12-day "pre-retirement" seminars. Contact: Ecotours, 3325 Wilshire Blvd., #504, Los Angeles, CA 90010. (213) 386-1215, FAX (213) 385-4405.

Lifestyle Explorations, Inc. has 13-day tours to investigate retirement and investment. World Trade Center, Suite 400, Boston, MA 02210. (508) 371-4814, FAX (508) 369-9192.

Ecotourism Examples

Listed below are a just a few examples of ecotourist facilities and prices advertised where available. The rates listed were for the 1991-92 summer season and probably will be a bit higher for 1992-93. Unless otherwise indicated, prices are per person, double occupancy, and usually include meals. Most of the following are places I've never visited; they are being listed for your information and investigation, should ecotourism appeal to you.

Arenal Lodge. High on a mountain with a view of Arenal Volcano, with good food and a comfortable atmosphere with library and even a pool table. Convenient for fishing and trips to volcano. $60 a day plus food.

Bosque del Cabo. Located on a 100-hectare farm on the Oso Peninsula, about a one-hour drive from Puerto Jiménez. These are said to be rustic accommodations in an area of beaches and forest frequented by scarlet macaws and other wildlife. Tel: 22-45-47. $55 per person.

Corcovado Lodge Tent Camp. Located on the beach on the southern border of Corcovado National Park. Ten large tents with two cots, shared bath, family-style meals. Reservations through Costa Rica Expeditions, Box 6941-1000, San José. (506) 57-07-66.

Drake Bay. Near Corcovado park, comfortable lodge near rain forest and beaches. $55 per person in cabins and $38 in tents. Tel 22-55-33.

Ecoadventure Lodge. See Chapter 10 for details.

El Gavilan Lodge. In the north, near Puerto Viejo de Sarapiqui, on the Río Sarapaqui which empties into the Río San Juan, a true wilderness area. Rooms are $25 per night, with meals extra. Tel: 34-95-07.

La Paloma Lodge is nearby, featuring thatched-roof cabins, private baths and a club house. Tel. 39-09-54.

Las Imagenes. A large ranch north of Libera with a combination biological station and ecotourism facility. Horses for rent and volcano tours. Reservations: Hotel Las Espuelas, (506) 33-99-55. $120 per couple.

Los Inocentes. A large cattle ranch located On the slopes of the Orosi Volcano. Tours to the volcano and horses for rent. Tel.: 39-54-84. $100 per couple.

Monteverde Lodge. In the Monteverde Cloud Forest. Three-day, two-night tours offered to the lodge, with meals and wildlife tour with naturalist guide. Reservations through Costa Rica Expeditions, Box 6941-1000, San José. Tel.: 57-07-66. $349, 3 days/2 nights.

Rainbow Adventures (Arco Iris). See Chapter 10 for details

Rainforest Living. A small place with no more than eight guests at a time, advertises "majestic jungle trees, wild fruits, rare flowers, exotic birds, magnificent butterfles, quiet borrks and roaring waterfalls in a secluded paradise." Box 241, San José 1017, FAX (506) 31-09-80.

Rancho Naturalista. Near Turrialba on the Atlantic slope, a 125-acre reserve with a lodge and meals for $85 per day, or $550 per week. Tel: 39-71-38.

Rara Avis. Combines tourism, research and forest harvest to prove that rain-forest conservation can also be profitable. On the Selva Biological reserve. Rooms are $140 double. Tel: 53-08-44, FAX: 21-23-14.

Tierra Buena. Accommodates no more than eight people at a time on a 1,500-acre rain-forest reserve in the northern part of the country. $450 per person for three days. Tel./FAX: 31-09-80.

Books

Adventures Abroad, by Allene Symons and Jane Parker. Gateway Books, 13 Bedford Cove, San Rafael, CA 94901, 1991. A guide to living overseas, includes sections on many other countries as well as Costa Rica.

Choose Latin America, by John Howells. Gateway Books, San Rafael, CA, 1986. Covers most Latin American countries, with emphasis on Costa Rica. (Out of print, but available in many libraries)

Costa Rica: A Natural Destination, by Ree Strange Sheck. John Muir Publications, P.O. Box 613, Santa Fe, NM 87504. A guidebook for those interested in ecology.

Costa Rica Guide, by Paul Glassman. Passport Press, Box 1346, Champlain, NY 12919. Information on travel in Costa Rica, with regional maps.

Costa Rica Reader, by Mark Edelman and Joanne Kenen. Grove Weidenfeld, New York, 1989. An excellent background source.

The Costa Ricans, by Richard Mavis and Karen Bicsanz. Waveland Press, Box 400, Prospect Heights, IL 0070. Book about Ticos and their country.

The Costa Rica Traveler, by Ellen Searby. Windham Bay Press, P.O. Box 1198, Occidental, CA 95465. Covers travel in Costa Rica and descriptions of various attractions in the country.

Frommer's Costa Rica, Guatemala & Belize on $35 a Day, published by Prentice Hall Press, 1991. Comprehensive guide to hotels, transportation and tourist attractions, focused on budget travel.

Investor's Guide to Costa Rica, by the Costa Rican-American Chamber of Commerce. General information on investment, banking, finance and business opportunities.

Living in Costa Rica, published by the United States Mission Association, 1989. Writen and produced by employees of the U.S. Embassy in JS. Excellent information on rules, regulations, customs and shopping in CR.

The New Key to Costa Rica, by Beatrice Blake and Anne Becher. Ulysses Press, Berkely, CA. A popular travel guide for residents and tourists, and a must for anyone considering visiting Costa Rica for more than a short vacation.

Periodicals

The Tico Times, weekly English-language newspaper published in San José, Costa Rica. A trial three-month subscription is $16.50, six months $25.60, a year $45.26. From U.S. or Canada: Dept. 717, P.O. Box 025216, Miami, FL 33102. In Costa Rica: Apdo. 4632, San Jose, Costa Rica.

This Week, a newsletter offering news and analyses about Guatemala as well as the rest of Central America. Write to Apto Postal 1156, Guatemala City, Guatemala.

Aquí Guatemala, a weekly newspaper published by the American Society. Distributed free at stores patronized by North American community. Edificio Rodríguez, Diagonal 6, 13-08, Zona 10, Guatemala City, Guatemala. Phone 37-14-16.

Index

Our books are available in most bookstores. However, if you have difficulty finding them, we will be happy to ship them to you directly. Mail us this coupon with your check or money order (U.S. funds, please) and they'll be on their way to you within days.

Retirement

Wintering, Retiring or Investing
CHOOSE COSTA RICA..$12.95_____

Exploring the Travel/Retirement Option
ADVENTURES ABROAD ....12.95_____

Retire on $600 a Month
CHOOSE MEXICO: • *3rd Edition*..10.95_____

Leisurely Vacations or Affordable Retirement
CHOOSE SPAIN..11.95_____

Detailed information on America's 100 Best Places to Retire
WHERE TO RETIRE ....12.95_____

Strategies for Comfortable Retirement on Social Security
RETIREMENT ON A SHOESTRING ....6.95_____

Travel

The Complete How-to-do-it Book
RV TRAVEL IN MEXICO...9.95_____

A Guide for the Mature Traveler
GET UP AND GO:..10.95_____

A Hiking Guide for Active Adults
WALKING EASY IN THE SWISS ALPS ....9.95_____

$1.90 for postage and handling for the first book,
$1.00 for each additional one.. _____

California Residents add 8% Sales Tax_____

TOTAL ENCLOSED   _____

Credit Card Orders Only • Call our FREE number: 800-669-0773
For Information Call • 415-454-5215

Name_____

Address_____

City/State/Zip_____

Books should reach you in two or three weeks. If you are dissatisfied for any reason, the price of the books will be refunded in full.

Mail to: Gateway Books • P.O. Box 10244 • San Rafael, CA 94912